THE
LITTLE
COMMUNITY

—— AND ——

PEASANT
SOCIETY
AND
CULTURE

THE
LITTLE
COMMUNITY

AND

PEASANT
SOCIETY
AND
CULTURE

By ROBERT REDFIELD

Phoenix Books

THE UNIVERSITY OF CHICAGO PRESS

CHICAGO & LONDON

Separate clothbound editions of
The Little Community and *Peasant Society and Culture*
are available from

THE UNIVERSITY OF CHICAGO PRESS

THE UNIVERSITY OF CHICAGO PRESS, CHICAGO & LONDON
The University of Toronto Press, Toronto 5, Canada

The Little Community: First published in Sweden as
Volume V of the "Gottesman Lectures," Uppsala
University. *Peasant Society and Culture:* Copyright 1956
by The University of Chicago. All rights to both books
reserved. Published 1960. First Phoenix Edition 1967. Fifth
Impression 1967. Printed in the United States of America

CONTENTS

THE LITTLE COMMUNITY AS:

PEASANT SOCIETY AND CULTURE

v

The Little Community

ACKNOWLEDGMENTS

I thank the Gottesman Foundation and the University of Uppsala for the opportunity these two institutions gave me to deliver in the autumn of 1953 the lectures that have become this book. I am particularly grateful to Professor Ake Holmback, Rector of the University, for his many kindnesses, and to Professor Torgny Segerstedt, who took me into his office, his circle of colleagues and students, and his friendship. It was in a seminar, organized with Professor Segerstedt's efficient and whole-hearted help, that I had the pleasure of discussing some of the matters raised in the lectures with many people with good minds and with scholarly experiences and points of view differing from mine. The seminar included sociologists, ethnologists, geographers, historians, and students of Nordic folklife. In difference, generously explored, there is growth.

Before I gave the lectures, and afterward, Milton Singer of my own university helped me to think about the questions of method that are raised in these pages and steadied and guided my thinking more wisely and well than these results will show. I thank him. To Robert Pehrson I am grateful for giving me understanding of Swedish studies of community life. Edward Bruner read part of the manuscript and made good suggestions for improvement which I tried to follow. Melvin Tumin went through all the pages and made wise proposals for the improvement of the text; I wish that the book that now appears were more nearly like the book he imagined that it might be. My wife, too, shared much of this work with me, and has given me much counsel. To Rosemary Witko I am grateful for much effective help in preparing the manuscript for publication.

I

THE LITTLE COMMUNITY AS:

A WHOLE

Humanity presents itself to the view of common sense in just a few kinds of integral entities. A person is one such kind of entity, a separate and unique human individual. Another is a people, *ein Volk*: the Navaho, the Lapp, the Latin-Americans. Yet another, characteristic of our times but not of all, is the national state. A fourth, more difficult to delimit and to characterize even than these others, is a civilization. Person, people, nation, and civilization are forms of humanity, each kind of which constitutes a great and easily recognizable class, and each separate one of which is describable in its own characteristics as a whole.

The small community is another of these prevailing and conspicuous forms in which humanity obviously comes to our notice. In all parts of the world, in all of human history, there are and have been little communities. We think now of the Neolithic settlement of fishers and farmers built on piles in a Swiss lake, of the nomadic band of hunters in the Bolivian rain-forest, of the medieval English or Swedish village, of the camp or village of Sudanese cattle people on the Upper Nile, of the Persian pastoral tribesmen moving camp and cattle every year across the mountains, of the hamlet or village or small town in present-day Dalecarlia, Provence, or Missouri.

This book is about some of the several ways in which the organized life of man can be viewed and understood. The subject is the forms of thought for understanding humanity; it is a book about "method," if one means by that word not merely the techniques of observation and analysis, but also the conceptions which allow us to characterize and compare. The point of departure is a certain strain or struggle, so to speak, between the claims of the human whole—person or village or civilization—to communicate to us its nature as a whole, a convincing complex entity, on the one hand, and the disposition of science to take things apart and move toward the precise description of relationships between parts and parts, on the other. Human wholes persist through time, each one preserving, for years or centuries, a certain unique character which one may come to know through personal experience or reading. Each person, each stable human settlement with an organized way of life, each historical people, even each art or body of literature associated with such a people, has a sort of integrity which is recognized both by common sense and by much scholarship, humanistic or anthropological.[1] Yet each of these entities arouses the disposition to make acquaintance with such things into more strictly controlled knowledge about them. We want, also, to compare one community or one personality with another. What shall be the forms of thought that will help us toward this more strictly controlled knowledge, a knowledge that will preserve some of the holistic qualities of the things compared?

The small communities that will appear, briefly but frequently, in the following pages are here to provide illustrative comparisons. They are not the subject matter of the book; the purpose is not to provide a description of any community or of any class of communities. The materials illustrative of the several forms of thought to be reviewed will be drawn solely from small communities for the reason that this investigation of related yet different conceptions can best be attempted, in the first place, in terms of just one kind of human whole. The little community has been chosen because it is a kind of human whole with which students of man have a great deal of experience, and because it is easier to develop a chain of thought in relation especially to villages and bands than to try to do so also in relation to personalities and civilizations and literatures. Some of the conceptions to be examined are relevant to other kinds of human wholes, and the student of personalities or of historical epochs may possibly find something that bears on his work in the pages that follow. But the discussion here will be with reference to small communities only. The generalization of the problems to other kinds of human wholes is a further and much more difficult problem.

Illustrations will come to our aid as they are suggested from such studies of village and band life as I know. I shall refer often to the

Maya Indian villages of Yucatán, because I have lived and worked there. As what I have done there, or failed to do, is a principal part of the experience that contributes to the effort to make some order in a variety of conceptions that follows, the exposition will have a certain personal character. Four other communities, to be mentioned more particularly almost at once, will also provide material, but there will be no point-for-point comparison of these four or five. The order of the book is provided by the relations among the more or less holistic conceptions for describing and comparing the community, not by any systematic comparison of cases.

But because the source of illustrative materials, the focus of interest, is to remain with small communities, the reader should be provided with some identification of them; therefore the first part of this chapter tells about what small communities are and where they are. The point to be made is that these relatively simple and widespread forms of organized human life constitute no closed class but shade into communities with other qualities. And this is to be helpful to us, for we shall find that as we begin to shift the focus of our attention from the kinds of band or settlement studied by anthropologists in remote parts of the world to other and perhaps more "modernized" societies, the conceptions, the forms of thought, that are our real topic here, undergo changes and developments that are interesting to us. In the next pages we identify these human societies of our first interest; later in the chapter return will be made to the holistic viewpoint that we are to maintain throughout the book.

The small community has been the very predominant form of human living throughout the history of mankind. The city is a few thousand years old, and while isolated homesteads appeared in early times,[2] it was probably not until the settlement of the New World that they made their "first appearance on a large scale."[3] To Tocqueville, the village or township was "the only association ... so perfectly natural that wherever a number of men are collected it seems to constitute itself."[4] One estimate[5] is that today three-quarters of the human race still live in villages; and to these villages are to be added the relatively very few who still live in nomadic bands or other unstable small settlements.

In the development of systematic investigation of human life the small community has come to provide a commonly recognized unit of subject matter. Anthropologists have done most of their field work in little communities, and no small part of empirical sociology derives from the investigation of villages, small towns, and urban neighborhoods. In several parts of the world, the studies of small communities have become so numerous that regional groups of studies have been reviewed and criticized: this has been done for community studies in Mexico,[6] China,[7] Japan,[8] and India.[9]

What, then, do we mean more particularly by a little community? I put forward, first, the quality of distinctiveness: where the community begins and where it ends is apparent. The distinctiveness is apparent to the outside observer and is expressed in the group-consciousness of the people of the community.

Second, the community we are here concerned with is small, so small that either it itself is the unit of personal observation or else, being somewhat larger and yet homogeneous, it provides in some part of it a unit of personal observation fully representative of the whole. A compact community of four thousand people in Indian Latin-America can be studied by making direct personal acquaintance with one section of it.

Third, the community to which we are to look in these chapters is homogeneous. Activities and states of mind are much alike for all persons in corresponding sex and age positions; and the career of one generation repeats that of the preceding. So understood, homogeneous is equivalent to "slow-changing."[10]

As a fourth defining quality it may be said that the community we have here in mind is self-sufficient and provides for all or most of the activities and needs of the people in it. The little community is a cradle-to-the-grave arrangement. A club, a clique, even a family, is sectional or segmental contrasted with the integral little community.

These qualities—distinctiveness, smallness, homogeneity, and all-providing self-sufficiency—define a type of human community that is realized in high degree in the particular bands and villages to be mentioned in these chapters. But the qualities are present in them in different degrees. Furthermore, we may in a preliminary way arrange them in a roughly descending order according to the degree to which the qualities are present. The band of Siriono

Indians of the Bolivian forest, described by Holmberg,[11] is a little community very small and distinctive. Much the same can be said of the Skolt Lapp community, homogeneous and all-providing, described by Karl Nickul.[12] The pastoral Nuer tribesmen of the Sudan that Evans-Pritchard[13] has described live in communities in which most or all of these four qualities are marked, but are not so marked as in the case of the Siriono band. With these pastoral people who also sow and harvest, we are moving up a scale of societal complexity and of diminution of the four qualities I have mentioned. The villages of Maya Indian peasants of Yucatán[14] represent a further advance on this scale and in diminution of the four qualities. Finally, a rural village or small town in a modern state presents a still further position away from the very small, distinct, homogeneous, and all-providing band or settlement with which we began. By adding to the list of particular real communities to be considered here the rural village in Missouri described as "Plainville" by James West[15] or the Swedish town described by Allwood and Ranemark as "Medelby,"[16] we introduce communities that notably fail to realize the four qualities, while yet retaining them in significant degree.

In the succeeding chapters questions will be raised as to thinking about human societies with reference to these communities just mentioned, and also to other communities in which the four characterizing qualities are present in lesser degree. There are, on the one hand, communities of peoples yet more urbanized than is Plainville or Medelby. About these little will here be said. There are the various kinds of agglomerations of residents to be found within the modern city. There are also the little communities to be found in frontier regions: the lumber camp, the settlement of laborers drawn to some mine or dam or plantation. These last communities are small, perhaps, and distinct, but they are in many cases heterogeneous.

In these frontier communities and also in the communities of the city, new characteristics of human life appear: impersonal institutions; what has been called atomization of the external world; perhaps a new kind of character structure. The present examination of little communities begins, and on the whole remains with, a type of human aggregation that prevailed long and widely. It may be expected to provide understanding of the newer types in so far as the questions raised prove irrelevant and give rise to different questions as one begins to think beyond such a relatively distinct and homogeneous modern community as Plainville to more industrialized, urbanized, or otherwise heterogeneous communities. The way to understanding of the emergent conditions of human life in modern cities and industrialized rural communities may not be through study of the small community, for as defined here such a community ceases to be. Other ways to study these emergent conditions may take the place of the study of little communities.

For a few pages let us turn away from urbanized and heterogeneous groups to such communities of the less civilized or less urbanized peoples as are, for different reasons, not fully little communities in the sense of our preliminary definition. These bound our illustrative examples on another side. Consider those rural communities that are homogeneous but that lack compactness or other clear delimitation. In many parts of the world where agriculture is carried on under such peaceful conditions that families are not compelled to live closely together for protection, the houses are distributed through the countryside and there may be no town, hamlet, or village in which a common life is lived. Professor Erixon has shown[17] how varied were the patterns of early settlement in Sweden. In south Sweden compact clusters of several homesteads were usual, but in north Sweden there were commonly to be found diffuse settlements of irregularly distributed farms. Settlement in scattered homesteads may be illustrated from many parts of the world: Ireland, the West Indies, the American Middle West. In some of these cases the village or the market town is absent, or plays no important part in the life of the rural population. Writing of such a kind of settlement in Wales, Alwyn D. Rees tells us that there the diffuse form of rural community not only is able to function without a unifying social center, "but seems to be opposed to all forms of centralization."[18] The hearth of the lonely farm is the only center. There is no community centering upon town or village; there is only a double network of kinship connection and neighborly connection to hold together, loosely, people who dwell separate from one another. One group of farming co-operators overlaps with many others; there are no fixed groups. A population of five hundred may have thirteen churches and chapels. A burial is the occasion that brings together the largest number of neighbors.

It may reach a hundred. In this rural countryside there are hamlets, three or four houses together, but these are not unifying centers of any delimitable rural group.

Among isolated mountaineer peoples of the Appalachians or Ozarks the little community is defined plainly enough, but by the very separateness of the little valleys the community is not much of one. Near Washington, D.C., in 1928 Sherman and Henry[19] found separate and distinct settlements, each in a mountain pocket, of people with much abraded culture. The community here consisted of perhaps a dozen or so scattered families, each with its cabin and cornpatch, in some cases without school, church, or other centralized institution and without any organized group life. Outside such a hollow, as they call it, lay other such communities, and beyond these a small town to which the people occasionally went to make purchases or rarely for employment. Marriage between hollows was infrequent. Each hollow was, then, pretty much a world to itself, although there was little to make a community of the families that lived there.

In partial contrast to the diffuse and nonnucleated societies just mentioned are those rural dwellers who have, one might say, a part-time nucleation. The Indian people who live about the western Guatemalan town of Santo Tomas, Chichicastenango,[20] live in widely scattered households. Among the thirty thousand people who live a common life, there is no hamlet or village settlement, but the common life centers for certain purposes in a town, where are the market, the offices of civil administration, the churches, and the little buildings in which the Indians house their saints and celebrate their rituals. To this town the Indians come frequently. On the most important festal days most of them are in the town at the same time; some of them, and especially those who for a year are required to fulfil some public office, rent a town house where they spend many nights when they are compelled to be in the town center. This sort of settlement is both less than a village community and also more. A people live scattered over a wide area, and the one notable town is not the permanent residence of any particular small, integral local society.

Something like this and yet distinguishable appears among the Tarahumara of western Mexico.[21] There, too, the community is not constant but is intermittent. The day-to-day life is one in which each family lives isolated from all others and with small exception dependent on itself alone. Several miles of distance separate one family from another. The mountain gorges are deep and trails are difficult. Among these scattered people there are two latent little communities, loose, shifting in personnel, and almost entirely without formal institutional organization. There is, first, the neighborhood. Ten or a dozen men will come together to help each other in plowing, cultivating, or weeding. Such work parties usually end in a drinking party to which the women come also. These are occasions of relaxation and sociability. Slightly larger groups assemble to perform what they call curing ceremonies to assure the health of cattle or to avert sickness and lightning. Such groups come together for the purposes of the ceremony and for as long as the ceremony lasts, no longer.

The second and larger kind of intermittent community is that centralized in the pueblo, a center for government and for the performance of rituals fixed by the calendar of the Catholic church. Every Sunday some of the Tarahumara of an area perhaps fifteen miles in radius assemble to hear a sermon and perhaps to listen to the trial of a lawsuit. Several times a year many more Indians come together at this center for the performance of ceremonies lasting several days. In the intervals the center is empty of human occupation.

The life is, thus, one of diastole and systole, in which two rhythms, one dependent on the agricultural necessities and perhaps also on the gathering impulses to sociability, draw people together for a few hours of work and play. The other rhythm is the annual cycle; its pulses draw together Indians from more widely scattered homes for a variety of interests and purposes. On the whole, nevertheless, we may say that these people do not live in distinct little communities.

These dispersed rural communities with part-time nucleation that have just been mentioned are all communities of agriculturalists. A man lives at or near his fields, or some of them; and other men do the same. The land owned by any one is not great in extent. Pastoral and hunting peoples, on the other hand, require large tracts of land to maintain their herds or to provide fish and game. So it is common among such peoples to find that the little community consists of a band of related and friendly families each of which controls and makes exclusive use of a family territory. So it is among Athapaskan hunters of Canada: each family hunts over a hereditary family territory. So too among the Skolt Lapps, where Nickul has described in such detail the boundaries of each family territory used for hunting and fishing. These Lapps lead a life divided into two parts: that greater part of the year in which each family is much to itself on its territory, and those few months of the winter when the families gather in the winter village, and, as Ernst Manker writes, "from time immemorial tradition has pulsated regularly with the seasons, driving the blood—the people— out toward the periphery in the spring and back again to the heart in the winter."[22]

The several instances of more or less dispersed rural communities that have been mentioned could be ranged in an order according to their approach to the little community that meets our initial definition. Most unlike village or nomad band are those scattered rural dwellers such as the Welsh countrymen without any town serving as a nucleating force. Next are such rural peoples, also without villages or towns, but drawn into separable and distinct communities, though of scattered households, by the effects of valley and mountain, island or cove.

Third, represented by the Tarahumara, are scattered rural peoples with established centers of occasional assembly, and after these such peoples as the Indians of Chichicastenango, who make part-time use of a fully developed town on the whole occupied and operated by another people, different from themselves, who do not share the other aspects of their common life.

Let us now return our attention to the villages and nomad bands that lie well within the area of our interest. Up to this point we have been asking, what is it that we are to consider? What kind of human society will help us to think about characterization and comparison? From this point on in this chapter we ask: What is the viewpoint which we are to adopt? The answer is that we are to consider any one community as it remains in our view in its entirety, as a whole. What does this mean?

It means that a band of hunters or a long-established village is unified, as is a personality, and has its own character, as does a personality. We say easily, "That village over there in the valley has a long history," and we so declare that the village is one thing, distinct from all others, with its own story to tell. In western Guate-mala, each settlement has words with which to characterize each of its neighboring settlements: that people are rude and dangerous; this other village is regarded as more open, friendly, and amiable. And the unity and distinctiveness of the little community is felt by everyone who is brought up in it and as a part of it. The people of a band or a village or a small town know each of the other mem-bers of that community as parts of one another; each is strongly aware of just that group of people, as belonging together: the "we" that each inhabitant uses recognizes the separateness of that band or village from all others. Moreover, to the member of the more isolated band or village the community is a round of life, a small cosmos; the activities and the institutions lead from one into all the others so that to the native himself the community is not a list of tools and customs; it is an integrated whole.

In the development of science it is usual and necessary to break up the wholes we encounter into parts. It is the way of science to find small elements that can be more precisely described and related to each other than can such complex wholes as are communities and personalities and civilizations.

So, in the ordinary way of going to work, one looks first at a peasant or primitive village as an assemblage of items: artifacts, customs, institutions. To make a beginning with precise knowledge, one turns attention to some one or few of these items. One becomes interested in the form of the house or the betrothal customs or the tales the people tell one another. From this interest in some one of these elements one may be then easily led to the resemblance to the house-type or betrothal custom in some other village. In anthropology this leads to distributional studies or to the raising of questions as to the historical origins of some separated element of the whole. We may then become interested in the events that explain historically how it is that this artifact is now made here or this custom followed.

Such a way of thinking about the little community breaks up the whole. It turns the attention to parts of the whole, part-systems within the total system that is the community. We may study the economic system of the community, or the technology, or the system of kinship. Any of these subsystems will give us plenty to do in understanding what is there in the immediate community, its relations to other such subsystems elsewhere, and its historical development.

Such analytic or atomistic studies of the little community constitute much of the scientific work that is done in them. The study of particular artifacts and customs, and of such special aspects of the community life as the economy or the kinship institutions, is necessary and important. The resemblances and connections, historical or sociological, that customs and institutions in the village have with things outside that village are proper and inevitable subject matter of a great deal of growing science and scholarship. By limiting our view to just some parts of the whole in their connections with one another we may learn something about process, as did Nordenskiöld in his study of the modification of artifacts in South America,[23] and as did Boas in his study of the play of imagination on the formal features of the bone or ivory needlecases of the Eskimo.[24]

The restriction of interest to something less than the community, little or great, may direct our minds to groups within it, to subgroups of it. We may study a family, or a streetcorner gang, or a clique of adolescents, or the working-team in one corner of a great modern factory. All these things have been done. The study of such groups has a name: "small-group sociology." The small group appeals to our minds when we want to consider human relations as the central subject matter; when we want to learn about how people act with regard to one another and become related to one another in situations so simple that the relevant factors may perhaps be seen and precisely described.

Our present interest is directed at one level of human living more complex than is the small group. We begin by looking at groups that provide for all of life's needs for all the kinds of people needed to keep that way of life going. We ask how such a group can be thought about as a whole.

Of course it should be said quite plainly that no words describe all that a community is. We are going to consider some words that attempt to represent a great deal of the systematic whole that is there. We are to become interested in concepts that cover much of what goes on throughout all of the human life for everybody in that community. We are to review some of the terms and propositions that purport to declare the essential and all-pervading characteristics of the little community. The phrases "ecological system," "social structure," "human career," "personality type," and "world view," with some others, all offer, in one way or another, to comprehend the community more or less as a whole. They are the first beginnings of a scientific language for the description and comparison of this one of the several human wholes—the little community—as a complete and integrated thing.

As we shall see, each of the ways of conceiving the community more or less as a whole which we are going to pass in review leaves a great deal about it unsaid, while each brings something into the forefront of attention which others do not bring there; yet all of them retain a hold on the community as something that retains identity and completeness. Even when, as will be the case in the eighth chapter, account is taken of peoples and institutions outside of our community, the community as a whole is kept in the center of our attention and is related as a whole to that which is outside of it.

This is perhaps the place in which to say something about present wholes and past wholes. One may describe a community not as it now is but as it once was. N. S. B. Gras[25] wrote a detailed account of an English village, as it was in the Middle Ages, and Professor Sigurd Erixon[26] has reconstructed the early mode of life of a village in Kila, Sweden. Such accounts of bygone conditions are relevant to our present undertaking too. But in these chapters I shall confine myself fairly closely to the village or band that is known to direct observation by living there, and this because I am used to it and because of a certain confidence that more can be learned about a present community than about a past one. The questions to be asked should be more nearly answerable in the case of a contemporary than in the case of an ancient community.

The course on which the reader is perhaps persuaded to set out has direction but no one defined terminus. As some of the different kinds of wholes or near-wholes in terms of which human life can be conceived are taken up, questions will be raised which will go unanswered. These chapters present no report of thought completed. They exhibit some thinking just begun. This is an exploration, not a finished map. But a course has been laid, and this should be announced before the journey begins.

Various ways of conceiving communities are to be taken up in an order that is obedient, although not too closely, to two concurrent lines of development of thought. First, we begin with those views of the community which see it as if it had no development in time, as if it existed on the flat, temporally, and we move toward views which strongly emphasize the historical or full diachronic aspects of the reality. Although time-changes will appear in the next three chapters, they will not concern us much until the fourth chapter, and there it will be a sort of a permanent or perpetual time-change, namely the time-change of the typical human life in that community, which will provide the temporal axis. We might say that this fourth chapter will be concerned with the biographic dimension of the community.

The fifth and sixth chapters return to an essentially static conception, but the seventh, as appears from the title, adopts the temporal organization usual in the work of professional historians. In the ninth chapter again we will encounter, but now only in a place of secondary emphasis, still another time-line, that of acculturative change, or the time-line of the transformations from primitive or precivilized life to urban civilization.

The second very general principle of order of sequence which is here to be made explicit arranges the several expositions so as to bring forward first those conceptions which choose *relations*, the kind of connection between this or that, as the materials of the system, as the parts of the whole. We consider first the ecological system and then the social structure. These are conceptions of people in relation to things or to other people.

In the fourth and fifth chapters the reader will hear, surely not for the first time in these pages but now more insistently, about beliefs and ideas and ideals. By that point in the book the subject matter will have undergone something of a transformation. In the early chapters the word "society" will come easily to mind, but by the middle of this series of chapters it will be "culture" that will suggest itself more naturally. The sixth chapter, which is concerned with world view, has to do with this polymorphous reality of ours in plainly cultural rather than societal terms. It will be in that chapter a culture seen, so far as possible, from the inside out.

Of course, it is a little artificial to confine ourselves to one conception, to one of these alternative forms of thought at a time, in this way. In most published work about communities one finds a combination or mixing of conceptions. One sees a village partly as an ecological system, perhaps partly as social structure. One writes an account of the prevailing personality type of this or that community, and then puts down something about the customs and beliefs that seem to have some connection with the kind of personality one finds there.

I have not designed these chapters in order to convert the students of small communities into separated battalions of overspecialized workers. I am imaginatively separating ideas from ideas, kinds of wholes from other kinds of wholes, holistic from analytic viewpoints, not to cause myself or other people to think just one way or to work only one way at a time, but in the confidence that the effort of imagining this separation will help us to understand two things: what a human society is and the variety of ways of thinking about it. I have a hope that an examination of some of these conceptions will show how some of them are naturally, in the reality of the community itself, related to others and at what points.

The ideas to be taken up successively will be found to differ in a number of respects. They will first differ as to the degree to which each purports to describe all of the community. And they will also differ as to the preciseness with which they describe it. Common language about peoples and communities prepares us for this. If I say that the community is one in which the people are careful not to eat with the left hand, I do not say very much to stand for the whole. If I say that the Chinese are a people in which family connections are of first importance, I say more. If I say that the Americans are a people of technological abundance I become increasingly vague, and yet somehow what I have said seems to stand for a great deal of it; and if I say in connection with the United States, liberty, equality, and the sovereignty of the people, the vagueness is now of course very great indeed; and yet these resounding nouns do in a way stand comprehensively for this nation. So it is with the more formal language for characterizing cultures or communities; we shall find that "ecological system" is more precise but less inclusive than is "world view."

Further, in the coming review, we shall be impressed with differences among the conceptions as to the element of reality that is brought forward for special notice. One will be concerned with the relationship between man and nature, a second with social relations and corporate groups, and a third with ideas, ideals, or even passions.

Third, we shall find that these ideas differ as to the viewpoint from which the whole is described. Where do I stand who assume to characterize that village there? He who describes the social structure of a community describes the relationships as the member of the community lives them, but in terms and in more abstractly conceived relations, as *he*, the describer, sees them. In contrast, a description of a world view of a community reproduces more of the conceptions and categories of the member of the community himself.

A fourth kind of difference among conceptions for describing a community as a whole lies in the question whether it is described as something changing through time, or is described without reference to change or to history; and a fifth difference has to do with the recognition or the failure to recognize the systems of relationships which lie outside of the community and are connected with it.

There is a sixth kind of difference among the conceptions we shall consider useful on which some words need particularly to be set down because with it we are brought into a somewhat different realm of thinking. This is the question as to the logical form of the idea, the concept, itself. The general question here is: What is the form of arrangements of the parts of the conception to one another? Or, to what model, present to experience from some other source than the human community, does this chosen holistic concept tend to conform? In the next chapter we shall imagine ourselves describing an ecological system. The question then is: Do we now think of the community of the African Nuer as if it were a kind of machine, the land, the water, and the cattle and the people interacting with each other, conditioning the movements of each other as do the parts of a machine? Or perhaps do we think of the Sudanese community as if it were a vast organism, conceiving the movements of cattle and people as if they were the respiration or circulation of a single living body? Later, when we come to think of the community as a system of moral norms, will the model of the machine or the organism serve us there, or will we then find ourselves thinking forms of thought that approximate quite other kinds of models of organized wholes known to our experience? Perhaps then we shall find ourselves conceiving the community in terms of values or basic assumptions about life and experience, and imagine these as arranged in a sort of hierarchy of propositions, not like a machine or an organism at all, but rather like a textbook on formal logic. Perhaps, in thinking about the way the people of a small settlement, long established on the land, look out upon the life of man in the cosmos they know, we shall find ourselves using words and thoughts that do not readily find acceptance in the natural sciences but rather are appropriate to drama or other forms of literary art. There may be models for conceiving the community that come to our minds from sources more artistic than scientific.

We shall be required, then, as we proceed, to accustom ourselves to thinking at two levels. First, we look at an Indian or African village or a peasant settlement, and we think about it. We think about it, as far as we are able, as a whole. We find what there is to say about all of it. And then we turn to the form of thought we have used in thinking about it so, and we think about this thought. The kinds of thinking about communities as wholes become the second and derivative subject matter of these chapters. This is an invitation to consider the mental apparatus for characterizing human societies.

II

... AN ECOLOGICAL SYSTEM

We are interested in the little community as a whole. Where does that whole begin? When do I understand a community as a whole? Do I see it as such only after I have lived and worked there for a long time?

Some things are seen as wholes at once, at first view. If I look for the first time at the Mona Lisa or at Picasso's painting "Guernica," I have in the first few moments of my vision an impression of one whole thing, not a sum of parts. The impression that is made on me, whatever be the content of that impression, is made by a something which at once I take into my comprehension in its entirety. At this first view, I am not aware of the balance of the design, or, in the case of Leonardo's painting, of the subtle harmonies of the painting of the face and of the background. The whole comes first.

Later, perhaps, in studying a painting I may see the parts and relationships among them. Out of this more analytic knowledge perhaps new wholes will suggest themselves to me. Perhaps the first impression will be much modified. My own first impression of "Guernica" was of discord and terror. Later I saw a balance of parts almost musical, and I saw compassion for humanity. Others probably see other things in that painting and later find other wholes.

The face of a living person is such an immediately apprehended whole. And, even more in the case of the painted work of art, does the holistic impression which the face first makes on me give way later to other impressions as I come to know the man or woman behind that face. The first impression, itself a whole of unanalyzed parts, gives way to understanding of the personality of my friend. This too is a whole: I can think of my friend as a personality and I call to mind the total impression. His unique character is one thing. Yet, reflecting, I can identify parts of this whole: he is a seclusive man, a man unusually sensitive, a man slow to form judgments, and so forth.

A village or an encampment of nomads also has its face, and the first view of a human settlement, if the habitations and other structures be at all visible, may be attended with some immediate attribution of significance to the settlement and its peoples. As I first saw the Mexican village of Tepoztlán, I was moved by its beauty. As I first saw Chan Kom, Yucatán—I think I recall rightly —my first impression was one of a certain raw bleakness, from the new-cut streets like scars upon the land, and from the wide and stony plaza, partly leveled and cleared of trees.

The first impressions of any human community are often clear and—at the moment—very convincing. The time to write a book about the national character of a people other than one's own is in the first weeks of the first acquaintance with them. Never again does one have so vivid and compelling an impression of them.

If one does not write that book it may be because a certain amount of scientific training and sense of responsibility prevent one. And one knows that in Sweden or in Yucatán one's first impressions give way to understanding based upon deeper knowledge of particular fact. After knowing the whole as one thing, intuitively, one begins to know particular things, critically, and, it seems, less surely. Then the student of a human community begins to put pieces of knowledge together to make new, larger organizations of understanding. Little by little he builds new forms of thought about at least parts of that community. He makes new wholes, understanding as he goes the ways in which parts are connected with other parts, and seeing, from time to time, new wholes or part-wholes. The intuitive apprehension of wholes does not cease; but now it is limited and controlled by particular knowledge subjected to testing and proof.

This common experience may be stated in more formal terms. We have before us a problem of the relations of intuited wholes, particular facts, and systems. An intuited whole appears in the immediate and unconsidered apprehension of the unique character of something recognized as complex but taken as one thing. A system, on the other hand, is another kind of a whole: it is an analyzed whole; the entities that compose it and their interrelationships are understood. It is such an arrangement of related parts as may be seen separated from other things about it. I see a community first as an intuited whole. I then begin to understand particular things about it. From connections now discovered among these parts I conceive of systems. We shall become interested here in considering the possibility that very much, perhaps all, of the life of a community may be conceived as just a few systems, possibly as one all-encompassing system. Can an intuited whole give way, as study proceeds, to one equally comprehensive analyzed system?

In moving to understand the systematic character of the life of a community the student cannot begin everywhere; he must begin at some point. What shall that point be? Commonly the beginning is made with the things immediately visible. Prominent are the houses, the tools, the work of the house and of the forest, the field or the byre. If we look at the published accounts of primitive or peasant life, we are likely to find descriptions of the work on and with the land in the first pages or chapters. It is safe to say that almost any student of any simple community probably attended early in the course of his work to just this subject matter: the land and the work upon and with it, the things taken to eat or otherwise to consume, and the material objects made. These things are visible, and understanding them is relatively easy.

This was my own case when I began to study the Maya Indian village of Chan Kom. I began where it happened to be convenient to begin. I went along with a man to the field he had cleared in the forest for the planting of his maize. I watched him cut poles and with them build a little altar in the field. I saw him mix ground maize with water and sprinkle it in the four directions, and then kneel in prayer. I watched him then move across the field punching holes in the shallow soil with a pointed stick and dropping a few grains of maize in each hole.

From this, I naturally followed forward the activities involved in the further development of the maize and the harvest. The corn sprouted. I saw the agriculturalist cut away the weeds. Later in the summer one could watch him bend over the ripening ears to protect them from destructive animals. When the ears are ripe, the men tear them from the stalk and carry them to the house, or else store them, stacked close together in granaries built out in the center of the maize field.

As I witnessed such things done, I talked to the people about the earlier agricultural preparations, made before I came to the village. My mind was thus led backward to the activities which preceded the planting: back to the burning of the fallen trees to make a clearing in which to plant maize; and back of that to the felling of the trees to make possible the burning and the planting. My mind could as well be said to move forward to the next felling of trees, the burning of the trees felled, and the next planting. For this is of course an annual cycle. It is repeated (almost) every year. Soon after the harvest is in, the Maya agriculturalist begins again to choose a spot in the forest where he may cut down the trees there to make new milpa, as he calls it.

While my attention was upon this series of activities, necessarily interconnected in the same invariable order, I was recognizing one particular system within the whole that is the life of Chan Kom. What is the nature of the order among the parts that make up this system of agricultural activities? Plainly, the parts are related to one another as links to a chain, or as means to an end, each means leading to the next means, and so on. Thinking of it as a chain, one sees that many links are connected with subsidiary related chains of means and ends. The system could be extended and complicated by adding the activities of marketing, or by attaching to the right link in the chain the activities which convert the maize into the food for the agriculturalist's family.

The course of my thoughts as I worked in Chan Kom did not, I suppose, follow only the simple lines of connection offered by the cycle of agricultural activities. As I worked I learned things other than those I have already mentioned, and as I learned, the organization of ideas about the life of the village changed. New systems presented themselves to me, and systems I had already apprehended became modified and complicated.

First, I began to discover complexities of the linked practical activities. Retaining my interest in the agricultural cycle, I began to discover that the cycle was compound. Most of these farmers had two kinds of fields: fields that had been cleared freshly that year by felling timber, and fields that were planted for a second or in some cases a third time, having been cleared in previous years. I discovered that the practical series of acts was not the same in one class of fields as it was in the other class of fields. At least two chain-like systems were going on simultaneously.

A second development of the organized systems in terms of which I strove to understand occurred as I became more attendant to features of the natural environment which were involved in these practical activities. In short, I changed the system in my mind to make it include features of the land itself. When it came to considering more carefully the choice of the site of the cornfield, I learned the differences in soils, the indications by way of the kinds of trees growing there and other signs on the land which would enable the agriculturalist to choose tracts which might be more fertile than others. I came to understand the hazards and uncertainties attendant upon the first coming of the rainfall, and how this uncertainty affected the choice of the day on which the felled trees for the new cornfield were to be burned.

In short, I began to see that the activities of the Indians were in part reflections of the regularities and irregularities of nature: of the invariably changing seasons and of the variable weather. I became more attentive to the land and to the heavens above. Gradually I came to see that these Indians dwelt in a very simple landscape in which a few features, some natural and some man-made, limited and expressed the activities of the community. I saw four of these principal features. One, the bush, the thorny, low forest covering all of the flat limestone shelf on which the people lived. Two, the natural wells, called cenotes, places at which the limestone has fallen away to leave deep dark holes down to the ground water; these cenotes provide all the water for the people; there are in this land no rivers, streams, or lakes. These two features, forest and cenote, are nature's provision. The cenote is a fresh, green punctuation in a dry monotony of thorny bush; only at cenotes may men make their settlements. Three and four of the major features of this land are man-made: the maize field or milpa, and the village itself. Man clears the forest to make the milpa; man goes to the cenote to build his house. One might almost state these relations as a proportion: the milpa is to the bush as the village is to the cenote.

In this consideration of these relationships a new form of thought for organizing particular facts into systems was beginning to grow in my mind. It would be possible to group much of the life of

Chan Kom around the prominent pattern of the land itself and man's making-over of that land. Such a system would not be chainlike; it would not take the form of a series of linked means to a particular end. It would take the form of a map. Around the bush, cenote, milpa, and village one would group the activities of the peoples and the ideas the people have of their land and of their activities upon it. Such a system would be a topography of the people's doings and ideas.

A third way of thinking about the practical activities of the people also presented itself to my mind at some stage in my work, for I find it expressed in the book about the community which I wrote with the help of Alfonso Villa Rojas, then the village school-teacher. This third kind of system arose out of the recognition that maize, the plant and its products, was of central interest and importance to the people of Chan Kom. When, later and after my first visits to the village, some Chan Kom people for the first time traveled to the swampy sea coast and gazed out upon the vast ocean, one of them remarked, "But how do people live here where there is no maize?" For to them maize is life itself. The maize provides most of their food. It is sold to provide goods bought from outside. And it is central to the religious ideas and practices. The pagan deities are protectors of the maize; the important ceremonies addressed to the rain-gods and the earth-gods are prayers for rain and for good harvest of maize, and the Virgin is addressed in prayer as "the protector of the young maize plant." The good man, the moral man, is he who grows maize and is reverent in doing so. A few men who support themselves in trade nevertheless grow maize, because not to do so is to cut one's self off from the community of good and pious men.

So I began to form another way of conceiving parts as related to one another in a system of activity and thought. This third system is neither chainlike nor maplike. It is radial: maize is a center and other things are grouped around it, connected to it in different ways, some by a series of useful activities, some by connections of symbolic significance. The mind goes out from maize to agriculture, from maize to social life, from maize to religion. Maize is always the center of things.

This third way of thinking about the productive activities makes them component parts of a system of conceptions and practices in which other parts, not productively practical at all but religious or moral or of a sort having to do with relations among men, are important. My mind was moved to conceive of such another form of thought as I came to understand that aspect of the life which was not merely practical work but had to do with faith and hope and the people's ideas as to the nature of the world around them. I came to see that the decision when to set fire to the trees felled to make new milpa is attended with much anxiety, for if the Indian sets fire to the trees too early they will not burn, being as yet not dried, but if he delays too long the first rains will fall and so wet the wood that he will have to let it stand for another year before trying again to make milpa there. I came to follow his efforts to decide when to burn the trees; I studied the ways of divination used by the shaman-priest; I learned what I could about the prayers offered by the agriculturalist for help from the supernaturals. And from this I went on to investigate the religious and cosmological ideas. Villa and I recorded the prayers used in the ceremonies, watched the ceremonies performed, and persuaded the shaman-priest to tell us something about the meaning of these prayers and ceremonies.

This direction of the investigation resulted in our recognition of the presence of general and comprehensive patterns of thought in the minds of these Indians. These offered themselves to my mind, my ethnographer's mind, as still another way in which to organize the parts into analyzed systems. It seemed that the activities of the people were obedient to a limited number of prevailing and influential general ideas about the nature of things. The investigator might then recognize a fourth kind of system. This fourth kind of system takes the form of variations upon a theme. I will merely illustrate this fourth kind of system with one example: the idea of pious contract.

I came to see that in a great many different and yet similar situations the Maya villager has the idea that whatever he takes from nature by his effort is loaned to him by the gods, and that it is his obligation to express his part in the sacred contract by returning to the gods some portion of what is loaned him. The successful hunter does not eat of the meat until he has left some part of it for the supernatural protectors of the deer. The agriculturalist does not cut down more trees than he needs for space to plant; if he leaves part of the forest cleared but not planted he has taken wrongly from the guardians of the bush. When he has his harvest, he does not eat the young maize until he has first offered the best ears to the deities of the maize. Indeed, he keeps a sort of running account with the gods; if he misses his payment one year, he is expected to pay double the next.

Such an idea provides a new kind of organizing principle. The idea becomes the basis for an analyzed system that is not chainlike and that is not maplike. It is a system depending from a categoric idea that finds expression in many activities and in several spheres of life.

In suggesting some of the different kinds of analyzed systems that appear in the course of coming to understand the life of a little community, I do not ask that a choice be made from among them. I want only to suggest some of the dimensions of the problem of characterizing a community more or less as a whole. As we have brought forward first one system and then another, we add to the totality that we are seeking to understand more analytically than at first view of it. The systems, so far as here suggested, do not connect themselves one to another by any rule or principle that I can see. And they crosscut or overlap one another: things seen in one systematic context are later seen again in another.

I do not pursue further the problem of relating these systems to one another and the very difficult problem of representing the whole community by an ordering of part-systems. Instead I return to the productive work of the little community and the relations of that work to the land in which the community is established. Let us see, if we can, what parts of the total life of the community can be described by beginning with the productive activities, or with the regularities that are both of nature and of man's life.

Our attention so far has been exclusively on the Yucatecan village of Chan Kom. Let us introduce into our thinking some materials from another community. I turn to the interrelations of man and nature described for the Nuer of the Upper Nile by Professor Evans-Pritchard. Here the central place in the system of activities and ideas is taken by the cattle. Evans-Pritchard writes:

It has been remarked that the Nuer might be called parasites of the cow, but it might be said with equal force that the cow is the parasite of the Nuer, whose lives are spent in ensuring its welfare. They build byres, kindle fires, and clean kraals for its comfort; move from villages to camps, and from camp to camp, and from camps back to villages, for its health; defy wild beasts for its protection; and fashion ornaments for its adornment. It lives its gentle, sluggish life thanks to the Nuer's devotion. In truth the relationship is symbiotic; cattle and men sustain life by their reciprocal services to one another. In this intimate symbiotic relationship men and beasts form a single community of the closest kind.[1]

This writer goes on to describe a typical day spent with the cattle by these people, the watching them, the driving them to water, the milking them, the cleaning them of ticks. He tells how they use cattle urine to wash in, how they drink milk and blood, sleep on the cattle hides, and burn dung for their fires. Every man knows all the personal qualities of each cow and the points of its grandparents. Some can tell the points of their cow's ancestors back five generations. Children's games and songs are preoccupied with the cattle. The poetry centers around the cattle. Names of boys and girls are drawn from cattle and their qualities. Raids on cattle are the almost sole cause of warfare. It is not too much to say that here cow and man have permeated each other; the Nuer view of the shape of the world, his values, his daily habits, are shaped by cattle and are expressed in cattle.

Let us use these two cases, the agricultural peasants of Yucatán and the cattle-raising Sudanese, to help us in carrying forward some of the distinctions already indicated. Let us now give names to two of the kinds of systems we have so far spoken of. Both of these systems start from the same beginning, with the tools and techniques of productive work.

One system to be recognized is the subsistence system. This is constituted of the acts and ideas that gain the people their livelihood. It is concerned with all of the functions of production. In the case of the Maya, it would include not only the all important maize and its production but also cattle. The Maya too have cattle, but their cattle are raised chiefly to make a show of wealth and have very little part in the religious ideas or in social organization. Indeed, if we are to describe the subsistence system of the Maya we should have somehow to show the relative separateness of the system of maize agriculture, for maize is central and religious; together with bee-keeping it is closely connected with religious and cosmological ideas. But animal industry, the raising of European fowl, the sale of eggs outside the community, are commercial and not religious. Thus the Maya subsistence system is in two parts, so to speak, one sacred and the other profane. The sacred part is powerfully unified by the religious and cosmological ideas which permeate it. The Nuer subsistence system, on the other hand, is one system in that these Sudanese have practically no commerce and in that the activities of animal industry, agriculture, and fishing form one whole of work. In contrast, subsistence activities of the Nuer are not shown in this book from which I quote to have such important religious ideas as those which unify maize and bee-keeping among the Maya.

But chiefly here are to be distinguished the subsistence system just indicated and the ecological system. Let us say that we mean by the ecological system the interrelationships of man and nature, the concurrent regularities, natural and artificial. This system starts from the viewpoint: man-nature. It is much more than the subsistence system. The interest the Maya have in the maize goes far beyond its interest to them as a means of livelihood and nourishment. Maize is involved, as I have already suggested, in their prayers, in their conception of manhood, even in their notions of political responsibility. Many of the thoughts they have about nature have no direct connection with their subsistence activities. Certain birds, it is true, are related to agriculture: they are believed to protect the maize by frightening away animals, or to encourage the maize to grow tall by singing to it. But certain elements in nature have no connection with maize. The Milky Way is a mysterious road across the heavens. The forest is important in a variety of ways because it is terrible, because man dares not go into it after dark alone. Among the cardinal directions the east is important without necessary reference to livelihood or subsistence; all holy things lie in the east and all things of mystery, because Jerusalem is there, and the rain gods are there. In the eastern forest are beasts that one has seen in dreams or that one's grandfather has seen.

If everything that the Maya thought or felt about parts of nature were put together, we should have a system much more comprehensive than the subsistence system and connected with it at some points but not at others. The same statement could no doubt be made for the Nuer. I mention the mosquitoes which during certain periods of the year are so ferocious that the Nuer must sleep in huts filled with smoke from fires of dung. This necessity only in an indirect way, like sickness, affects subsistence. Yet, as a part of the ecological system, it is certainly of great importance.

We have then at least two possible systems which overlap each other, interrelate with each other. The ecological system is larger than the productive system and has a different organizing principle, man-nature rather than productivity.

I pass now to another aspect of the problem of the definition and recognition of the system of thought which we shall employ as our guide in understanding as much of this whole of the little community as we can, provided we begin with the productive activities. I call attention now to the fact that the ecological system is not merely a system described as an interrelationship of statically conceived parts but is also a dynamic system in which occur regular transformations of its organization. We can become attendant to the regularities of the transformation of the system.

Consider again the Nuer. The important fact of nature in that part of the Sudan is the annual rainfall cycle. Alternately, floods drive the Nuer to high ground; alternately; annual droughts force them to seek water where it still remains in the shrinking pools and lakes. The land is at first a network of marshes and drowned rivers, and then it becomes an almost grassless savannah. In May, when the rains commence, older people leave the temporary camps by lakes and rivers for the more permanent villages built on high ground. They prepare ground for sowing. In June, the young people bring the cattle to the villages, and slowly camp life changes to village life. They must live in villages for protection against floods and mosquitoes, and plant and reap the millet needed to supplement the prevailing diet of milk. In late November or early December, the land dries out. Then the youths and girls take the cattle from the villages to the camps near the pools where range grasses have been fired to clear the ground. The cattle may be moved from camp to camp until January or February, when they settle in the final camp near some body of almost permanent water. In the period of village life, when the floods are over the land, fish are speared; and some wild vegetable foods are collected.

Thus the Nuer annual cycle is largely a repetition of the same activities with regard to the cattle. The activities are modified as rain and drought succeed each other, but milk and meat are obtainable throughout the year. The fishing and the planting are of much less importance. So the year has no single time of climax.

But the annual cycle of the Maya has a climax: the harvest. This climax depends on the rains and the favor of the gods. Anxieties and prayers are directed forward to this climax. Years are remembered, in their sequence, by the kind of harvest obtained, abundant or scarce, bringing happy security or threat of famine. The Maya annual cycle is like a play in which men and gods and maize are the actors; the play has a prologue, the felling and burning with a period of first suspense at the time of burning the felled bush; it has a development, the growing of maize, and a denouement, the harvest, good or bad. Here ecological time, as Evans-Pritchard calls it, has a quality like that of a dramatic literary composition. Every year the community lives that play, but its last act in one year may be different from the last act in the next.

I now call attention to a second kind of dynamic element in the ecological system of the Maya. This is the ecological control on the size of the little community. Another ecological process, operating over periods of years, limits the size to which any of these Maya bush settlements may grow. A first settlement is made at a cenote near fertile lands. As the population of the settlement increases, and as the lands near at hand are converted to milpa and again turned back to bush for seven or more years when they must lie fallow, the villagers are required to go farther and farther from the village to find lands on which to plant corn. When they have found places to plant that are remote, and near cenotes, they spend more and more of their time at these clusters of distant milpas, returning from time to time to their village. At last they come to think of the milpa settlement as their home and break off connections with the old village. In this way the growth of the old village is checked. The process is like the swarming of bees; it has been called "hiving off." But the causes of separation and of colonization are also to be found in the struggles of familial groups, of leader with leader, within the community, and in the issues and policies of the day. The dissatisfactions of individuals with either the social structure or the social policy also cause people to emigrate, sometimes to settle in another established village, sometimes to found new villages in the bush. If we were to concentrate our attention upon the cyclical process of "hiving off" in the Maya settlement, we should have to be attendant to both the ecological factors in the pure sense and the societal or structural factors also. An interplay of ecological factors and factors arising out of the strains within social structure is involved in this process, probably generic, of "hiving off," as it occurs in many little communities.

The concept of ecological system takes into account much of the whole community when that community is one that is closely dependent upon the land and the seasons. Primitive communities exist in such dependence; and in primitive communities we find it possible to describe concurrent regularities of man and nature in such a way as to include much of the life of the people and to describe the unique character of that people.[2] Evans-Pritchard succeeds in doing so for the Nuer. But as communities become more complex and more interdependent with other and distant communities it is less possible to use the concept of ecological system, as used by Evans-Pritchard, to describe and characterize the community holistically. It would have been difficult for James West to describe Plainville, U.S.A., as such an ecological system, because its people are only partly dependent on the natural environment around them, and about half of the people born in Plainville leave the village to go to towns or cities for employment or adventure. And for the study of urban communities, the ecological system is quite inadequate, so that the conception becomes there a very different one in the human ecology of American sociology: it becomes a study of the spatial and temporal orders of settlement and of institutions without much reference to animals, plants, or the weather.[3]

The conception of ecological system was first developed in the study of animals and plants. Animals and plants are affected by other animals and plants and by inorganic nature. Even where the activities of men enter into the ecological system of plants and animals, these activities, like the introduction of rabbits into Australia, do not require the animal ecologist to take into account the motives and sentiments with which the men introduced the rabbits, or lived to regret that they had done so. The ecological system of the naturalist is a system of organisms in a natural environment, not a mental environment.

But the environment of men is not only artifactual; it is mental. In towns and cities men build their environments into their very houses and streets so that the land and the weather are pushed outside of the system. And in every community, primitive or civilized, what most importantly surrounds and influences the people are the traditions, sentiments, norms, and aspirations that make up the common mental life. The world in which plants and rabbits live is made up of more or less adaptive responses to the natural features immediately around the rabbits and the plants. The world of men is made up in first place of ideas and ideals. If one studies the rise of urban communities out of more primitive communities, it is the change in the mental life, in norms and in aspirations, in personal character, too, that becomes the most significant aspect of the transformation.

Because the human environment is in large part mental, the possibilities of using holistically the concept of ecological system are greatly limited even in the more primitive communities. The possibilities and the limitations are both illustrated by Evans-Pritchard's excellent employment of the conception in his book about the Nuer. He points out that because the natural environment in that part of the Sudan provides for little specialization of product and as the Nuer produce little or no excess of food, there is little trade and so the people of village and camp "are drawn together, in a moral sense." He shows us that the land and water help to determine how huts are built near one another, how the byres of the cattle are placed, and how the people camp or make villages where ridges and bodies of water make it necessary; from this it follows that "the simple [nuclear] family is attached to the hut, the household to the hamlet, the village community to its ridge, and village communities are linked together by paths." "Herds of cattle are nuclei around which kinship groups are clustered, and the relationships between their members operate through cattle and are expressed in terms of cattle."

Commenting on this, we can surely admit that the ecology affects the social groupings of the Nuer. But it does not seem possible to connect with the ecology the complex arrangement of nuclear families, lineages, and wider social groups which make up the social structure of Nuer society. There is a sort of writing on the land of the vague outlines of a social structure; the content cannot be told from nature, nor connected with it in any well-defined relations of interdependence. There is a connection with the land in that it allows the Nuer to build hut, byre, and village, and each of these artifacts holds together a group of people who are a distinguishable unit of the society. That is all.

Apparent, and yet less close, is the connection between the ecological system and the values and character of the people. Evans-Pritchard says that the occasional scarcity of food and the narrow margin of sufficiency at all times is the cause of such an interdependence among members of the smaller local groups that there results in turn an ideal and practice of sharing food with one another. "Theirs is a habit of share and share alike." Because of an ecologically determined scarcity of food and dependence upon one another, Evans-Pritchard finds the Nuer character to include fortitude in the face of hardship and loyalty and generosity to kinsmen.

It is true that we can see the harmony between the natural environment of the Nuer and these traits of character. It does not, however, seem possible to predict the character of the Nuer from their natural circumstances. How much of a change in the natural circumstances would produce a change in the character? In Holmberg's account of the Siriono of the Bolivian forest we read of a people who live under conditions of occasional imminent want: these hunting Indians have a much more precarious food supply than do the Nuer. The Siriono hunters and food-collectors may eat well for three days and may be without food for as long. In this situation a character almost diametrically opposed to that reported for the Nuer is described for the Siriono. The Siriono are anything but generous. The members of the band go to great lengths to conceal, even from kinsmen, the food they collect. And demands for food give rise to much quarreling, suspicion, and hatred.

Human mental life has a structure of its own. It is difficult to describe it in terms of its connections with the land and the rain and the trees. The things that men think and feel are only partly connected with adaptation for survival. The land and the sky enter importantly into their thinking in ways that are not immediately adaptive. In part they are constructs independent of the forms of nature. The conceptions that the Maya have as to a four-cornered universe are discoverable not by looking at the world around them to find corners in it—for of course there are none—but by listening to the talk of the Maya and the prayers of their priests. The view of the Maya that a younger brother should be respectful and obedient to an older brother may be exhibited in the conduct of the two when working together in the milpa, but it is in no other wise connected with natural phenomena.

As the mind of the investigator of a community turns from the villager as one of a number of organisms in a natural environment to the villager as the recipient and creator of a changing organization of ideas and sentiments, the need appears for concepts to describe the little community which are not so exterior to that villager's mind as is the concept of ecological system. If we describe a community as an ecological system we describe it not as the members of that community themselves think of it. They are ignorant of a science of ecology. If what we want most to understand is their own view of things, we need concepts that will describe the inside view, as much of it as we can come to share. Later in these chapters we shall look into the possibility of developing such concepts.

III

... SOCIAL STRUCTURE

He who seeks a form of thought for describing much or all of a little community may center his attention not on the relationships of man to nature, but on the relationships of man to man. In any long-standing community the people who make it up are, of course, sorted out into kinds, and the connections each has with each of many other people are kinds too; fathers are a kind, a class, and paternal attitudes toward sons, or specifically toward elder sons, may be a class persistent in that society and susceptible of description. Further, we may find that these kinds of people and their kinds of relationships to others have orderly and coherent connections with one another. Now we are conceiving a system that may at points connect with the ecological system but that is different from it.

Among phrases used for this second variety of a more or less comprehensive system, "social structure" is one of the most used, and we will employ it now. The British anthropologists have brilliantly studied and described particular communities, especially those of native Africans, in terms of social structure. We will take instruction from them. But as they do not all use the phrase in quite the same sense—indeed, they are developing not one but several though related forms of thought for characterizing and analyzing small communities—we shall go forward more safely if we follow, for a time, the guidance of some one of these men. We shall certainly then receive all the advantage that could come to us from a fuller attention to the subtle and far-developed analyses of societies that have been achieved by men whose work can find little or no place in the elementary examination of social structure attempted in the few pages of this chapter. Social structure is a widespread, flourishing, and ramifying branch of the tree of community studies.

Professor Raymond Firth is one of those interested in kinds of people and their kinds of relationships to each other. He writes of "social alignment," "the ordering of the personnel component of the community."[1] And Firth limits our attention, at least at first, when he distinguishes, within social alignment, something more special to be called social structure. Social structure is that much of the social alignment, so much of the social relations, "as seems to be of critical importance for the behavior of members of the society, so that if such relations were not in operation, the society could not be said to exist in that form."[2] As example, Firth mentions the change in social structure that occurred in England when the common field system changed to private inclosure: relations among various social classes as to the land gave way to relations between laborers and employers and with local authorities. The social structure of England changed; it was no longer in form the same society. Firth adds, interestingly to us, "The ideals of many people were still much as before, and even some of their earlier expectations lingered on."[3]

With this much guidance, I will begin to imagine myself describing the Yucatecan village of Chan Kom as social structure. The reader may join me in looking at so much of the ordering of the personnel component of Chan Kom as seems to us to be so important as to make Chan Kom what it is. The elements of social relationship we are to recognize in our Maya village, Firth says, "must be more than of purely momentary significance—some factor of constancy or continuity must be involved in them."[4]

It may not be at once clear to us how we are to discover this quality of constancy or continuity. Must we reach back into the history of this Maya village to make sure that the elements of social relationship we choose to report were there many years ago? At any rate, we may proceed with at least two guides to use: We shall not include relationships that show themselves to us as of momentary significance. A brief friendship between this man and that is not to be reported, but if we find that friendships in general, with some characteristic content of accepted relationship as between all pairs of friends, are present in the village, we will report the generic characteristics of such relationships of friendship in our account of social structure. Perhaps the fact, if we do find it to be a fact, that older people as well as younger expect friendships to be formed may help us to see what elements of social structure are persistent. Probably we shall be able to apply also the test of importance, and imagine the consequences for Chan Kom if this or that social relationship were removed or changed. Thus we might assert with assurance that if the complex of relationships between husband and wife, and between each of these and sons and daughters, were entirely removed from Chan Kom it would be a very different kind of society; and so surely these relationships that constitute the nuclear family are important enough to be included. On the other hand, we might hesitate about including the relationship between that specialist, recognized in Chan Kom, who sets occasional broken bones, and his patients. We might exclude that relationship on the ground that to remove just that element in the assignment of personnel would not significantly alter the form of the society.

So far we have thought of the elements of social structure as if they existed independently of one another. But our mentor in this subject is clear in emphasizing that a social structure is a system. Firth says that we are to be concerned "with the ordered relations of parts to a whole, with the arrangement in which the elements of the social life are linked together."[5] These relations must be regarded as built up one upon another. "They are a series of varying orders of complexity," writes Firth. So we will describe the social structure of Chan Kom as the critically important and lasting social relations. We will think of the people of Chan Kom as personnel, as performers of functions and occupiers of roles, and consider the systematic interconnections of the enduring and really important traditional assignments of these functions and roles among that personnel.

As I now go forward in making this attempt I encounter difficulties and doubts. In trying to solve the difficulties and answer the doubts I may distort the concept of social structure as Professor Firth understands it. Let us hope he or some other will one day set me right. But it is possible that the difficulties and doubts come about because Chan Kom is not the same kind of community which Firth studied when he studied Tikopia. Maybe the concept of social structure undergoes a change as one employs it first to describe an isolated primitive community and then to describe a village of peasants in a modern state.

I do not know whether my task is simplified or made harder by the fact that Chan Kom is without many of the recognized forms of social groups that occur in many societies studied by anthropologists. There are no social classes which are named or otherwise identified by the people. There are no age-sets and no societies, secret or without secrets. We shall find it barely possible to recognize any of these bodies called in sociology "voluntary associations." There are no local, spatially defined subdivisions of the village which either the villager or the observer would find to be important.

At this point I may perhaps usefully introduce, if only at once to lay aside, one of the alternative meanings or emphases of meaning for "social structure" which British anthropologists have employed. As I want later to make other reference to the extraordinarily subtle and deeply considered studies of the African Tallensi by Professor Meyer Fortes, I here refer to the fact that in some contexts Professor Fortes, in discussing social structure, puts particular stress on the corporate groups of the society.

What are the corporate groups? They are those groups which form the never dying legal personalities of the total society. A lineage is such a group. I suppose that medieval guilds were corporate groups. Looked at from the outside, a corporate group is one of a number of equivalent groups making up the whole. You see it there generation after generation as people come into it and die or otherwise disappear out of it. For the man inside it the corporate group is that from which he gets political and legal status. It is defined, therefore, partly in terms of the permanence and clarity of its forms and partly in terms of its particular role in assigning rights and obligations to men and women.

Fortes and Evans-Pritchard have developed this conception in African societies where the principal corporate group is in very many cases the lineage, a unilinear descent group. The conception has been carried into other African societies where there are no lineages, and there Fortes finds the social structure in a system of politico-legal statuses attached to *titles*, traditional name-positions carrying authority and supported by ritual sanctions. In these bilateral societies social structure is something different from what it is in the societies with lineages.

The form of thought which Professor Fortes employs in describing a primitive society with lineages may be understood from his two remarkable books on the Tallensi.[6] He sees an arrangement of two kinds of parts. The first is made up of the lineage, the principal corporate groups. This is a permanent framework of the society. He calls it the "warp" of the social fabric. The lineages remain as people come and go. They provide a person with his political, jural, and ritual status. They keep going aspects of the society which are more emphatically collective or communal than personal or individual.[7]

Against this background, this stable structure, this warp, he sees the organized domestic life. This consists of kinship in the narrower sense, in the context of a man's relationship to this kinsman or to that. The relationships within the domestic group serve different, more intimate, and more basic necessities than do the lineages. It is in domestic relationships that the reproductive and primary economic needs are met.

The two elements of the whole system differ in that in the case of the lineages the entities of the system are the corporate groups themselves. In the domestic organization the point of departure is someone in a family and his relations with others. These keep changing as people grow up and die. Fortes thinks of these two components as a convenient analytic separation corresponding to reality. The whole system is conceived as an arrangement of parts in functional connection with one another. When he does not use the figure of warp and woof, he compares the two components to the blood and tissues of an animal organism; they are, he says, "interpenetrating media."[8]

In Chan Kom I do not find such a persisting warp of corporate groups into which the varying domestic and other ephemeral or occasional groups and relationships might weave themselves as varicolored weft. I should find it hard to designate the permanent framework of Chan Kom society. Perhaps the bilateral kinship groups, indefinite as they are, might be so regarded; I am not yet able so to regard them.

I leave this suggestion from Fortes and return to the lasting and important assignments of personnel in Chan Kom as indicated by Firth. It is of course true that without formal groupings, corporate or not, the people of Chan Kom are by custom assigned to this activity or that, this role or that, and true that these assignments form something of a system: one assignment is consistent with and connected with others. The British students usually begin their description of social structure with the assignments of personnel based on kinship. These are easy to see in Chan Kom.

There are kinship groups. A villager finds himself a member of a nuclear family: he is a child of parents, or a husband or wife in such a small family; each such family, as with us, is something of a unit. In a few cases, these families are inclosed within what some American anthropologists call patrilinear extended domestic families: married sons and their wives live in the same household and to some extent under the authority of the parents of the younger men. Furthermore, the native knows himself to be a member of bilateral kindred groups; his remoter relatives are in some degree interested in and responsible for him, and he to them. Here we are compelled to see a vagueness in the social structure. There is no certain degree of relationship at which the sense of membership in a kindred ends. It depends on what relatives are known to you, on who they are, and on where they are. If your father's first cousin in the patrilinear line is right there in the village he may be part of the native's kindred as he thinks of it. A man's father's relatives are a little closer to him than are his mother's relatives, but he recognizes the latter also.

Besides looking at these kinship groupings as part of the social structure of Chan Kom, we can look at the customary qualities of the relationships between any two kinds of relatives by kinship. As is done in the study of primitive tribal societies, in my first book about Chan Kom I attempted to describe how a husband and wife are expected to behave toward each other, and made similar descriptions for the relations of older brother and younger brother. There are other relationships which might be described, as those between remote collateral relatives, between father and son, mother and daughter, and uncles and aunts and nieces and nephews. The father's brother in Chan Kom is closer to one, more important to one, than is the mother's brother.

These are all relationships based on descent or on marriage. In addition to these, the villagers recognize important relationships arising out of the performance of the rituals attending three occurrences in the life of the individual: baptism; the first time a baby is placed astride the hip of an older person instead of being carried in the arms; and marriage. Each of these three rituals, baptism, *hetz-mek*, and marriage, is sponsored by one older person or by a married couple friendly with the parents of the individual for whom the rituals are performed, and these older persons become ritual kinsmen, godparents we would say, of that individual.

The three kinds of kinship relationship in this village—consanguineal, affinal, and ritual—form a recognizable system. The relationships interlock; for example, the relation of the father's brother to his brother's child is connected by rights and obligations which are part of that large system of thoughts and actions which define the relations of a father to his child; the father's brother is, in emergency, a secondary father, as the godfather is a supplementary father, to be turned to in certain circumstances even when the father is living. Furthermore these kinship relationships are obedient to certain pervasive principles that give a coherence to the whole. There is the principle of bilaterality: one recognizes one's father's kinsmen and also the kin of one's mother, but the latter in lesser degree. There is the principle that young people are subordinate to older people. A younger brother should show deference to his older brother. Here we have that fourth kind of system to which reference was made in the second chapter: a system made up of a dominating idea manifest in particular relationships and situations, a system with a form comparable to a theme with variations or a logical principle with correlates.

To these relationships of kinship it would be possible to add the relationships between the various kinds of specialists and their customers or clients or followers. Here we would describe the officeholder and his constituency, the artisan and his customer-client, the shaman-priest and the congregations or individuals that he serves. The relationships between the functionary who recites prayers in connection with Catholic novenas (which are not fully Catholic novenas!) are part of the social structure; and the relationships between a very important functionary, the pagan priest called *h-men*, the man performing the rituals for the supernaturals of the sky and the forest, and the villagers as a whole or organized in special groups, are, I suppose, parts of the social structure.

As I go on to think about the social structure of Chan Kom, I come now to aspects of the relationships which I am not so sure would be included within social structure were Professor Firth actually present to direct this endeavor. A question occurs as to whether the traditional assignment of personnel as between men and women is to be regarded as a part of the social structure. I do not recall seeing these relationships between men and men and women and women so included, but perhaps they might reasonably be taken into account. In Chan Kom, as in every community, men have functions and roles appropriate to their sex, and so do women. Men are by tradition assigned to certain social positions, as are women, and the separations and aggregations according to sex are conspicuous in the village. Men carry on all agricultural labor except that the women help a little in the harvest, while women do the gardening and men the hunting. I may add, as elements of the assignment of the personnel according to sex more special to Chan Kom, the fact that there bee-keeping is entirely in the hands of men—no woman would touch it—and the fact that only men make baskets while both sexes make candles. Here too it is possible to recognize the operation of certain major implicit principles. In all sorts of activities that have to do with public affairs—politics, government, and the principal religious ceremonies affecting all the people at once—the leadership is always by men. Women lead only in domestic activities in which small groups or neighborhoods are involved. The second implicit principle provides that in pagan rituals, whether communal or domestic, the leadership is by men, women having little part in the larger ceremonies of this kind; those of Christian origin, while led by men if public, are led by women if minor and women take important parts. Men are the shaman-priests, the marriage-negotiators, and the principal, but not the only, reciters of Catholic prayer.

It is hardly possible to think of men and women in Chan Kom as two corporate groups. A man does not think of himself as a member of an organized body of men that goes down through the ages like a clan or a guild. But it does seem to me reasonable to include the assignment of roles and functions, the traditional associations of men with men and women with women, as part of the social structure.

Another kind of doubt or difficulty arises from the fact that there are in Chan Kom groupings of people, kinds of social relationships, which are not constantly present but appear only at certain times. There are the groups brought together for ceremonies, pagan or Christian. Some of these ceremonies are annual and fixed by the calendar, others are performed at irregular occasions as the people feel a need. The personnel of these groups is always changing, but the roles and functions remain for the most part the same as sometimes the same individuals and then different ones fill the roles and perform the functions. We might speak of the latent aspect of social structure as contrasted with the constant or patent aspect. The work-groups and the assignment of men to serve as guards or messengers in an organization for occasional labor or to meet a public emergency might also illustrate this latent social structure.

From such occasional but traditional groupings the mind is carried to the groupings of people that are of brief duration and that are not prominently in the awareness and anticipations of the people. Shall we include the groups of children who form brief habits of playing together, the cliques of older people, and friendships, brief or long-enduring? Recalling Professor Firth's instruction that social structure consists of the lasting social relations of such importance that to remove them would bring it about that the society could not be said to exist in that form, I decide to exclude the play groups, cliques, and occasional friendships. They are part of the more ephemeral assignment of the personnel component of the society, but they are not part of the social structure.

But what of factions? In the life of Chan Kom, as I knew it over a period of about twenty years, factions played so important a part that it is almost if not quite true to say that had there been no factions the form of the society would have been notably different. For all those years there were recognizable in Chan Kom two groups of related families that were silent rivals or open contestants for authority and leadership. In the second book I wrote about Chan Kom in 1948, there appears some account of these factions, especially of the struggle between them to decide whether Chan Kom should carry on, in addition to its pagan religion, the traditional Catholic Christianity or the new Protestant cult. The factions of Chan Kom for at least a generation were a major assignment of personnel in connection with principal activities and decisions, political, social, religious. It may be that the factions in Chan Kom have been there so long that characteristic expectations have arisen with regard to them so that men live in terms of these groupings much as they live in terms of the nuclear family and the bilateral kindred.[9]

On the other hand, I do not think that the people of Chan Kom, asked to describe their social institutions, would have included an account of the factions. The villagers did not see factions in every community like their own around them. They did not think of factions as something that ought to be there, as no doubt they thought that families and kinship relationships ought to be there. This fact leads us into consideration of a question which I shall take up in the next pages: the question whether the social structure exists necessarily in expectations of the people as to what ought to be and to be done.

Before coming to that question I set aside the problem of the factions in Chan Kom with the help of another concept advanced by Firth: social organization.[10] For him, social organization is the way things get done over time in the community. It is the arrangement of elements for getting things done in particular action. The social structure is that important system of elements which lasts and which everybody takes account of. As Firth says that the people of the community may take advantage of existing structural principles in accomplishing social organization, so may we now say that the people making up a faction took advantage of the kin ties of social structure to accomplish political ends. But if this is what we say, then it seems to me that a very great deal of what we want to know about a little community is not represented in a description of the social structure alone. Then we need also to describe the forms and dimensions of what Firth calls social organization: we need to study aspiration and policy, both of the individual and of social groups composing the community, whether they be structural or more temporary.

Up to this point, in discussing problems of social structure in Chan Kom, I have neglected certain elements in the community of a kind that in isolated primitive communities are not there to make trouble for the student of social structure, but which are important in Chan Kom because Chan Kom has a long-established position as part of a modern national state. What is the relevance for our description of the social structure of the village of the fact that there are present in it institutions that originated outside of the community, that have been imported into it, and that have various degrees of loose or firm establishment in the life of the community? One of these is the school. The people of Chan Kom heard about schools, decided they must be a good thing, and got the Mexican government to provide them with a school and a teacher. The teacher (who was also my associate in our study) was partly inside the life of the community and partly outside: he developed a special and "untraditional" role of his own. There was a group called the *Liga*, an association of adult men organized by leaders from the town or city as a branch of the dominant political party of the state. The Indians conceived this as a sort of painful necessity; they had to have a *Liga* because modern people had *Ligas*, but its activities remained obscure to them. There was also an organization of the men of the village as agriculturalists; this group became the formal recipient of the communal lands when the national government got around to performing the legal rituals of that grant. And connected with these and other such groupings from outside there were new offices and officers; later the village came to have a registrar of vital statistics and a postmaster. Furthermore, for long periods of residence the village was honored or oppressed by the presence of school inspectors, land surveyors, rural community organizers, religious missionaries, and anthropologists.

It is all right to describe a very isolated primitive community solely in terms of what one finds within it, in terms of its indigenous institutions and its own internal relationships only. But very many small communities are related in important ways with communities and institutions outside of them. In the eighth chapter I will deal directly with this problem. Now I think of the institutions and offices brought into Chan Kom from outside in connection with our topic of social structure, and I ask: In describing the social structure what shall we do with these groups, relationships, and offices? If we ignore them, we do a serious violence to the reality. One possibility is to regard these newer assignments of personnel and groupings of relationships not as part of the social structure—because they are not fully traditional—but as elements in the social organization on a level with the weather, historical accident, the personalities of leaders and followers, and the interests and motives of individuals, entering into the way things actually get done. They are elements of the social life which the people come to understand and which, in conjunction with the traditional social structure, they use or adapt themselves to as they go through life.

On the other hand it is apparent that some of these institutions, relationships, and offices are entering and becoming closely bound up with the more traditional social structure. We might then regard them as parts of the growing edge of social structure, the cambium of the tree of social life. They foreshadow a social structure not yet in full being. These new groups and institutions are in their basis of relationship and in their origins different from the kinship and neighborhood groupings of the older settlement. The school might be seen as an enacted institution, the farmer's organization a more or less voluntary interest group, and the political party an organization formed under more compulsion. But the more important facts about these groupings are that at the time of the study they were only in part integrated with the pre-existing social structure, and that they were at that time firmly integrated with the structure of the national state. They were outliers of a much larger social system, penetrating into the local structure of Chan Kom.

To deal with these aspects of social structure, we might perhaps design a model of the traditional social structure of the old days. We could then in turn project the transformations we are witnessing in the coming of the school, the political party, and the farmer's co-operative so as to conceive the social structure that is coming about. In this future social structure school, party, and co-operative would be part of the expectancies of every growing child. With this second model to compare with the model of the older society, we might accomplish a description of Chan Kom, not simply as a static social structure, but as a social structure in intelligible transition. To this possibility I return in the eighth and ninth chapters.

Now I come back to the question that arose in connection with the discussion of factions when I set it down that the villagers presumably do not think of factions as something that ought to be there. Because they do not, doubt arises as to whether factions are part of the social structure. We are thus reminded that in any community people live partly in terms of what they think ought to be and partly in terms of what actually is. The two are not always in close correspondence, and in certain societies (as witness the Kinsey report) the two things may be far apart. Indeed, I suggest that there is at least one other dimension to the social life: the expectations of what one is likely actually to encounter in life. Thus, I think that it is desirable that men and women be treated with perfect justice; I desire that I myself receive justice; I realistically expect to get something a little less; and for all I know I shall some day experience grave injustice. Personal and social life is all of these things.

Professor Firth tells us that we are to include in the kinship structure both the ideals and expectations that people have, and also the actual forms that such relationships tend in fact to have. We need this advice in Chan Kom, for we find a notable discrepancy in Chan Kom between that picture of social structure which was given me by a conservative villager, a man advanced in years and with a feeling for the decencies and proprieties of life, and the actual facts in Chan Kom as I came to find them—and of course as he all along knew them to be. When I asked him about marriage and the family in Chan Kom, he tended to think about marriage and the family as he would like them to be. Of course I found out about as many particular families and marriages as I could, so as to come to understand the discrepancy between ideal and fact. In the first book about Chan Kom there appears an account of a theoretical kinship structure in which the nuclear family of husband, wife, and children exists within and partly subordinate to the man's parents, the wife's parents, and in further diminishing degree, the godparents. In this ideal system marriage is arranged by parents, with the active participation and advice of other elder kinsmen, there is a prolonged formality of petitioning for the girl, an elaborate betrothal ceremony, a complex and grave marriage ritual involving many relatives, and a period of service by the bridegroom in the house of his bride's parents before they set up their own household within or close beside that of the groom's parents. Similar ideal forms exist for baptism and for many aspects of familial life. In fact, this ideal structure is very imperfectly realized in the village. Many nuclear families are actually quite independent of older people. Godparental relationships do not result in the obedience and the responsibility that they are supposed to involve. Patrilocal residence is practiced in only a minority of cases, and some marriages—quite contrary to the ideal—are polygynous. And the rituals of baptism and marriage were at best approximated in the actual ceremonies that occurred when I was there. Sometimes the approximation was close; sometimes it was hardly realized at all.

Apparently we are now moved to consider social structure not only as a system of relationships, of existing kinds of ties between people and doings done by kinds of people, but also as a system of norms and expectancies. Social structure can be seen as an ethical system. It is an orderly arrangement of conceptions as to what good conduct is. So conceived, social structure is an important part or aspect—but I do not think it is all—of that conception which we shall meet in a later chapter and which I shall there call "ethos," or value system. But it is also necessary to recognize that related to and yet separable from this system of moral norms are the expectations of the people as to the realization of these norms. In so far as we now think of social structure not so much as knots—people—connected by the cords of their social network—social relations—but as the characteristic and interrelated states of mind of the people with regard to the conduct of man to man, it is well to include in it the ideal, the desired, the expected, and the realized.

From this point of view the social structure of a small community is a set of limiting conditions within which the conduct of individuals takes place. It is a system of ethical directives, a set of signposts to the good and virtuous life. But in any journey men are tempted to stray from the path, and furthermore in life's journey, even though it take place in the relatively orderly moral landscape of simple and stable communities, the signposts are not always fully consistent, nor do they provide for every contingency of life. Thus it happens that if we want to describe a little community as it really is, and not only as its ideal social structure says that it should be, we are required to take account of the kinds of circumstances that join with the social structure in bringing about the conduct of the members of the community. To describe the social structure of Chan Kom is one thing; to describe the usual social conduct of its people is another thing, though closely related.

One of the elements of every life that makes difficult and uncertain the moral instruction issued by the social structure is the presence within the social structure itself of conflicting moral imperatives. A man may meet a circumstance in which one rule of the social structure tells him one thing and another rule tells him another. Such a case is interestingly told by Professor Firth from the remote Pacific island of Tikopia.[11] In that community a requirement of the social structure is that a chief should pass on his sacred knowledge to someone so that the community continue to have the benefit of it. It is also required that the chief pass on the knowledge to his eldest son. In this case the eldest son had deserted the father and gone to live in another district. The son thus failed to fulfil a demand made upon him by the moral dimension of the social structure, for he had an obligation to remain by his father's side. Angered by this desertion, the father told his younger son what he should have communicated to the elder, and then died. Then, as the social structure required, the elder son was made chief. But of course at that moment he lacked the esoteric knowledge necessary to a chief. Then the younger son, responsive to the expectation that one who has sacred knowledge should pass it on to him who fills the role or office in which that knowledge is used, told his brother something of what he had learned from his father. But he was angered by his brother's conduct and by his own failure to become chief although his father had told him the knowledge appropriate to a chief, and so he withheld from his brother some of what he had learned. And then he too died.

As Firth says, each of the three parties acted differently from what would be normal according to the social structure. But each of the three had a reason for acting as he did, and each act seemed to the actor right, morally justified. We do not know what special circumstances justified to the elder son his decision to move away from the father. Perhaps, as Firth suggests, it was a family quarrel, or the advantages of working land in another district.

Once the older son had gone, the father had a reason, morally good, for passing the knowledge on to the younger son, and the younger son had a legitimate grievance when he failed to become chief after working so hard to acquire the qualifying knowledge.

Here the social structure seems to be a set of ethical paradigms, an exemplary; an ideal system of demands that men can follow only if all things go as the social structure provides. But things rarely do go that way. Somebody acts in a different way and begins a chain of consequences in the course of which other men are forced to make decisions with ethical consequences. They make these decisions always in terms of the moral rules issuing from the social structure, but as modified by the effects on them of special circumstances. Sometimes, as in the case Firth recounts, the special circumstances bring about a conflict between two rules.

Such instances of conflict between two moral imperatives of the social structure are not hard to find. Llewellyn and Hoebel[12] tell us of a decision that Cheyenne Indians had to make when an important chief committed murder. As a chief his ritual contributions to the common life continued to be necessary to the group. As a murderer he was ritually unclean and should have remained for years physically apart from all other Cheyenne. This conflict was solved by letting the chief function ritually because they had to have his ritual but by requiring him at ceremonies to sit apart from the others at the entrance of the tipi. In a similar way an American university solved the problem provided by the demands of the social structure that Negroes sit apart from whites in schools and colleges with the practical necessity to provide an expensive legal education to one qualified Negro, by having the Negro sit in the classroom near the door with a railing between him and the white students. (This soon disappeared.)

Professor Firth's incident shows us how the ethical demands of the social structure are modified as events make it impossible or at least difficult to obey them all. I think the case also shows how they fail to be fully realized as what we call "human nature" enters into the factors that determine a man's choice of action. You recognize that if you were a younger son who had spent years in learning from your father the sacred lore that would qualify you to assume his respected office, then, even though the social structure told you that as the younger brother the chieftainship was not for you, when you found yourself put aside for, of all people, your older brother, a man who had gone off and abandoned his plain duty, you would feel wronged. Anybody would, one declares, social structure or no social structure.

The social structure is forever making difficult demands on the common human impulses of people. Malinowski tells[13] us how a man in the matrilinear Trobriands sometimes favors his sons instead of his sister's sons, as he is supposed to do. The child a man has fathered and who is the son of his wife is humanly important to him whatever the social structure tells him to the contrary. William Graham Sumner wrote, "The mores can make anything right." Robert E. Park said, "But the mores have a harder time making some things right than others."

As here explored in the light of facts from Chan Kom, social structure is part of the whole community. It is a system with connections with other systems. It might be possible to examine the connections of the social structure with the economy, as one does in reporting how the obligation of a betrothed young man to bring food to his parents-in-law-to-be enters into the production and distribution of commodities. In the more primitive and isolated societies, at least, it is common to find connections between the social structure and the religion. In Tikopia each kinship group has its own spirit guardians, gods, and ancestors, arranged in a hierarchy corresponding to the hierarchy of rules and precedents among the kinship groups on earth; at death the senior man of the kinship group moves into the supernatural part of what might be seen as one hierarchy, one "social structure." "The future life of the spirit is in fact organized along much the same principles as on earth."[14] In the same way, in Chan Kom the hierarchical order of Christian and pagan supernaturals corresponds, although less closely than in Tikopia, to a hierarchy of earthly power as among members of kinship groups, and to some extent as between the leader-ruler of the village and less important people. The British students of social structure have done much to show the connections of social structure with, or the structural aspects of, the religions of those African peoples they have so much studied.

This brief review of some aspects of life in Chan Kom in terms of social structure would come out with different emphases and different forms of words were it made by Professor Firth himself, and it would come out still more differently if it were done by, say, Evans-Pritchard or Meyer Fortes. There is one distinction, from among many that might emerge from such comparisons, that I think will be particularly helpful to us as we proceed in this consideration of more or less holistic ways to conceive a small community.

Rather than regarding social structure as one of a number of interrelated systems making up the whole that is the village life, some parts of one system connecting with some parts of others, we may find it possible to make social structure the central, constant, organizing idea with which to examine all aspects of the life of the community. If I understand him rightly, this is what Professor Fortes does. "Social structure is ... the entire culture of a given people handled in a special frame of theory."[15] From this position social structure is the holistic concept: the central organizing idea in terms of which everything else in the life of the community, so far as proves possible, is seen. One does not move from social structure to religious system; one sees, for example, the rituals in Chan Kom wherein the rain-gods are asked by the people for rain and good harvest as an expression of the structure of interdependence that binds one agriculturalist to the others of the community and of their common connections with the supernaturals.

In the more primitive societies very much can be so included by examination in the light of the idea of social structure. Much of the economy and the religious and magical practices are expressions of social structure. An important part of morality lies in the conceptions of rightness attaching to the claims and obligations of kin and of other kinds of people and to the kinds of roles that make up social structure. It is not clear that all of what anthropologists call culture, examined in the light of social structure as a central and more or less holistic concept, proves susceptible of inclusion. Religious feeling and religious acts are in cases private and even solitary. The Maya agriculturalist mentioned in the preceding chapter who alone in his field built his little altar and made his lonely offering to the gods may be expressing aspects of social structure, but he is, for the time, not particularly close to its workings. A pious Maya refrains from cracking maize grains with his teeth, and in the maize field; a holy place, his conduct in isolation is subdued and seemly. Reaching such aspects of the life of the community from the concept of social structure, one has come out to meet aspects of the local life that might have been more immediately examined from a viewpoint provided by concepts other than social structure—ethos, perhaps, or ideology, or view of the world. And some parts of a local common life seem to have a freedom and an independence of social structure. The pattern of sound units of the language of a community is better reached from a purely linguistic concept of phonemic system than from social structure. The form of musical composition characterizing late Western society and known as the sonata form would be hard to reach from the social structure of the European community. In African tribes and in Indian peasant villages I suppose it to be true also that aspects of music and graphic art are hard to relate to social structure. The very general ideas a people entertain as to chance, fate, or causation might be examined—difficult though the task prove—and it is not at all clear that these are best examined through social structure. Of all forms of thought for characterizing and analyzing a little community, social structure, in its variant uses, has had the fullest exploration, the widest test in primitive communities. It will take us far into the whole. It is not apparent that it makes other forms of thought useless.

IV

... A TYPICAL BIOGRAPHY

Ecological system and social structure are alike in that both are ways to describe much of the whole community as a system of institutions and activities. As developed by Evans-Pritchard, the ecological system is made up of such of the conventional behavior as is adapted to the natural environment. It consists of such regular activities of men as reflect or respond to regularities in natural phenomena. In the conception of social structure, as it appears in the work of more than one British student of non-European communities, the band or village or tribe is seen as the functional inter-relations of groups and of institutions; it is the relationships of men rather than the men themselves that are thrown into bold relief by this concept. Whether we think of ecological system or of social structure, we think chiefly of the system or the structure. Individual men and women pass through it, but we hardly see them do it or see them affected by it. As Evans-Pritchard writes of these relationships conceived as a system, "Men are born into them or enter them in later life, and move out of them at death; the structure endures."[1]

In this chapter we consider a different and alternative way in which the community may be conceived as a whole. Let us do so by emphasizing the general and lasting character of the *way* that men and women enter and pass through a social structure. Particular men and women come and go, and make life's passage in varying ways, but in any stable community there is a characteristic passage. Very well; let us describe that characteristic passage. Let us bring forward the particular men and women who come and go as the structure endures; let us look at them and their life-experiences; what is general and characteristic about these life-experiences becomes our new subject matter. Ecological system and social structure are now background where in our earlier considerations they were the foreground. The newly conceived whole is the human career characteristic of that community. The social structure and the ecological system provide points of reference for the description of that career, but the form of our description is now not institutional; it is biographic. We are to describe the sequence of events characteristic of a man's life.

This choice of form for describing the band or the village provides us with a new temporal dimension and limitation. In description of ecological system or of social structure time enters too, of course. There are the recurrent cycles of human activity that in part depend on nature. There are the periods of change in the social structure. Of these some are cyclical, as in the case of the adjustment, again and again, of population and institutions to resources. This we saw in the cycle of growth and fission of the Maya village. And of course there are the transformations of social structure through time such as the changes in the social structure of England that were brought about by the enclosure acts or the changes in the structure of Swedish peasant communities that were brought about by the law as to redistribution of the land. Time enters into any description of change in a community, and at a later stage we shall examine the kinds of wholes that might be involved in the writing of a history, short or long, of a little community. But just now we are to accept as the time-line of our description the span of a human life. And we are to accept as the content of this description the events that a human life itself involves from birth to death.

The book that Villa Rojas and I produced about Chan Kom is not a developed account of either ecological system or social structure, and it can be said as emphatically that I wrote no considered description of the characteristic human career in Chan Kom. If one were to look for pages in the book which have something on the subject, one would find most of what I have to offer in chapter 9, entitled "From Birth to Death." Here appears an account of some of the things that usually happen to people in that village. The order of presentation is, roughly speaking, biographic order. First one finds some facts about what goes on before the birth and the treatment given to a pregnant woman. Like Tristam Shandy, my man takes some time to get born. Something is said about assuring the safe delivery of the child, and at this place I put in what little

I learned about the attempts of the people to control conception, and such facts as I gathered as to their knowledge of human gestation.

One sees, however, that such facts are not facts in the human biography at this point; knowledge of human gestation is acquired characteristically quite late in the human career. The order of presentation in that chapter is not, after all, strictly biographic.

I then say something about childbirth and tell about the seclusion of the mother, explain the father's role at the time of birth, and give an account of the midwife's ministrations. These pages include something about such customs as the burial of the afterbirth under the hearth of the house. I add a little explanation of the meaning of this custom to the people, again a diversion from the truly biographic line because it is the adult and not the child for whom this custom comes to have a meaning.

There follows something on how names are chosen and given, and then I describe the early rituals in which the infant is the center of attention. But again I do not really attempt to represent the order of developing experience as it occurs to the infant and child, for I give information on how the godparents are chosen—a matter which does not interest an infant a few months old. I even put in here the texts of the formal speeches used in asking some married couple to sponsor the baptism or some single individual to sponsor the ritual called *hetz-mek*. The fact, obviously, is that nobody bothers to learn these speeches until he is himself a grown person, and then the speeches of particular petitioners vary greatly in their formality and completeness. Moreover, the reader of my chapter then goes on to read of a ceremony in which the parents of a child just baptized formally express their gratitude to the new godparents. And at this ceremony the child, whose developing consciousness of the world around him might have been the subject of the exposition, is not even present. The parents leave him at home when they come to the house of the godparents. Again, what little I have to say about weaning and toilet training is said as it appears to an adult. But in the short description of the first participation of boy or girl in the adults' activities and in what is said about the sorts of knowledge as to sex that is communicated to children or withheld from them, I come a little nearer to following a truly biographic line.

The account I give of marriage is once more a mixture of statements about what young people come to experience as they pass puberty and as it is suggested to them that they should now marry, and as then they are married; and in part it is an account of the exterior formalities of betrothal and marriage, as known by older people. Immediately after the passages on marriage the reader is carried at one jump over all the rest of the individual's human life, for in the next paragraphs that typical villager is already dying or dead. The next following description has to do with the treatment of the dying and the dead, and tells about the beliefs as to the life after death. But it is not when one is dead that one has such beliefs; their importance in the human career comes about as the growing individual hears of these beliefs and begins to take account of them in his conception of life and his own career through it. Thoughts about death may be most important in childhood.

The account of the human career in chapter 9 of that book can be supplemented by other information on the subject presented in other parts of the book. In the chapter on the division of labor one finds something about the domestic activities of women and about the agricultural and other activities of men. One meets with the roles men and women occupy in the religious ceremonies and in government in the chapters in which I deal with religious ceremonies or with government.

Nevertheless, it is evident that that book uses no single intellectual form for the description of Chan Kom. It conforms to none of the models of description which I have ventured to consider somewhat separately in these chapters. And as an account of the human career in Chan Kom, it is merely some fragments of fact about that career, presented in the course of viewpoint shifting from young people to old people, and on the whole as seen from the position of the observer outside of the individual whose life it might be one's purpose to describe. It is the old ethnological category of "crisis rites"—birth, puberty, marriage, death—which provided me with a few usual pegs on which to hang some observations.

Having taken so many pages to tell what I did not do, I will now take as many more in trying to say what I might have done. Could one write a book about a little community in the form of a generalized biography? What would be the difficulties in doing so? And what advantages and disadvantages for the total understanding of the community would follow from the adoption of such a form of description?

In considering these questions we lack the help of such a well-developed and tested mental form as is social structure. There is no group of students of small communities who are hard at work describing such communities as generalized biographies. Dr. Morris Opler, in his book about the Chiricahua Apache,[2] certainly came very much closer than I did to describing the round of life of a community in terms of the career of its typical individual. Making up his mind to tell his story that way, he presents most of his facts about the life in the order which a human life defines. His chapters follow the sequence: birth, childhood, maturation, adulthood. But with the chapters on adulthood the biographic order is in part abandoned because so much does happen in adult life, and at this point Opler found it necessary or desirable to introduce chapters on folk beliefs; medical practices and shamanism; the maintenance of the household; marital and sexual experience; and the round of life. Yet Opler's book does show the people of a little community as any one of them moves from the cradle to the grave. If I should look seriously for other guides in connection with the present endeavor, I think I should find some parts of human biographies typical of certain communities in the accounts published in recent years by those anthropological students of the formation of personality who see in the early experiences of the child much of the explanation for the kind of personality he develops. In the next chapter we shall consider these latter studies more directly.[3]

Without a perfected model of this kind of study to help us, I proceed as best as I can to conceive a description of a community in biographic form. The first major principle of composition would be to present every aspect of life in the order and in the way it appears to the individual at the time he encounters it. Taken too literally, this principle makes nonsense of the endeavor, for everyone encounters things around him not only once, but again and again throughout his life. Yet, though this is true, it is also true that some things are encountered importantly at some times and other things at other times: breast feeding is important in the first months, but the experience of fatherhood is not realized until much later.

In accordance with the principle, so far as it is realizable, one would describe the technology not as an organized system of operations in which perhaps many men, women, and children take part. One would instead describe the way the child begins to enter into the work and play of the home or the labor of the cornfield—how gradually he comes to assume activities and share understandings about the use and meaning of practical acts and objects. In the same way the organization of the village community would be presented, now not as a social structure of permanent and functionally interrelated parts, but as a succession of added comprehensions of the meanings of those acts which express kinship connections or public life. In the account of Chan Kom that I now imagine, one would see a boy helping his father, a little later assuming his first public office under direction of the village authorities, and then fulfilling the roles and statuses now seen as he experiences them and comes into them. It would be the regular transformations of act, mind, and personality that one would describe. The new system would be unified in the form of a course of development in one generalized person.

A community is, then, among other things, a characteristic human development. To present it as such would have consequences for the progress of our understanding of man's life in society. To choose this form would make it difficult if not impossible to state clearly, and in their systematic connections, most of the other more or less holistic concepts which we have already taken up or are yet to take up in these chapters. Ecological system and social structure would appear only as the experiences in which the growing human individual encounters some element of one or the other of these two systems. A description in terms of human development alone would make almost impossible a comparative science of the adaptive relationships of men to nature, let alone a comparison of human societies with plant and animal societies. The very concepts that prove important to the student of social structure could not emerge from a study of generalized human careers alone. We should not find ourselves talking of "equivalence of siblings" or of "the lineage principle" as some of the students of social structure have done.

So, too, the attempt to reach other kinds of descriptive syntheses of small communities, to which I come later in these pages, would be checked or prevented by an unqualified commitment to the biographic form. Later I shall consider outlook on life or world view. Then I shall try to think of the ideas people of a community have about the world around them in so far as these ideas tend in their own minds to have categoric or systematic character. Such a conception requires us to look at the world as the villager sees it at any one time, all of it together. The biographic form would here too meet with the other conception, the conception of world view, only as the growing person encounters it. In the generalized biography I imagine for Chan Kom we would get glimpses of that great canopy of the universe which people are always more or less aware of. In the first book about Chan Kom one reads in the account of the rituals of life how the midwife sees to it that someone in the household takes the severed umbilical cord and buries it under one of the four crosses that stand at four of the many paths entering the village. This little event in the child's life has reference to one of the great ideas of the world view of these Maya. They conceive of their universe as four-cornered, with protecting deities at each of the four corners of the milpa, the village, and the earth and sky. The supernaturals that watch over the village guard the people at the four crosses set on four paths coming to the village from the four cardinal directions. The umbilical cord of the child, placed under such a cross, commits the child's life to the protection of these supernaturals. But if one began to tell all that is implied in the small order given by the midwife as to the disposal of the umbilical cord, one would soon stray from the telling of the typical Maya biography to the study of the systematized ideas about things which are world view. So it would be with many elements in the biography. When the grown person in Chan Kom mourns at the funeral of one dear to him, he should not weep; the reasons for this restraint lie in the conceptions of the people as to the road taken by the soul of the departed to heaven and the unwanted delay that would be occasioned by the tears of the mourner upon this road; when a man dies, a hole is made in the thatch of the roof; again it is the speeding of the soul along its road that is implied. A human career intersects world view again and again; but to describe world view is another task, different from the description of the community as a human career.

On the other hand, the description of a community as a typical biography would direct our attention to questions and problems that are not so easily brought forward by way of the study of social structure. To tell the story in this form would most emphatically require us to recognize the several modes of human social life which were distinguished in the preceding chapter. To tell of a human life and its development it is necessary to tell of the changing states of mind of the person who lives that life. So the generalized biography would tell something of what people think ought to happen, of what they expect to happen, and of what actually happens. The biographic form should make it possible for us to study the influence upon men's actual lives of the ideals that may prevail in their society as to what these lives should be. Does the Hindu ideal of a man's life as a passage through certain stages—disciple and student of Veda, father and householder, hermit and wandering ascetic—shape in any way or degree the lives of people, peasants, or scholars, who do not, of course, literally fulfil that ideal? In some societies ideals as to the good life take definite forms, taught by teachers or expressed in myth or literature.

In developing the biographic form we would try both to look at the typical person of the community as we, observers on the outside, see him and also as he sees himself. And in trying to find out how he sees himself, we would strive for insight into how he would like to represent himself to outsiders and of how he may feel about himself, privately, somewhere deeper down. As soon as our attention turns from a community as a body of houses and tools and institutions to the states of mind of particular people, we are turning to the exploration of something immensely complex and difficult to know. But it is humanity, in its inner and more private form; it is, in the most demanding sense, the stuff of the community. While we talk in terms of productivity, or of roles and statuses, we are safely and easily out in the light, above ground, so to speak, moving among an apparatus we have ourselves built, an apparatus already removed, by our own act of mind, from the complicated thinking and feeling of the men and women who achieve the productivity or define and occupy the roles. But it is the thinking that is the real and ultimate raw material; it is there that the events really happen. And the choice of a human biographic form for describing the whole turns us to it.

In such a mixed dish of reporting as is illustrated by the early book on Chan Kom there is very little record of this inner stuff of the villagers' minds. There is a short and rather shallow autobiography written at my request by one of the older Indians. In this one finds something of that man's thoughts about the good life. It holds hints as to the ways in which his career had or had not realized his own expectations of it. In accompanying paragraphs I attempt some evaluation of the use of that Indian's autobiography as a statement of two aspects of Chan Kom life, the life that was thought desirable by that man's peers during the time of his youth, and his own personal attempts to see the actual events of his life as consistent with the desirable.

In the second book I wrote about Chan Kom seventeen years after the first, there is a little more information as to what the people of the village expected would happen to it and to themselves. The same man who many years before had written for me an account of his early life told me in 1948 a great deal of the new fears he had come to have as the things and ways of town and city were coming closer to his village. In 1933 this man was all for progress; he led his people in their effort to get roads, schools, and all modern advantages for the village. But in 1948 he was thinking mostly of the evils that were soon to come to the village as a result of this same road to the town which he had earlier struggled to bring about. Now he saw that the road would bring problems and vices; that new standards of living would result in discontent; that his children would want the pleasures of the town; and that the old way of life, which after all he thought good, was threatened.

From this little experience and from other facts, it seems to me that the biographic form of description provides a direct entry into problems of social change. The respects in which a community is not one stable and self-consistent structure, but is changing from one manner of life to another, appear most plainly in the changing states of mind of people, or in the differences between what older people think and feel and what younger people think and feel. We might therefore attempt a comparison of the careers of older people and of younger. This could be done by obtaining the life stories of representatives of each generation. The little autobiography I obtained in Chan Kom in 1933 is insignificant beside the many long and critically examined autobiographies of individuals from primitive or modern societies that have now been recorded and published. But even the little one from Chan Kom would be of greater value if I had also got some young people to write for me their own life stories—and their hopes and desires. The autobiography of the older man that I did publish represents the problems and aspirations of the village people in Yucatán in the first and second decades of this century. That was a time of struggle to build new villages in the bush, of revolution and of war, and a time in which the strong purpose of the villagers was to achieve material security and political independence. But the problems and aspirations of the 1940's were very different. They were problems of coping with the rapidly advancing town-civilization, and of what to do about a population growing too rapidly for its agricultural resources and so turning to the town and the city for a livelihood as well as for a new and exciting kind of experience. In a changing society the way in which one generation conceives of life and that in which the next conceives it become different, and this difference is most directly to be studied through the biographic form of description of the community.

One of the shortcomings of a description of a community in terms of its social structure is that it does not clearly bring into our understanding the prospective dimension of a man's life. A man does not always look back on the past or around him at the immediately present. Also he looks forward to what will happen to him and to others. So it should be possible, through the study of a community in its biographic form, to get understanding of the relations in that community between what a man thinks ought to happen, what he thinks will happen and, of course, what we who watch the careers of the people develop find does actually happen.

There seem to be several possible kinds of relationship between the norms and expectations of a people on the one hand and the realization or failure of realization of these norms and expectations on the other. In the isolated band of hunters such as Holmberg describes for the Bolivian Siriono, there is presumably no important difference between the ideal career and the career that men realize. What a man thinks is good is what happens to him and his sons— allowing, of course, for the differences in luck or in individual personality. The same is probably true for the Nuer of the Sudan. The anticipations that men have are as to the return of the conditions already experienced. It is easy to suppose that the Nuer, when he is camping by the shrunken river in the time of drought, looks forward to village life to be experienced when next the rain comes; and when he is again settled in the village he looks forward to the breaking up of the village and the making of camps with the cattle by the river. In the sequence of expected events which is provided by the life cycle, there is again a consistency between the approved expectancies entertained by a young person and the experiences that come to him later. Evans-Pritchard describes the age-sets of the Nuer: the associations of young men of similar age. He describes the transition from childhood to manhood; for the Nuer this transition is abrupt and important; surely the boy looks forward, with emotions not yet reported, to his entry into manhood. But there, as with the Siriono, the career that a man sees for himself is a career for the most part realized when the time comes, and the career that a man sees for his son is also the career that the son desires and that he, in his turn, for the most part realizes. The desirable, the expected, and the realized are much the same in stable and consistently integrated societies.

In societies which have experienced considerable change of life conditions we shall find, in contrast, kinds of human careers in which expectancies are regularly created only to be regularly defeated. We shall find kinds of people who are taught to look forward to a career which they are not allowed to fulfil. A young man I know is studying the typical human career among college-educated people of African descent in the Union of South Africa. He is doing this in part by getting some of these Africans to write their life stories. He finds that, eager for the opportunities that education seems to offer them, they acquire college educations only to find that there are few places in the society of the native Africans which are there to fill with their educated competence and no places for them in the society of the whites. There is an important inconsistency between the desires created and the realities that the social structure provides. Much the same, but in lesser degree, could be said of the situation of many educated Americans of African origin. It could be said, I think, of many women in many parts of present-day western European-American society. Women are taught to expect an equality of treatment and opportunity; equality of opportunity is an expressed ideal norm of their society; but the desires and expectations are not realized when they come to later life. The actual social structure does not provide for the kind of woman that is made by education and early experience.

Among the Siriono and the Nuer and the Maya there are of course great differences in the typical career of men as compared with the typical career of women. (Though I have not as yet expressly said so, to describe even the most stable and isolated small community in terms of human careers would require generalized biographies of more than one kind of person, a man and then a woman, if not also biographies of certain kinds of occupational specialists.) But in the isolated and stable small communities the career of each sex is the recognized and accepted complement of that of the other; in such a society a woman and a man realize the same ideals and purposes through the fulfilment of different roles.

The more important characteristic of the human career in societies that have changed rapidly and are continuing to change is that the career of any one kind of person, man or woman, factory worker or business man, becomes within itself inconsistent and inconclusive. The purposes that are created in early life as to material success are not always the purposes that the individual finds he can realize; or the ideals and purposes of mutual help and sacrifice for the community are not the ideals and purposes which he may be called upon to realize in his working life. The ends of life become obscure. Educated women find themselves doing many things which are immediately necessary but that do not seem to be directed toward significant ends. People develop wants whose satisfaction brings no satisfaction. Such characteristics of the human career in the more modern societies demand a view of the community that is more than its conception as social structure; the biographic dimension is a form of description and investigation which exposes these characteristics to our notice and that calls upon us to devise ways more precisely to define and to explain them.

The turn of thought in this chapter has brought us into much closer concern with the sentiments and motives of men, indeed also with their judgments of good and evil. Somehow we are now more on the inside of people than we were when we thought of the little community as an ecological system or as social structure. Of course it is a matter of the side of the whole that one turns to. The student of social structure must understand, for instance, the sentiments and judgments of a father toward his son in order to describe the ordering of personnel in that community. But in the case of the student of social structure the investigator does not stay long inside the mind of any one person to find out very much about it; for him the "insideness" soon yields to a formulation from the outside point of view; the inside states of mind of the villager are not the stuff of the terminal characterization.[4]

Now, in seeking to describe a human career typical of a community we have lingered over this insideness. We insist that a human career is not only a course run over; it is also the villager's thoughts about the past, present, and future of that course. The stuff, the subject matter of our growing knowledge, is that stuff which we constantly recognize within ourselves. We assume the responsibility of saying true things about that stuff as it occurs in the European villager, the hunter in the Orinoco forest, or the Maya Indian of Chan Kom. If, in describing ecological system or social structure, we take with us any theory about human nature, any set of assumptions as to how men think and feel always or in certain circumstances, we do not need to bring it forward. Such assumptions lie buried somewhere underneath the descriptions of the activities on land and water, or of the institutionalized relationships between kinds of people in the community. But when we try to explain the course of development of a man, from the inside, we are compelled to reflect as to the assumptions we make about how, in general, men do think and feel. "It ... is the presence of psychological theory, that is, the inclusion of intra-psychic processes in the descriptions of members of a society, that differentiates the culture and personality approach," writes Margaret Mead.[5]

If there is to be a theory, there must be some explicit statement of testable relationships and some way to test them. Common knowledge of how men think and feel will not provide these things. If we have now ventured inside the mind, even, perhaps, inside the mind as it first develops in infancy and childhood, as the biographic form demands, where shall we find the theory and method for proof? The requirement is inexorable and not easy to meet. As students of communities have come to consider the inside development of people, they have looked about for such theory and such methods. To meet the need appears, looming most impressively of all the conceptions of human nature as yet put forward, the ideas set going by Sigmund Freud, that "triumphant argonaut of the human mind." Here are some ideas, coherent, original, directional, for making order of this deep and difficult inside stuff. Indeed, it was in freshly creative reaction to Freud's view that there developed, especially among American anthropologists, that effort to show that there are culturally delimited biographies other than those postulated by Freud, which came to be known as the "culture and personality approach." But in developing the biographic form for the study of a small community one may take a simpler view of human nature than did Freud, and perhaps make some list of universal needs or wants or wishes.

And as for methods for proving whatever theory of "intrapsychic processes" one may adopt, we are offered from another side various kinds of formalized investigating of the hidden mind, especially those procedures called projective tests which call upon the individual to make known mental states of which perhaps he himself is unaware. These, being tests, seem to offer a means of proof of the existence of mental states conceived in terms of whatever ideas we take from Freud or from others as to the nature of human nature. But whether we are here guided by this psychologist or by that, as we turn from institutions to kinds of men, some ordered ideas, applicable and testable, as to human nature become necessary to us. The human community is an analyzable system of tools and institutions; it is also an analyzable kind of person.

V

... A KIND OF PERSON

In discussing the possible relation of ecological system to personality or character, I remarked that both Holmberg, describing the Siriono, and Evans-Pritchard, describing the Nuer, had something to say on this subject. The former found the Bolivian hunters quarrelsome, often sullen, ungenerous, unco-operative and notably indifferent to the unhappy fates of their fellows. The English anthropologist found his Sudanese people generous, courageous, patient, proud, loyal, stubborn, and independent. It appears, then, that these two students of men in small communities, while they worked, came to know two different ecological systems and social structures, and also came to know two different kinds of man.

If their experience was like mine with the Yucatec Maya, they were aware of tools and customs before they had formulated anything very considered about the character of the man with whom they had to deal. When I first went to the villages of Yucatán, I saw people doing things: a man felling trees in preparation for planting maize, or a woman washing clothes on a raised wooden tray. My first attention was to the things they did and the things they used. I did not at first have much impression as to the prevailing character or temperament of these Maya. I found myself writing out considered statements about their social organization and religion before I set down anything about them as a type of character or personality.

Tools and technology, institutions and beliefs, personality or character, was the rough sequence of the movement of my mind. On the other hand, I was very early aware of the differences in personality and character as among the individual Indians I came to know, and these personalities continued to seem to me very distinct and different. I saw much more difference as between

66

any two Maya men I had come to know than between the Maya peasants as one type of man and any other type. This impression I never lost, and when I returned to the village of Chan Kom after an absence of seventeen years, I met with a rush of familiar feelings the same score or more of men and women I had known well in the earlier years; they seemed still the same people to me; each was a distinct individual, a unique combination of personal traits. Some of these men strongly reminded me of persons I had known in America or in Europe. The resemblance of any one such man to someone personally like him from another and distant society seemed closer to me than his resemblance to his fellows in Chan Kom.

And yet I see now that all of the time I was moving toward a characterization of the Maya Indian as one generalized type of human being. By 1948 I had come to understand a great deal about the way in which the customs and the beliefs, the daily life of work and of prayer, the aspirations and the fears of these people, were interrelated and tended to constitute a more or less coherent view of the good life. I was striving to express in compact terms the general directions of effort and value toward which this conception moved this people.

Kroeber writes in his *Anthropology* that "formulations of the total pattern of cultures contain both strictly cultural and psychological characterizations."[1] And he goes on to say: "A formulation begins with the former, with institutions or folkways; and as these more and more weave themselves into a larger coherence, it gradually becomes evident in what directions the culture is faced, what ends it looks toward and what qualities it is occupied with and prizes most. In short, its characteristic values and orientations become comprehensible."[2]

This was my experience. The characteristic values of the people of Chan Kom became comprehensible to me. I tried to write down the ends toward which the culture of the community looked. It seemed to me, after a long acquaintance with these Maya, that not only had I met before other particular Americans or other people resembling some of my individual Maya friends, but that I had met before this people of Chan Kom as a whole, as a type toward which the separate Maya persons tended to conform. As I reflected on this impression, it appeared to me that I had met the like of these villagers in what I read about the commercial Puritanism of New

England, and in certain pages by Max Weber. Thus, in writing the later book about Chan Kom, I set it down that the Maya had the Protestant ethic. I noted that they regarded industry, frugality, and productive effort as ends in themselves, condemned idleness, and viewed the increase of capital as a good thing in itself. To work and not to waste was the strong injunction they put upon themselves. From describing Chan Kom as a system of productive technology in significant interdependence with the land and the weather, I had come by irregular movements and through a confusion of un-perceived distinctions to describe the institutions of the village and then, toward the last, to describe the village as if it were one man viewing the kind of life that is good, as if it were one single personality.

Have the words I have just written—the kind of life that is good; the community as if it were a single personality—named one form of thought for conceiving the community as a whole, or two? What are the relationships between a conception of a good life and the characteristic personality of the people who have that conception? In describing a community, how in terms more closely connected with the individual than with the collectivity is it possible, ne-cessary, or desirable to distinguish between the two conceptions? And if one can and does distinguish them, what are some of the problems one encounters in using the one or the other to describe the whole before us?

There is another passage in that section of Kroeber's *Anthro-pology* titled "Content and Form; Ethos and Eidos; Values" that closely links the two conceptions as I have just linked them. Having introduced into his discussion the word "ethos," and having said that it carries an implication of what is sanctioned and expected, Kroeber writes that "however, when we speak of the ethos of a culture, we ... refer not so much to the specific ethics or moral code of the culture as to its total quality, to what could constitute disposition or character in the individual; to the system of ideals and values that dominate the culture and so tend to control the type of behavior of its members."[3]

A code of conduct; a kind of human being: two things. But the code or system of values dominates the culture and so controls the type of behavior of the people, makes the type of human being, and corresponds to character in the individual. In some sense the two ideas are one, or, if they are two, it is easy for the mind to pass from one to the other. In writing about the ethos of Chan Kom in the last chapter of the second book about the village, I passed from the one conception to the other, or blended them, unreflectingly.

I wrote: "The ethos of Chan Kom is practical and prudent; it stresses sobriety and obedience; it takes honesty for granted." I described the Chan Kom morality as "sober and prudent in its tone,"[4] but as making "much more place for the life of pleasure than did Puritanism."[5] The subject of these sentences is the ethos or the culture itself. "We are here," writes Kroeber, "getting into metaphors that personify culture as if it had a will and purpose of its own."[6] True. But how else shall we describe the "pervading differences of character and outlook" that distinguish a people? Elsewhere in the same pages of my little book I seem to be describing not the system of values but the kind of human being to be found in Chan Kom. I wrote: "The people feel disgust or fear at the suggestion that the children be seated together, girl and boy, in the school," and I put it down that in the dutiful way of these villagers "there is little passion and no turmoil of the inner life."[7]

In these passages I am saying things about people, including the very subjective feelings of people. Values, ethos, do not have feelings; they are abstract qualities. And here and there, in a sentence or two, I seem to be expressing a sort of causal relation between the values or the ethos on the one hand and the kind of person on the other: "the wasteful, violent and self-indulgent"—nonconformists, by the way—became, with the aid of the Protestant missionaries, as sober, or more sober, *than their own ancient ethos told them to be*"[8] (italics added).

Now that we are attending to the distinction between a community seen as if it were a single personality, and a community seen as a system of values, of signposts toward the good life, it should be possible for us to make the effort to keep the two conceptions separated in the next pages. I will first imagine myself attempting to characterize Chan Kom as if the village were one human being with aspects of personality distinguishing it from other such imagined beings. While I never did such a thing as a serious study, there are many who have, and from them you and I can now learn.

The problems divide into two. How shall I convince other people that what I say about the Maya personality is so? And, what will be the nature of the concept, the generic idea form, which I will use to describe the Maya personality?

The question as to proof or validation raises all the troublesome matters as to the nature of scientific method as one kind of validation. We may say that among the methods for commanding assent through evidence, the method of science is that one which offers confirmation in the form of accessible, specific, objective procedure. Outside of science, our assent may be evidentially commanded without such procedure. What Lafcadio Hearn wrote about the national character of the Japanese commands my assent, as does what Balzac wrote about the provincial French bourgeois, and both Hearn and Balzac gave us plenty of evidence. Indeed, the command of my assent to the truth of those characterizations may be more powerful upon me than the command exercised by many a scientific study of group personality. Science is not able in every situation to do the best job of validating understanding; we regard it so highly because faith and experience tell us that its methods in many fields of knowledge are susceptible of the greatest degree of perfection; in the long run it will work conviction through its own special kind of demonstration of proof.

While I was writing down observations on Maya customs, others were working at the characterization of Maya personality. Sylvanus Morley went at the task from the simple beginning of his own thirty years of close association with the Maya and with no pretensions to procedure of any kind. His characterization will be found in his book, *The Ancient Maya;*[9] and is summarized by Kroeber in his *Anthropology*, at page 587.

Morley's characterization is too long to quote here. It is a list of personal traits, some quite abstract, like conservatism, sense of justice and fatalism, and some more concrete, like being fond of practical jokes. A portrait of a person does emerge. Does it command my assent? Speaking for myself, I answer, in a general way, yes. Kroeber says that to him it seems an adequate rough description of Indians in general, "except for being somewhat sunnier."

I know that Dr. Morley enjoyed and liked the Maya Indians even more than I did, and although much of what he tells me to be true about Maya personality agrees with my own impressions, such assent as I give to it rests on Dr. Morley's impressions and their coincidence with my own. And I know how subject these impressions are to bias. Both of us, saying what we could about the Maya personality, were swayed by I do not know what uncontrolled personal experiences.

If I took what Morley wrote about the Maya and compared it with what somebody wrote about other Indians, or about white Americans, I should not be making progress in science. As two recent writers on the techniques for studying group personality put it: To compare one investigator's "description with that of the description of another society by still another investigator using a similar impressionistic technique would consist in compounding a felony."[10]

Dr. Morris Steggerda, physical anthropologist, tried to study Maya personality by more objective methods in the 1930's while I was reporting customs and institutions in some of the same communities in which he worked. Unfortunately, he made his attempt too soon. The Rorschach test had, I believe, not yet crossed the Atlantic, and Henry Murray was still to make known his thematic apperception test. Dr. Steggerda tried in several ways to make his procedure scientific. Instead of asking just one Dr. Morley to give his impressions of Maya personality, he asked twenty-nine educated North Americans to do so, and he caused them to report their impressions on a five-point scale; thus, each was asked to say whether in the life of the Maya superstition played a part of Tremendous Importance, Great Importance, Moderate Importance, Little Importance, or No Importance. Furthermore, Dr. Steggerda gave several score of Maya Indians standardized performance tests such as form-board tests and the use of the Goodenough drawing scale, designed by psychologists to measure intelligence or particular aptitudes. The results of these investigations were summarized and related to such incidents of actual behavior as had come to Dr. Steggerda's notice in Yucatán, and which seemed to him to give understanding of the Maya personality. Provided with these more specific data, Steggerda wrote an extended account of the Maya character which is detailed, anecdotal, and freely compounded of propositions about personality and propositions about custom.[11]

The result was, I must in frankness declare, not much to increase the command of the critical reader's assent. The techniques employed, while objective in form, involved a very great amount of uncontrolled subjective judgment. Even the most formal proce-

dures, the so-called intelligence tests, could not be soundly compared with the results of the same tests given to people of other
traditions; and the outsider's impression of Maya character remained still impressions, even when set on a five-point scale.

Since the years in which Steggerda and I were working, near
each other but separately, new and important procedures for the
study of group character have come into use. The procedures vary
a great deal, depending, for one thing, on whether the investigators
are interested in the group personality of a village or a primitive
tribe or in that of a modern nation. The procedures for studying
national character have been recently discussed by Dr. Margaret
Mead,[12] and to attend to them now would take us far from the
little community and its problems. The essential change in technique, with regard to characterizing the people both of villages and of
national states, is the use of documents coming from people
themselves and analyzed by the student from outside for what
those documents express of the temperament and other traits of
personality of those who made the documents. Such documents
may be novels, court records, autobiographies, cartoons, jokes,
proverbs, interviews set down, or words recorded as spoken in
comment or on an ink-blot or on a vague and ambiguous picture.

In using any of these classes of documents the assumption is
made that through them people express something about their
personal natures. In certain of the formalized procedures known
as projective tests, the form of the experience eliciting an expressive
response is fixed: it is a standardized ink-blot, or picture, or design
to be copied. In others, for which also rules for interpretation have
been established, the subject expresses himself more freely: by
playing with dolls or by drawing a picture of anything he likes.
Both kinds of projective tests, "are believed to elicit from him
responses representative of his thoughts and *feelings* about himself
and the world around him."[13] The projective test is claimed to
reveal the inside man in outside form.

If I were today attempting to describe the personality of the
village Maya, it would be these tests of which I should make use.
I should have to learn a great deal about how to administer them;
I should have to learn even more about how to analyze the products:
the inferences as to character and temperament I might fairly
draw from the records of the responses. And if I were at all wise

about their use, I should have to attend to many questions that are still unresolved as to the worth of these tests in establishing scientifically the facts about the personality of a group. There are doubts as to whether these tests, designed for use in Western society, can be used safely to learn something about the group personalities of very different peoples. Some of the tests have been modified, both in design and with respect to the rules of interpretation for particular primitive or exotic people, but we are not yet sure what inferences from the results can be safely drawn.

Furthermore, I should be required to study the use made of these projective tests in cases where they have been used to correct or confirm impressions as to group personality derived from the more varied and imprecise observations of the ethnologist or sociologist, and see if I could devise a way to use the tests which would in fact amount to a check upon such impressions from an independent source. In many of the published studies the man who interpreted the results of the tests already had heard a great deal from the ethnologist about what the people who took the test were thought by the ethnologist to be like.

These remarks on the projective tests have led me from the main road of these chapters. I have just been writing of techniques to get particular facts that will carry conviction as to the truth of generalizations made about the personality of an entire community. It is helpful to consider the techniques so used in close connection with the forms of thought employed for characterizing that group personality. But my principal concern is with the forms of thought, and I turn back to a consideration of ways in which the mind may move in reaching a characterization of a community as if it were the character or personality of one man.

One way to reach the characterization is to begin with the customs and institutions and try to derive the kind of man from them. This is the way my mind moved in the years I was studying Chan Kom. If one goes at it this way the terms used in the characterization tend to be the names of virtues, ideals, goals, or purposes. I found myself writing of sobriety, obedience, honesty, industry. And, as I said before, my account slides back and forth between an account of a good life and a description of one generalized personality. But if I should go at once to testing the Indians with ink-blots and ambiguous pictures, especially if I did so under the guidance of the professional psychologist whose language has developed out of the study of particular human individuals, each considered more or less by himself, I should find myself describing the psychic constitution of first this Maya and then that, and then generalizing what I had learned still in the language appropriate to the description of a single personality. I should describe the desires, frustrations, shames, adjustments, or maladjustments of the average or typical Maya Indian. In this case I should be pretty clearly concerned with the kind of person to be found in Maya villages and should not so much confuse that conception with a description of the good life in terms of virtues and other ideal ends or purposes.

Nevertheless, the two conceptions—group personality and value-system or ethos—are difficult to separate. I might write of Maya culture as if it were a person. I might say, "Maya culture is prudent and sober." And this (see Kroeber) is to speak metaphorically or by analogy. Strictly speaking, a culture cannot be these things; only people can. But it is sometimes convenient to think of the institutions and customs all together as if they were one undifferentiated collective personality. Ruth Benedict wrote, "Cultures ... are individual psychology thrown large upon the screen, given gigantic proportions and a long time span."[14] And when she described Kwakiutl, Zuni, and Dobu culture it was as if she were describing three very different human individuals one might come to know. One may make substantially the same assertions only substituting for "Maya culture" as the subject of the sentence the words "The Maya Indians of Chan Kom." Then one moves toward the examination of these particular human beings who are these Indians.

Whether one writes of customs or of people, one has a range of possibilities for the form of characterization of the little community as a kind of person, and it is at this point I get back on our main road. From Professor Milton Singer I have learned much of this range, but not enough to do justice to his thinking in the following remarks about it. Let us think again in terms of Chan Kom. I might, as did Morley and Steggerda, assemble psychological traits and ideals of the Maya and set them down one after the other. A sort of verbal portrait of the Maya results. The portrait convinces or does not by its total effect, as compared with whatever experience the reader has himself had with the Maya. There is no demonstration of systematic arrangement among the parts of the characterization. Second, I might do as I did at the end of my work in Chan Kom, and as Benedict and many others have done: select what I take to be the *dominant* characteristics of these Maya people and characterize them in terms of these characteristics—prudence and sobriety, perhaps. Here I have a choice as to the kind of qualities I select for the characterization and also as to the locus of these qualities. I may emphasize the affective, the temperamental dispositions of the people, as Montesquieu wrote of ruling passions and as Benedict described Dobuan culture as paranoid and Kwakiutl culture as megalomaniac. If I had been differently influenced or prepared, perhaps I could have characterized the Maya village culture as inhibited or even anal erotic. Such a characterization would command assent, if at all, not by any demonstration of proof acceptable to those used to laboratory experiment, but by the degree to which the reader found persuasive correspondences between the connotations of "inhibited" or "anal erotic" on the one hand and particular facts about the life of the Maya on the other.

It would not be necessary that the Maya Indian himself find these persuasive correspondences. This is what Benedict means in writing[15] of the "unconscious canons of choice" of a culture; she means that neither chiefs nor anyone else in the society sees how all phases of life are organized by and conform to this same motive. Such a characterization is from the outside view. On the other hand, I can attend particularly to the ideals of which the people are conscious, and describe their explicit purposes in life. Now I have moved back to value-system and to more of an inside view.

A portrait in words is not an analyzed system. Nor is a characterization of a culture or of a people in terms of leading goals or in terms of temperamental traits likely to be a system of parts fully analyzed. It may be only a suggestive analogy or metaphor. It may be accompanied with such a demonstration of fact about the people, either facts of custom or facts of behavior of particular individuals, as to make the characterization something more than an analogy and very much less than demonstration by experiment. I suppose the reader of my second book about Chan Kom is more or less persuaded that the dominant ideals of the Maya are sobriety, industry, prudence, and the rest, by the show of consistency

between these general assertions and the particular things I reported as having happened in the village. The resistance of the
villagers to propaganda and teaching contrary to these ideals is
perhaps particularly compelling evidence. But there is in this
book no explicitly conceived intellectual form for the understanding
of the personality of the group. I just throw out a short list of
characteristics or virtues.

More considered intellectual forms have been conceived by other
students of other peoples in the effort to make the characterization
of a kind of person systematic. If one should be making a more
serious attempt to characterize the Maya group personality, one
would have now available a little tool box of concepts that have
been forged in the interaction of comparative ethnology with
psychology, especially psychoanalytic psychology. One would notice
the increasing use of the phrase "modal personality," and see that
it denotes a simply statistical conception: it refers to the kind of
personality that in fact occurs most commonly in that group. As
the means for characterizing personalities, one by one, improve
through the development of projective tests and other procedures,
students are ccming to have so many equivalent records of so
many individuals that the indicators of personality they contain
are actually reduced to means and modes and standard deviations.

The concept "modal personality" is descriptive; its use would
tell me that this is the kind of person that one coming to Chan
Kom from the outside world would find to predominate there.
Using it, I should also discover those individuals departing most
in their descriptive personal characteristics from the modal personality. So there would be suggested to me questions as to how
it had come about that the one kind of person predominates and
how then to explain the deviants, and how perhaps to predict the
consequences for Maya personality of changes in the Maya world
external to the personality. But the concept of modal personality
alone would not give me the answers to such questions.

What is to be the intellectual form that will help us to get beyond
description to explanation? The conceptions that students of group
personality are now using combine elements of the human career,
as we thought of it in the last chapter, with elements of a descriptive
system enlarged to include customs and institutions, with qualities
of developed personality, and with elements of assumed universal

human nature. The personality, individual or group, is seen as developed in the course of the human life, especially in its early stages. The intellectual form employed is a system of parts in which a kind of person is made by a kind of experience with people and institutions. The biographic form of characterizing a little community combines easily with that form which describes it as a kind of person. The system of thought is now much more than analogical or suggestive; it is functional and mechanical. The human career is now conceived as a machine for turning out the product, modal personality.

There is a considerable variety of available functional-mechanical intellectual forms that might help one to explain the personality prevailing in Chan Kom. Some that lean strongly toward a classical Freudian view use a conceived system of which the parts are assumed universal elements of impulse or desire in interaction with relatively few kinds of experiences very early in life. Other conceptions include in the structure of ideas much less of assumed universal human nature and much more of the interaction, later in the human career, with more kinds of institutions. Some students have attempted to make use of simple mechanical conceptions in which certain experiences or interactions are supposed to bring about certain kinds of personality. The emphasis that occurred earlier on weaning, swaddling, and toilet training as explanations of personality produced a very simple deterministic form of thought. This kind of conception is not often brought forward today.[16] Its place is taken, I think, by one of two kinds of intellectual forms about which I now speak.

One of these, developed by Kardiner and Linton,[17] although modified and employed by not a few others, is the conception of basic personality in systematic interrelation with two kinds of institutions distinguished as primary and secondary. The basic personality is not a statistical concept; it is nothing directly perceived; it is not descriptive but explanatory, and it is a construct inferred from the facts of custom and institutions. It is that arrangement of personal qualities which, it is concluded from examination of primary and secondary institutions, is established in the individual in the early months or years of his life. The form of thought here is strongly functional and mechanical: the primary institutions—on the whole the treatment accorded the infant—are the

cause of the basic personality. The basic personality is in turn
the cause of the secondary institutions, which include the religion
and the art. There results a form of thought about the kind of
person in the community which is wide enough to include description of most of the things that go on there and which offers an explanation of how some of the principal components come about
in such a way as to exhibit to the student a congruence of the parts.
The conception is markedly scientific in the sense that it offers
apparent opportunities to reach conclusions of the form: if this,
then that; it promises predictability.

Whether the conception does attain these ends of science is open
to question, and Milton Singer has written an extended criticism
of the work of Kardiner and Linton, and of *The People of Alor*
by Cora Du Bois and others, in which the conception is employed.[18]
The conclusions reached by the use of the conception depend upon
transfer to exotic cultures of inferences drawn from the experiences
of psychiatrists with the neurotics of our culture, and the argument
as to the cause-and-effect relationships of basic personality to
primary institutions on the one hand and to secondary institutions
on the other may prove to be circular. My task here is not to consider the validity of the conclusions reached by this form. I contrast, now, the complex causal and functional conception for understanding personality and culture with the kind of conception now
employed by certain other students of group personality. I think
now of the work of Ruth Benedict and of the many studies of
national and other group character pursued by Margaret Mead
and her associates.

If in going to Chan Kom to make a study of the personality
prevailing there I should follow the lead of these workers, I should
conceive the whole before me very simply but very comprehensively. I should conceive of the way of life of the village as an
assemblage of institutions, beliefs, practices as to caring for and
raising children, religion, and material productions and type of
personality in many kinds of mutual interrelations. There would be
no one cause producing an effect in personality. There would be
no necessary separation of institutions into primary and secondary,
and I should not have to separate out from the typical finished
personality a primary phase at once effect of some institutions
and causative of others. The circularity of the system now becomes
its virtue. In Dr. Mead's words, "The student of cultural character

recognizes ... a circular system within which the newborn child
or the adult receives, perpetuates, and stimulates behavior in others
in terms of the entire cultural tradition, so that the method of child-
rearing, the presence of the particular literary tradition, the nature
of the domestic and public architecture, the religious beliefs, the
political system, are all conditions within which a given kind of
personality develops."[19]

Such a form of thought for characterizing the little community
may be called a unique analyzed system. As far as it alone takes us,
it allows us to understand how it is that the parts of this system
fit together. The system differs from the usual "functional" ethnographic description of a small community in that facts of typical
personality are introduced and emphasized. Indeed, the institutions
tend to be grouped around the person and his biography; the
developing personality is the axis of the system; one thinks of the
customs and institutions as they communicate meanings and values
to the individual and make him a kind of being in which these
are internalized. But each system—so far as this conception goes—
is *sui generis*, and in it no one cause achieves a single and certain
effect. The scheme of thought, while it remains accessible to the
advances of more analytic and precise science, lies closer to portraiture than does the conception of basic personality and its
developmental relationships.

And what of ethos or system of values? In this chapter, devoted
to group personality, ethos has been the head of King Charles,
intruding unasked into the discussion, and yet not really considered.
What form is taken by this conception?

World view, temperament or group personality, and ethos are
(remarked Milton Singer) all on the self-axis. All represent the
shift of description from products of culture to psychological
characterization. Our examination of ways of conceiving the little
community has led us through points of view corresponding to
kinds of scientists and scholars. We first looked at the little community as people getting a living in relation to natural resources;
the geographers might have been our guides then. In describing
the little community as social structure, we emphasized terms,
aspects of reality, especially employed by sociologists. Now we
have come to describe the whole as a psychologist would, especially
a psychologist concerned with personalities, for personalities are
the human wholes of psychology. Further, the group personality,

and the temperament of a people, are conceptions on the self-axis that emphasize feelings. Also, let us now recognize that these conceptions describe the reality—after taking a long deep inside look—in terms appropriate to the outside student. Modal personality is what people are however they think they are or ought to be. The concept of ethos is on the self-axis too. But the essential meaning of ethos lies in norm, in the conceptions the people have as to the good. It is what is to them desirable. It is a psychological characterization in that the conception looks at these norms as they exist within the human being. It is conduct looked at in terms of standards felt and believed in. Included within it are the standards as to relations between one's self and other people and between one's self and God. If contemplation is a good, contemplation, as an internalized norm, is part of the ethos. Modal personality is a description of the kind of person seen by the outsider who has looked inside the people. Ethos is a description, written by the outsider, of the way the people there see and feel the rightness and wrongness of things. This may be in part formulated by the people. In great part, it is implicit in the drift and struggle of their inner life. Ethical system is then a special case of ethos. Ethos is the system of judgments, implicit and explicit, characterizing the group. And included among these judgments are the judgments as to how people ought to be, but not the conclusion of the outside psychologist as to how they really are.

The further movement of our thought from modal personality to ethos carries us a little away from the kinds of ideas and interests characteristic of psychologists. Ethos is a value-system internalized, and it is not the psychologist who talks most of value-system. It is the philosopher. We expect philosophers to be interested in norms. We have reached a segment of our great circle of vision upon the real community that is appropriate to the interests of the philosopher. And thinking of this, we remember that value-systems are but one of the great interests of the philosopher. The norms that rule people are only one of the philosophical provinces. Another is the ideas held as to the nature of things and the nature of knowing. If ethics is one standardized philosophical area, metaphysics is another. There are ultimate problems of the good and there are ultimate problems of being. One might look at the little community as a way of conceiving the universe and man's place in it, a way **and a** product of knowing and conceiving.

VI

... AN OUTLOOK ON LIFE

Throughout these chapters occasional reference has been made to the "inside view" in contrast to the "outside view." It has been recognized, but only incidentally and by the way, that the student of the community has two positions to assume in communicating to other students what he has learned about the community. He must first take the position of the nomad or agricultural villager or citizen of a small town in a modern state and look out on something as that person looks out upon it. The investigator has to see the meaning, understand the valuation, and feel the feeling connected with object or act in the mind of the native. Only after he has seen it from the native's point of view may the investigator change his viewpoint and look at that object or act—together with the meaning and the value it has for the native—as an object of scientific interest now to be described from the outside and related by the investigator to other things according to the demands of a more detached and abstract understanding.

This necessity to see the thing first from the inside and then from the outside arises in understanding anything personal or cultural; it is true in understanding a pot or a plow or a sledge, for one must take the viewpoint of the native at least long enough to see that to him the object has the uses and other meanings that are suggested by our words "pot" or "plow" or "sledge." If one is studying a religious ritual the necessity first to take the native's point of view is all the more compelling because the meanings and values of religious rituals are complex and subtle. Much of the advance of anthropological wisdom has come with the more discriminating and careful assumption of the inside view of things. Thus, the concept of totemism seemed a simple and uniform conception in early anthropology when the acts and objects called totemism were looked at pretty much from the outside. Then all totemic people seemed much alike, but as inside accounts appeared of Australian totemism and of totemism in other parts of the world, the very great differences in meaning of the things once called totemism became apparent, and the concept changed its nature and its usefulness.

This necessity to take the inside view mediately on the way to systematic understanding is the peculiarity of the study of the personal and the cultural. The student of star or starfish, of chemical element or of atom, does not have to enter sympathetically into any of these things to learn what these things think and feel because, of course, they don't think or feel. The student there can begin with the outside view. He can describe the star or the starfish at once as it looks to him. But the sentiments, ideas, and judgments of good and bad that make up the mental states of other people are the very stuff of the personal and cultural studies; they are the data out of which such science is to be made as its students can make. On the other hand, these mental states of other people do not become data, do not enter into abstract and general knowledge, until they are looked at from the outside and given names that relate them now in the minds of outside students to other such data. If I should come perfectly to share the inside view of the Maya Indian villager, to share all his thoughts and feelings, and yet could state these thoughts and feelings only in his language, in his gesture and act, I should have triumphed over the difficulty of getting the inside view, but of course I should have failed as completely as a scholar or scientist. There was a student of the Zuni Indians years ago, Frank Cushing, who assumed the inside view so perfectly that he became in effect a Zuni Indian and was made, I believe, a Priest of the Bow in their religion. But after that he told outsiders nothing more about the Zuni.

This tension between the inside view and the outside view, this obligation to manage correctly the relationship between them, is the central problem in studies of culture or of personality. Let us examine the problem as it occurs in the more holistic descriptions of little communities.

Looking back at the forms for such descriptions that we have so far considered, I seem to see that in each case the propositions we have employed are in part in terms of the inside view and in part in terms of the outside view. Further, I seem to see that as we have moved along the arranged order of conceptions, from ecological system to ethos or system of values, we have tended longer and longer to put off the moment for leaving the inside view in favor of the outside view.

When Evans-Pritchard writes about the ecological system of the Nuer he begins with a paragraph[1] in which he tells us that to the European the land of the Nuer, with its endless marshes and wide savannah plains, has no favorable qualities, while to the Nuer it is the finest land on earth. When he writes of the Nuer and his cattle as the parasites of each other, he is telling us how the relationship between man and cattle looks to him, Evans-Pritchard; and it is again the outside view of the scientist that is expressed when he reaches a six-point description of Nuer ecology in terms of symbiosis, cycles of transhumance or seasonal migration, and delicate balances of an economy in equilibrium. This is the scientist speaking to other scientists; Evans-Pritchard does not have to ask the Nuer if that is the way they see themselves in the world around them.

On the other hand, when Evans-Pritchard describes how Nuer men wake at dawn in the midst of their cattle and sit contentedly watching them till milking is finished, how they compose songs about the cattle as they watch them graze, how they again contemplate their beloved cattle in the evening, he is helping us to understand the absorption of the Nuer people in their cattle, and the warmth, interest, and joy which these Africans experience in connection with their beasts. The young Nuer "often at night ... walks among the cattle ringing an ox-bell and singing the praises of his kinsmen, his sweethearts, and his oxen."[2] In such passages we are helped to see the Nuer world as the Nuer look upon it. These are almost the words that Nuer might frame if, in English, they were telling us directly about it.

The student of social structure also has this problem of combining the inside and the outside views. Professor Fortes, in his study of the Tallensi, took the inside view when he talked with this native or that, coming to share his thoughts and feelings about his kinsmen or his lineage. He has learned what the native has in his mind about how he should or may behave as to one relative or another. Then Professor Fortes has constructed that systematic description of Tale institutions in terms of a framework of persisting organized groups interacting, like warp and woof on a loom, or like blood and tissue in an organism, with the more intimate domestic life of the native.

Does the Tale native see the world as it is described by Fortes in terms of social structure? It is better to say, I think, that he lives that world. He could not state it the way Fortes does. There is no claim in Fortes' description that the native has any words or ideas corresponding to Fortes' classes of functions, jural, political, and so on, or that he conceives the whole social structure in the formal and abstract way in which Fortes presents it to us. Fortes has attended to that part of the native's view of things that bears most nearly upon a mental structure descriptive of certain emphasized aspects of the whole reality, emphasized by Fortes, not by the native, and has built in his outside mind abstractions of complexity at considerable remove from the way the native sees the world.

Ecological system and social structure do not call upon the student of a community to remain for long inside the mind of any particular native. Rather, these conceptions call for understanding that many natives think similarly about just this one kind of situation or relationship. The scaffolding of ideas that guides the investigator is composed of relationships, groups, institutions. As we now move to human career, group personality, and system of values or ethos, we move to conceptions in which the self is the axis. Now the investigator must stay with the states of mind of somebody in the community as these states of mind range over many experiences and many phases of a single human life.

At the same time, the student of typical human career or of group personality is driven by the demands of science to find words that will describe that career or that personality as it appears to the outside student, however the native in the community studied may look on it.

That summary of the Chan Kom character that appears, *passim*, in the later book about that village, is offered the reader on *my* warrant. I do not know or assert that the native sees his own character that way. On the other hand, in so far as the language I use tells of the virtues extolled in Chan Kom, in so far as it says that the Chan Kom people think a man ought to be prudent, industrious, and sober, I am describing something seen from the inside view: the conception held as to the good man and the good life. Again there are to be reported two dimensions of the reality:

the native's own view of the good life and the good man, and the outsider's description, in the language of Freud or Kardiner, or in the categories found in the Rorschach protocols, as to the kind of a man that he is. It is because we have moved from conceptions developed from a consideration of institutions and institutionalized relationships between kinds of persons to conceptions that lie on the axis of the self, that the management of the relationship between inside and outside views has become so difficult and subtle. There is the inside view of what a person is. There is that view of what he ought to be, his own inside view. There is our outside view of what the person there is. (What we think he ought to be is, by the declared rules of science, excluded from our subject matter.) And there are our formulations made in terms admissible to science, of these three things. All this without adding the relations among what people think they are or should be and what the outsider finds them to be, or the developments and explanations of these things!

Ethos too is a conception on the axis of the self. But now the self of the Chan Kom villager, for instance, is no longer the central object of the outsider's description. That place is now taken by the normative system characteristic of the villager's view of things. The self as a whole thing is a little to one side, so to speak; the entire meaningful world around the villager is nearer the focus of attention than it is in the study of group personality. If I report the ethos of Chan Kom I may claim to describe the whole culture, but I describe it as it lodges in the thoughts and feelings of the typical villager. In describing ethos one describes the cosmos within, but it is that cosmos as felt and judged to be right or wrong, good or bad, desirable or not to be desired by the human being of the community studied. Ethos requires the investigator to take an inside view that is very deep and very broad. It makes him share the intimacies of conscience and the villager's feelings of shame or guilt.[3] It sends him to consider the views and feelings of people about all that is around them in so far as values are attached to these views and feelings. Ethos holds the student to the inside view until a whole is reached that comprehends all the range of life, seen now not as a personality or a developmental sequence, but as an ordered position of the insider as to the good life.

The good man, that was the inside dimension of the conception of the group personality, is now one segment of the internalized view of things which we call ethos. The student of ethos or value-system adopts such a language moving him toward science as refers to the whole culture conceived as a moral orientation. The words that now appear for parts of this presently conceived whole are taboos, sanctions, judgments, guilt feelings; or, in that aspect of ethos that is seen not so much as private life but as explicit ideals, the corresponding words are virtues, standards, manners, morals.

In these remarks about ethos a kind of phrasing has crept in that was not used in what was said earlier in this chapter about ecological system or social structure, or even in the statements about group personality. I wrote that in turning to ethos as the organizing idea the whole meaningful world of the villager comes nearer to focus. I put it down that ethos has reference to the whole range of life. I recognized that with ethos it is possible to take into account the whole culture from the inside view as it is not so immediately possible in considering ecological system, social structure, or group personality.

The conception of ethos borders on a conception of the whole of the community which we might now call "outlook on life" or "world view." As ethos borders on group personality and tends to blur with it for the reason that both conceptions require attendance to the whole inner structure of the person, so ethos borders on world view and, I think, tends to blur with that concept, because both call for an inside view of the whole meaningful world of the native.

Have we now reached another intellectual form for the understanding of the community as a whole? May we not mean by "outlook on life" or "world view" the whole meaningful universe seen from the inside view? If such an idea is conceivable and useful, its distinction from ethos must lie in this difference: Ethos is a precommitment by the outside investigator to look at values as the leading mode of the personal and social life. Ethos is a conception in which the normative aspect of human experience is in advance given priority, allowed at the outsider's decree to give order to the whole.

What if one attempted to maintain the inside view over the whole range of the native's life without a preliminary commitment to value? What if one put one's self in the native's place without such a commitment at all, attempting to see the world as the native sees it, not with reference to even so large a thing as personality or system of values, but with reference to everything, just as everything comes to the native? That would be a commitment to the inside view to the uttermost.

Looking back on the accounts of the little communities on which these discussions have been largely based, we shall not find a full and consistent presentation of a world view. Holmberg tried to get the Siriono to tell him what they thought about things about them; he reports: "The Siriono conception of the universe is an almost completely uncrystallized one. My Indian friends never voluntarily talked about cosmological matters, and when I attempted by questions to get some insight into their ideas about the nature of the universe I almost always met with failure."[4]

And in his account we meet with the merest hints of Siriono attitudes toward things: that there is no grouping of the stars into constellations and no records of time; it is thought that animals are to be hunted and evil spirits to be avoided, and so on. That chapter in Professor Evans-Pritchard's book that describes time and space as the Nuer live and conceive them is a fragment of Nuer world view, and also a description in the outsider's terms.

I wrote a little sketch of the world view of the Maya villagers in the fifth chapter of the *Folk Culture of Yucatán*. There one finds something about the structure of the natural and supernatural universe as the Maya see it. I report that these people see the cosmos as quadrilateral, with importance attached to the four corners of things—house, cornfield, village, earth and sky. This four-cornered universe is, I write, conceived of as in layers, with underworld below and heavenly world above, and within this layered cube exist or move supernatural beings that have hierarchical relationships as well as special functions and responsibilities.

Further, I tried to represent the villager's view of the moral structure of the earthly life that reflects or expresses the structure believed to exist among the supernaturals and in the seen universe. I tell of the familial structure in this connection, and mention the expression of the corresponding heavenly hierarchy in the arrangement of ritual foods as placed on the altars in ceremonies. There is something in this chapter about the symmetry of the man-god relationship and the conception of a sort of sacred agreement between man and the supernaturals.

So far the account has to do pretty much with what is thought to be, by the Maya, but the normative element of this world view is also strongly present in what is reported. The connections of the ideals of piety and industry and prudence with the religious rituals as expressions of the attitudes toward deity, the connection of sobriety and moderation as ideals of conduct with the belief as to the avoidance of immaterial principles or beings called "evil winds," and with the management of the opposing dangers and benefits involved in the categoric distinction made by the native between foods, plants, and remedies called "cold" and those regarded as "hot"—all these matters indicate a view of things in which the existent and the normative are both present to the villager. Things are and things ought to be, being such as they are. That is the nature of world view. But in my short chapter a very great deal of the outlook on life of these people gets no attention at all.

It is the attention to the native's conceptions of the cognitive along with the normative and the affective that distinguishes the world view from other conceptions for describing the whole reality. World view is the philosopher's approach to the whole. In attempting to describe a little community in terms of world view the outsider withholds his suggestions for systematizing that whole until he has heard from the natives. The outsider waits. He listens to hear if one or many of the natives have themselves conceived an order in the whole. It is *their* order, *their* categories, *their* emphasis upon this part rather than that which the student listens for. Every world view is made of the stuff of philosophy, the nature of all things and their interrelations, and it is the native philosopher whose ordering of the stuff to which we, the outside investigators, listen.

Apparently the Siriono have not had the time or patience or interest or whatever may be the causes of reflective thinking to begin their own philosophy. Yet perhaps there is more reflection and ordering of things there than we know from Holmberg's account (which is, incidentally, a remarkable ethnological achievement).

Clyde Kluckhohn has written: "Speculation and reflection upon the nature of things and of man's place in the total scheme of things have been carried out in every known culture. Every people has its characteristic set of 'primitive postulates.'"[5] And in the paper from which I quote these words Professor Kluckhohn gives an account of the world view, although he does not use that term, of the Navaho Indians, a people he has studied long and well. The account is of the way Navaho conceive experience and things, of all sorts. It gives the "implicit philosophy"—the "underlying premises," the "laws of thought"—again his words. Kluckhohn has sought to find the basic ways in which the Navaho arrange their experiences, to identify the categories in which the Navaho group things, and to relate these cognitive aspects of their outlook on life to their emphasis and ordering of values. The account begins with the ways Navaho think, moves to the ways they conceive things—evil, the sacred, property, personality, and so forth—and continues with an account of their value-system, their normative life, their ethos.

In writing about the world view of the Maya I was very conscious of the presence of native philosophers. Perhaps I was prepared for the possibility that there were such by the important work of Paul Radin[6] in this field of study and I knew one such philosopher well, a villager of a strongly reflective turn of mind. In trying to set down something to represent the world view of all the village of Chan Kom I could not ignore the fact that there were some villagers who apparently thought little about the nature of all things and looked on a world with very little order in it of which they were conscious; that there were reflective laymen like my friend who conceived much more of the whole in a much more ordered way; and that, finally, there were specialists in esoteric knowledge, those who had memorized the traditional prayers for use in the pagan rituals, who had a view of certain aspects of the Maya universe which was not shared with other people in their community. In describing world view there is always the question, Whose view? Among all the variants of culture, those connected with world view are, I think, among the most variable.

To stress this truth and this difficulty, let us imagine ourselves opening two books, two existing books, each a record of one man's view of things in a community unfamiliar to us. Each is a long report by a native of that community who set out to tell outsiders about the world around him.

Johan Turi, a Lapp, sets out to make a book[7] through the ethnologist, Mrs. Hatt, that tells everything about Lapp life and circumstances, his own declared purpose. Turi knows he is talking to that world outside the Lapps, that world which crowds upon the

Lapps and makes new difficulties for their nomad way of life. He
wants the Norwegians to understand how Lapps live. For Turi life
is action and action is mostly with regard to reindeer. His inside
view is of reindeer, the care of reindeer, and about fishing, wolves,
and usually about work, the work as it changes with the seasons.
Turi has tales to tell. They are little tales about men doing things,
or about the underground little people, the Uldas, and how they
take away Lapp children from their cradles. But Turi is no historian.
When asked about the origins of the Lapps he says, "There are all
manner of tales, but it is not certain that they are true, as they have
never been written down."[8] Nor do Turi's stories and his accounts
of practical action fit into any pattern of the universe about which
Turi is able to speak. They make no epic of Lapp origins; they do
not link the Lapps in any consistent way with the physical universe;
the tales and descriptions of the activities provide no set of coherent
symbols for the understanding of existence. This is an outlook on
life with great richness of meaning and feeling, but with very little
intellectual structure. Turi is no philosopher.

Down in the north central Sudan, in the great bend of the Niger
river, Professor Marcel Griaule[9] found a primitive philosopher
named Ogontêmmeli, an aged African diviner, initiated into esoteric
religion and knowledge by his grandfather and later instructed by
his father. Then, having become blind, Ogontêmmeli sat in his
darkness and thought through the orderliness of the outlook on life
of his mind's powerful eye. And what came out, in the accounts he
gave Professor Griaule in thirty-three long meetings, is wonderfully
coherent in structure. It is an intricate linkage and fusion of form
and meaning, of symbol piled upon symbol, a marvelous primitive
system of thought about the origins and the nature of the world
and man's place in it.

The account has several dimensions of organization. It provides
a historical organization of existence, for the first beginnings of the
world at the hand of God are described and connected with all the
little parts of the contemporary life of this people, the Dogon.
Everything—houses, weaving, pottery, the human body—has some
connection with the line of events going back to creation. The
conception has also a meaning of similar parallel forms. The village
is laid out as the parts of the body lie with regard to one another,
and so forth. The conception has, third, a moral order; human

conduct is defined, the significances of human life are revealed in this same system of symbols, at once geographic, depictive, and historical.

These two books declare the problem of the variety of world views. We cannot say, from these accounts alone, how much of the difference between Turi's account, that of a man of action, and the account of the Sudanese philosopher represents differences in culture and how much differences between the two men as individuals. Probably both kinds of differences are present here. The life of the Lapps does not give the philosophic temperament as much chance to develop as does the settled, more complex life of the Dogon. On the other hand Turi and Ogontêmmeli are plainly two different kinds of men.

The books raise also the problem of the effect of informing or of stimulating information about world views on the intellectual structure of the world view. An outlook on life is a construction, whether it is the native's or mine. No man holds all he knows and feels about the world in his conscious mind at once. Presumably the Maya villager is frequently aware of a four-cornered structure of things and other principal co-ordinates—rain, protecting deities, the need to keep one's account with the gods—such things come easily and often to his mind. Further details, deeper relationships, emerge to awareness during the ceremonies when the meaning of things is dramatized before him, and if the native is induced to sit and reflect, if he finds it interesting to arrange his thoughts so as to communicate them to someone, perhaps an ethnologist, the structure of the world view grows and develops. Every account of a world view is therefore a temporary construction, a precipitation of a crystal from thoughts that from day to day are carried in the flowing solution of life's doings. It might be useful to recognize this distinction between these two aspects of the outlook on life and to find a term for each. We might mean by "world view" or *Weltanschauung* the total inside view of a cultural community as it is learned about and assembled by the student on the outside of that community. In describing the world view, the student would take account of such categories of experience as he finds implicit in the conduct and language of the native, whether or not the natives as a whole state these categories to themselves. The word "cosmology" might serve to refer to such formulations of their own world view as are accomplished by the natives, especially by the more reflective natives. We know of communities in which a distinction between two levels of world view is recognized by the people themselves. Among the Maori of New Zealand there was a more esoteric and complete view of the origins and nature of things which ordinary Maori knew, that was understood only by certain specialists. Ogontêmmeli probably achieved a cosmology in reflecting upon a world view already more than commonly coherent and ordered.

If in conceiving of outlook on life, a form of thought for describing another's culture as a holistic inside view, we have reached a limit of possible progression away from external view and cultural product to inside view and content of thought, we have also come closest to the horns of the ethnographical dilemma. We seek now to present the world of the villager as he sees it, entirely so, but we also seek to describe that world to other people like ourselves who are not of it; and to do this we have only the words of our language and the groupings of experience that have been developed in our kind of life, not in Lapp life or Dogon life. When we were describing the life of an exotic group in terms chosen from the equipment of our science, like "symbiosis" or "social structure," we frankly claimed the necessity to describe the unfamiliar way of life in our language and forms of thought.

Now we are conceiving the possibility of using the terms and forms of thought that the native uses for ordering all of his life. If we use only his terms and forms of thought we merely become natives like those we study, speaking and thinking as he does—imagining for a moment this impossibility could be achieved—and no communication to outsider would result.

I remember my feeling of achievement when I thought I had come to understand that a certain Maya word had a complex meaning of considerable subtlety, only to realize that no English words would do justice to the meaning of the term I had come to share with the native. I had, of course, encountered the inevitable problem of translation. I gave up, in this case, the translation as too difficult, and put the Maya word right into my English account. But to do this consistently would have resulted in a work written in Maya, to do which I was certainly not competent. And that way lies a permanent solipsism of the cultures.

The "ethnographical dilemma" is the scientist's form of the problem encountered in our common-sense life as the problem of "intercultural understanding." How are we to understand another people through definitions of experience that are different from those we are trying to understand? Ultimately it is the problem of communication and understanding between any two human beings. In all these cases it seems to us that in some circumstances understanding is in fact reached. And in all of them the way to understanding seems to lie through an alternation of talking and listening. One talks to the other, expressing one's self to him so that he may interpret your signals to him through a projection of himself into you. And then one listens to him with the best projection of one's own sympathetic feelings and thought about the other that one can achieve, held in suspense and made subject to correction.

The simple fact seems to be that to study and to report the way of life of another people one must begin by assuming, as common sense assumes in trying to reach understanding in talking with another person, that something is the same in that way of life and one's own. One cannot listen meaningfully to another without supposing that there is something in his way of conceiving things and of judging that is the same as one's own. The concept, the scientist's effort to make this explicit, is a kind of hearing device. It states these assumptions as to what may be the same in the outlook of that other and in my own outlook. Even the most external view of another's culture, in terms perhaps of his observed habits of work, contributes something to scientific knowledge and to "intercultural understanding" too. A developed concept of world view would attempt to represent much more of that other's understanding of things. But that concept too assumes that there is something in what I am trying to find out about that is the same as that which I already know in myself, in my own view of things.

Our neighbors are a little different from us, the peasant peoples of Macedonia a little more different; in India, in New Guinea, there is something more alien; and yet we cannot go so far as to reach entirely beyond the familiar. I may at any moment find in a distant people something very familiar, as seemed to be my experience when I rediscovered the Protestant ethic among pagan Catholic Maya Indians.

The outlook on life, or world view, is one dimension of the

common human. Group personality, moral life, social structure—all concepts—require that we see something to be the same in that which is otherwise different. World view differs from these others only in that we seek to share as much of the other's total vision as we can, and attend especially to his formulations of relationships within his conception of the nature of things. Yet to this task we bring whatever forms of thought, whatever possibilities of such arrangement as have been conceived by our philosophers, linguists, and other scholars and scientists. The outsider cannot wholly withhold his suggestions as to how the inside view is to be organized.

So we find it useful in studying world view to attend, for example, to the work of Whorf[10] and other students of language who tell us that the inside view of experience may be in part learned about through attention to the syntactic patterns of the language spoken by the people who have that view, and we see in the way F.S.C. Northrop[11] goes about consideration of alien cultures in his studies of the Orient and the Occident a suggestion for understanding of world view. He sees the conceptions of being, the ontological order of the native, to be the basic and determining mode of world view. This is to conceive a possible universal structure of world view: a system in which the conceptions of being are primary and all the rest is derivative.

Today the characterizations of world view that we find in the literature are for the most part shorthand, connotative descriptions of wholes that remain in large part unanalyzed, and that lack any generally applied structure of thought to guide such little analysis as has begun. It has, for instance, been said by Bunzel of the world view of the Zuni Indians that it "is a remarkably realistic view of the universe. It is an attitude singularly free from terror, guilt, and mystery."[12] Such a characterization tells us something, and if we read further about the Zuni we recognize that such a general characterization covers a great deal of particular fact about them. It would be a development of our procedure in the direction of science if we were able to make use of some generally applied structure of thought for conceiving of all world views.

The little attempt I once made[13] to suggest how such a general structure of thought about any world view might be developed begins with the assumption that all world views are visions outward from the self; in other words, it supposes that in every human community everyone distinguishes his own self from all other things (though there may be differences in the quality and degree of separation) and sees all else from this recognized fact of self. Further, I made the supposition that the scene of their lives upon which all men look is conceived by them as having some order: that chaos is not a possible vision of the world for anyone. Still further, my little universal plan of life includes the assumption that this order includes elements that in my own language are connoted by the words "man," "nature," and "god," however these elements may be connected or distinguished in other world views; and finally, that for all men existence has some structure of direction or possible consummation, so that there are characters, theme, and story in every world view.

Such an attempt to state abstractly and somewhat formally the common characteristics of all world views will be found to have such value as may appear from its use in characterizing and comparing the world views of particular people. Other attempts, already made[14] or yet to be made, may well turn out to be more useful than this of mine I have just briefly summarized. Any such scheme, like every concept or set of theoretical assumptions, always does some violence to particular reality. So my little generalization may be found to leave out too much of what appears in any one world view, or to bend too much out of shape the real visions of the universe that there are. At least let me claim that more than one investigator has sought all-inclusive concepts for the description and comparison of world views. World view does not start from any choice of a particular segment of cultural life. It does not emphasize economy or social structure or personality or even ethos, system of moral norms. It enters seriously into the possibility of devising a form of thought for general use of the real whole of the little community that awaits the insider's total vision and conception of everything.

VII

This consideration of the available alternative forms for thinking about the little community has reached its seventh point of attack. We have gone this far without looking squarely at the possibility— perhaps the necessity—of conceiving of a small human settlement as the subject of a history. Yet it is obvious that one may make deliberate effort to give an account of past events in a village as in a nation or an empire, and some writers have done so. Local history is encouraged and written by professional historians, the study of Nordic folklife is in great part historical, and many an ethnological description includes something about the past of the community that is otherwise described in the present. What are some of the possibilities and limitations of the history of little communities?

One quite unprepared by training to write a history is disqualified from saying how it should be done. Certainly I shall not attempt to do so. But these chapters express an effort to learn what might be done by looking at a few things that have been done: by reading and thinking about some published studies of other men, and by reading and thinking about some published studies of my own. Now I may bring forward the little experience I have had with the writing of history about villages, and make the comment on it which seems to me to move us along the road to understanding the holistic nature of the small distinct societies that are our subject matter.

There are aspects of history, illustrated in special form in small communities, to which I do not propose to give thought here. There are great general questions with which historians are concerned that shall have no mention here. Nothing shall be said about causation in history, and very little about how motives and influences are to be established in past actions. There will be nothing about the schools of historians or about philosophies of history; and I shall not ask the little community to reveal to us the final answer to the question as to what the present may learn from the past.

At another extreme of range of problems of history lie the questions as to historical method in the narrow sense: the critical examination and analysis of the records of the past; the questions as to kinds of sources and as to how they are judged and used by historians. It would be interesting and constructive to examine, as I shall not do, how the ethnologist, studying a present people, is like or unlike the historian, studying a past people. That quality of mind called "historical-mindedness"[1] by which a historian, studying a document, sees events and personalities with the eyes, standards, and sympathies of individuals of other times, is very like the quality of mind by which a student of a living but unfamiliar people sees events and personalities with the eyes, standards, and sympathies of those other people.

One might explore the consequence of the fact that the historian's people are no longer there to talk to. There is a great difference in that the ethnologist, talking to living people, makes from what they say records of which he is the writer. On the whole, this making of records from interview and observation by ethnologists has been casual and even irresponsible as compared with the critical canons for treating sources that the historian has developed.

The ethnologist has two parts to his primary task: he has to think about what to ask about of whom, and he has to think about how to make his record of what is said and done and how then to interpret it. The historian must take the document that is left him. The student of a living community is directly within the universe that he sets out to describe and explain; therefore, he faces directly the problems of sampling and the difficulties as well as the opportunities of getting the people to say and do what will most reveal those aspects of their lives in which the ethnologist is most interested. The problem of judging the truth and relevance of what an ethnologist's informant says to him is not entirely unlike the historian's problem of interpretation of an old document. The ethnologist is helped by at least two advantages that are denied the historian: he may direct his inquiry of his informant as *he* chooses and so make a record along the lines of his interest; and, second, he may come to know directly a great many, perhaps all, of the people and households and common events of the community. The trustworthiness of a good ethnological account lies in the high degree of consistency among the many incidents and many pieces of information which the ethnologist reports. The ethnologist is closer to his materials than is the historian, or than is the sociologist with a questionnaire, and as he knows so much of the whole that he studies directly, in many particular cases the absence of a statistical proof, if no statistics appear in his proof, may be a less serious weakness than it looks.

All these interesting matters I put aside. I look now not at the ethnologist while he is observing and noting down things about the little community, but as, afterward, he writes history. I consider only the historiography of little communities. If the student of band or village sets out to write, whether from documents left by other writers or from the interviews he has with older people in the settlement, a history of that community, how does he form an imaginative reconstruction of the past?

The question is still too broad. It should be limited so as to direct it along the lines of interest of these chapters. So let us ask, if one begins with the desire to understand a community of living people as a whole, what historiography of that community will contribute to our understanding of it as a whole? We have seen that our whole is many kinds of a whole. Of the kinds of wholes we have considered in looking at the contemporary community, which can enter into the history we write of it? What account of what arrangements of events will have relevance to our understanding of the community as ecological system, social structure, a characteristic kind of person and the life experiences needed to form it, or as outlook on life? Or, in the writing of a history of a little community, shall we discover new kinds of wholenesses, or perhaps find that the wholenesses we thought we saw in its present life disappear as we write the account of the events which led up to its present?

Three times in my study of Chan Kom, Yucatán, I made something of an imaginative reconstruction of the past. No one of the three attempts was a well-considered piece of historiography. The three attempts differed greatly. Now, however, looking back on them, I think that from them something can be learned.

In the book about Chan Kom written in 1933 appears a chapter entitled "History." It consists, although not formally, of two parts.

The first part is an account of some events that took place, not in Chan Kom, but in southeastern Yucatán before the Spaniards came there, and of events of the sixteenth to nineteenth centuries. These facts were drawn from histories or archeological accounts already published of Yucatán. I simply read such books and took out assertions of fact about the part of Yucatán where Chan Kom must have been if it was there in those times. There is not much in this part of the chapter that appears directly relevant to understanding of the village as I myself saw and described it.

I do show that Chan Kom lies near a frontier between two ancient rival native principalities, and suggest that the attachment of Chan Kom to lands east of it rather than to the country west of it may have been historically rooted in this old political division. And I do let the reader know something about the war between the Indians and the whites that helps to explain both why the territory in which Chan Kom now lies was an unpopulated frontier into which the founders of modern Chan Kom went, in pioneer spirit, to make a settlement, and also why it was that the very similar Indians to the south of Chan Kom were, as descendants of unreconstructed rebels, unknown and even hostile to the founders of Chan Kom. The second part of the chapter tells of more recent events as recounted to me by the people of Chan Kom themselves. In this part something is told as to the purposes of the founders to win for their settlement material security and political power. This part of the account is more coherent and more closely relevant to the ethnographic description which follows.

Nevertheless the account of the past given in this chapter is meager, superficial, and ill organized. It cannot be seriously regarded as a history of anything. It is rather a collection of statements about past events some of which have a bearing on present-day Chan Kom and others of which do not. In these respects my chapter II is much like many another brief historical introduction which is made to his description of a community by an ethnologist or a student of folklife.

If one has only very fragmentary historical knowledge of a small community, it is perhaps better not to assemble that knowledge in one chapter or group of chapters, but to introduce the historical facts wherever they are relevant in the ethnographic account.[2] If one is able to make a serious study of earlier conditions, using, one hopes, not only the recollections of old inhabitants but also such documentary record of the community as exists in libraries and archives, then one may be able to make a considered and fruitful comparison of the same community at two different times in its history. But this I have not myself done.

In my studies in Yucatán, I paid attention to history for the second time when in 1940 I came to compare the results of studies of four communities of the peninsula of which Chan Kom was one. Then it resulted that, "to the degree to which the investigators obtained information as to earlier custom in the communities they studied, there appeared a certain rough overlapping of the courses of history of each, so that, if their accounts are superimposed on one another at the points where the past conditions of one community coincide with the present condition of the next most isolated community, there results a single historical account, although a very rough one, of culture change in Yucatán."[3]

I did not write that account. In one chapter (III), I did compare the definitions of ethnic and status groups, Indians vs. mestizos, upper-class people vs. lower-class, and so on, with a result that a generalized account emerged as to the sequence of changes in a society whereby two very different and separated peoples, Indians and Spaniards, had entered into relations with each other so that through a series of transitions the society of Yucatán became one of culturally similar social classes rather than one of distinct and hostile ethnic groups.

This procedure has of course been frequently used in providing a history of development of some material tool or other trait of culture: the more ancient form is found in the more remote and less modernized community. We may use this method in inferring historical development of farm vehicles in Sweden or of outrigger canoes in Oceania.

Anthropologists on the whole recognize the procedure as a poor substitute for a history based on documentation. It is not likely that a convincing history of a village as a whole would be written by such a method, and we may leave without further consideration my own little experience with it in Yucatán.

In 1949, I wrote a little book about Chan Kom[4] that is, if anything, a history. It is an account of events in that village between 1917 and 1948, an expansion and development of the second part of that second chapter entitled "History" that appeared in the first book. It covers a period of thirty years within the memory of the leading men of the village. The materials for this little history were chiefly what these men told me about those thirty years. I used also the reported observations and interpretations of my colleague, Villa Rojas, who lived for almost three years in the community as a school teacher, and some notes made and statistics compiled by other visitors to the village. Because this is a history made on the whole, not of records written by other men or by men long dead, but of my direct experience with the community over periods of time from a few days to many months at intervals during seventeen years, and also of the things said to me by men of the village who had lived the experiences told about, the little book raises those important questions of the use and control of observation and interview in the making and writing of histories. For one thing, Villa and I were in the community so much that we were not insignificant parts of the events I later came to write about. Some, at least, of this I saw and part of this I was.

What sort of historiography appears in this little history of thirty years of Chan Kom? Of the historical facts I collected, which did I select to put into my little history and why did I select them to put into my little history, and why did I find those relevant? Why did I emphasize some events and not others? Did my history have a subject? What was it? Why did I begin with 1880? Was there any reason for concluding the account in 1948 other than that that was the year in which I made my last observations? And especially I now ask, is there a unity in my history of Chan Kom and if so of what does that unity consist? Does the history tend to satisfy the expectation of historians or does it make some recognizable contribution to social science—or fail in both respects?

It would perhaps be more enlightening to have someone other than myself offer answers to some of these questions. The reader will form his own judgments on these points, if they interest him. Here are mine for what value they may have.

This book of mine seems to be a history of an accomplishment. It is the story of how these villagers, leaders and followers, made up their minds to do something and then did it. The unity of the history lies in the central fact of the conspicuous collective effort of these people to make their community the progressive chief community of their region. This is a small history with a central theme: a purpose of a people and its outcome. I do not know if this theme was chosen by me from others possible or if it forced itself on me as the only possible or acceptable theme. I incline to the latter opinion. It seems to me that from the first of my acquaintance with these people I saw this purpose and its uncertain outcome to be the axis of interest in the community that any persistent observer would have. The villagers I associated with most closely were the men most committed to this effort. But then they were the leaders of the community, and I found them the most interesting men.

As this purpose and its accomplishment are the theme of the history, its central unifying proposition, so the questions of relevance were determined by it. I attended particularly to the events which led the villagers to make this effort to become modern, progressive, and politically powerful. The sequence of steps by which they attained their end became the beads on my historical thread. The first settling of the community, the establishment of the school, the struggle to receive from the state the communal lands, the coming of outsiders—traders, city people, Americans—the opening of roads, the attainment of political municipality—these are the signal events. I really do not see today what other significant line of organization might have been chosen.

This theme determined also the temporal definition of the history and its inner structure, so far as it has any. I began necessarily where the village began: with a first settlement around a natural well in the forest in the year 1880, and I ended, where I took leave of the village in 1948, with a people who had attained success and had come to find the fruits of victory turning ashen in the mouth. So the small work has a dramatic form: the years up to 1931 develop the theme of aspiration and policy. In 1931–33, there is a crisis midway in the course toward victory. The community is torn by religious schism, and unity is with difficulty regained. Then follows climax in the form of political independence, wealth, and prestige; and anticlimax follows in the weariness of a generation that has exerted itself and finds the achievement only the prelude to new dangers and new decisions to be faced and made.

The reader's interest, if it is caught at all, will be caught by the aesthetic unity of the tale, by the suspense and resolution of the

problem the people set themselves, and by the human interest of
the little story. A reader may also respond to the overtones of
comparison with his own situation as one who has himself experienced, or has known, through recent history, a shaken confidence
in material progress and reform, and has come to see the difficulties
and complexities and dangerous outcomes of this view of the
human career. The book, toward its close, is explicit about this
dimension of its possible significance; it is offered as a *multum in
parvo*.

The overtones of comparison sounded by this little historical
work constitute, I think, a contribution that it makes to social
science. In this book it is as if I had taken the advice of such a
writer on the historical method in social science as Professor M. M.
Postan, of Cambridge, who asserted in his inaugural lecture that
the "microscopic problems of historical research can and should be
made microcosmic—capable of reflecting worlds larger than
themselves. It is in this reflected flicker of truth, the revelations of
the general in the particular, that the contribution of the historical
method to social science will be found."[5] The struggle of the
villagers of Chan Kom with the problems brought upon them by
new technology, increasing commerce, fresh ideas, and breakdown
of the old traditional way of life, is a microscopic account of what
may be seen as a microcosm: a great world represented in a small
one. This way of looking at my small history in its possible relation
to social science calls for a look at history as a whole. It is the entire
tale of the Maya villagers that stands for the much larger tale of
modern man, that pulls the big problems down to village size, so
to speak.

I think it is also possible to look at little histories like this with
an eye to what may be told that relates to the more special problems
of social science. Thus, a student of human ecology might find
relevant to his general understanding of ecological process what is
reported in my book about the effect of soil exhaustion on the
development of new kinds of wealth in cattle and trade, and in the
effect of new roads upon the reorientation of the community from
east to west. Or, he might find, as I suggested earlier, the way in
which the Maya villagers make new villages by settling around
distant milpas, an instance of a general process of formation of
communities by "hiving off."

This book contains something about the effects of technology on other aspects of life: the adoption of the Spanish form of town brought about in the village new forms of association. Women went to wells instead of to the central cenote. Women now were walled off from one another in new neighborhood groupings. The conspicuous difference between indigenous hut and Spanish masonry house resulted in new differences of status among the inhabitants. Moreover, there is something in the little book about the effects of adoption of this form of town-building on the conception the people had of themselves as modern leaders of backward neighbors. There is also something about the development of individual property rights, even against the influence of the national government exercised in confirming communal lands, through the digging of private wells, the building of valuable masonry houses to which strong sense of ownership attached, and the fencing and continuous use of tracts of land out in the bush. There is a tiny history of the rise of individualism in my pages.

I call attention to these connections between particular facts I reported and some general questions not, of course, to recommend my book to social scientists as something in these respects remarkable. I just say that, like other historical accounts, there is something here that might relate to general problems set by more scientifically minded workers.

It is as much true and as little that there is something in the book that relates to the interests of professional historians. A student of the Mexican revolution of this century may find a worm's eye view of it here: something about the effect of a great movement on a remote people. The change in state of mind, from acceptance of the traditional ways to a zeal for progress and reform, which I report in Chan Kom, may be looked at from the point of view of one who writes about modern Mexico, or even about the popular and agrarian movements of the twentieth century in all parts of the world.

But neither social scientist nor historian has been given much help by me in the writing of the book, for I have related the story of Chan Kom explicitly neither to the history of the Mexican "real revolution," nor to any chosen general problem of social science. Historian and social scientist will find in the book a "reflected flicker of truth ... revelations of the general in the particular," but they will have to look for themselves to see the flicker. There is in those pages no explicitly declared unifying central question. As I have said, the unity of the book lies in the kind of human interest which might interest a dramatist or novelist. There is no description of a single demonstrated abstract process.

Yet, clinging for a few moments longer to the book of 1949, I say there is, after all, a chosen emphasis. There is a central subject matter: the collective mentality of the community. I wrote a few pages back that I reported the "change in state of mind." It is the transformation of states of mind that interested me the most. As a history, my book is not so much a history of the products of the cultural life that I describe as it is the "psychological" dimension of that life. I tell something about the tools and the economy, and about the relative stability of the social structure, but I present what happened to these things pretty much in terms of the villager's own view of the changes. And, having become interested in the shifting viewpoints and judgments on the people, I try then to describe these changes to outsiders. The book begins with examination of the question as to why the people changed their minds from an isolationist position to a progressive, go-forward-to-join-other-people position. Then, after using three chapters to describe the material and institutional changes of seventeen years, I try to describe the struggle of minds involved in the religious controversy; then in the sixth chapter report something of the moral judgments of older and younger people upon modern clothes, dancing, schools, and sport. Finally, I offer a general account of the persistent values and ideals of character prevailing in Chan Kom throughout these struggles and transformations. I describe the ethos of Chan Kom, the emphasis on industry, frugality and productive effort, the familial controls, the earthy ethic unconcerned with salvation, and the world view including pagan and Christian beings in a sort of hierarchical common family sharing responsibility for mundane affairs. This ethos and this world view were, on the whole, stable, while other states of mind changed greatly.

As I look at it now, it seems to me that as soon as I become interested in the transformations of village life through time, as soon as I venture into history, while retaining my interest in the more psychological and philosophical aspects of the inside view of the life of this community, I need words to distinguish newly recognized parts and dimensions of the states of mind of the people.

In the book, I used the term "ethos," but I found no words for the less stable parts and dimensions. Nor have anthropological students of group personality or value systems offered much in their published studies with which to describe the transformations and the more ephemeral aspects of collective states of mind. But since I wrote last about Chan Kom, some terms have been suggested to me and I bring them forward now.

Against the relatively stable ethos and world view, the mind of the people changes. They form a decision to progress. The decision is attended with a conception of a glorious future, of building "a village just like the Americans." Let us say that the people formed aspirations.[6] The usual account of a culture, a value-system, a group personality, does not say much about aspirations.

Aspirations are conceptions as to how the future will be or can be made different from the past. The concept is called forth when we attend to people whose states of mind are changing under changing circumstances. If we study a stable and isolated community, we shall probably find, as I remarked earlier, that the future is conceived to be like the past. Such people have no aspirations. But the people of Chan Kom, like people in thousands of other little communities all over the world at the present, have formed aspirations. So we need the word to describe an element of their state of mind that is distinct from ethos and world view, though of course related to both. The old way of conceiving the norms of conduct and the nature of all things persists, but now aspirations to make things different lead the way toward change, and we are required to examine the effect of the old ethos and world view in limiting the aspirations, or the effect of the aspirations in modifying the ethos and world view.

Aspiration corresponds to myth. It is a vision of the desired state of things. But it is prospective, and it is more closely related to action than are the retrospective myths of the little-changing communities; the past cannot be lived; the future must be. So aspiration gives rise to policy at the point where the people formulate means to realize the aspirations. The people of Chan Kom formed a policy to accomplish their aspirations to become a modern town. They determined on ways of appeal to the state government. They adopted a program of leadership among the neighboring villages. They imposed on themselves obligations of work and service that would make their community something different from what it had been before. Policy is the servant of aspiration, the expression in real life of a dream of improvement. Policy is primarily political; it has to do with controls and influences on action, internal to the community and external, domestic and foreign. Policy, like aspiration, is a conception that is needed in the characterization of changing communities.

Aspiration and policy connote things thought about. And they refer to thoughts about the future. Not all the changes of states of mind of which we need take account in describing the history of a little community are provided for by these two terms. In the little history of Chan Kom I tell how, when the new school building collapsed during construction, the state of mind of the people changed at once from confidence and determination to dismay and despair. The whole emotional tone of the collective state of mind was instantly reversed. Let us say that the mood changed.[7] "Mood" is a word that suggests the affective component of the changing states of mind. And mood is a very fluctuating component. During the struggle over the choice of religion, Catholic or Protestant, the mood of the village ran through changes running from deep anxiety and even bitterness to harmonious sympathy. I suppose that in little-changing societies there is also mood, but moods must be stronger and more variable where important changes are conceived or are under way and conflicts are realized. And moods get involved with aspirations and policies; an aspiration to become a pueblo or to achieve national independence is sustained by the more persisting optimistic moods and endangered by the moods that come with doubt and defeat. Mood is the more subjective aspect of morale. If I were turning again to writing the history of Chan Kom, I would look more closely at the interrelations of aspiration, policy, and mood, and try to relate these dimensions of the collective mental states of the people to the more persisting aspects recognized as ethos or world view.

There is thus a way in which the later book about Chan Kom can be seen as a history of some of the wholes which little communities are. It is something of a history of the ethos as related to aspiration, policy, and mood, even though I did not use these last words and did not really examine their interrelations. Perhaps then the book does contribute to our understanding of the more psychological kinds of wholes represented in little communities.

But certainly the book is not a history of the wholeness of the community. It does not ask the question: In the course of these seventeen years did the community become more or less of a whole, and why? If the community disintegrated in these years, I could hardly have escaped the necessity to report the changes in wholeness. But it did not disintegrate. The social structure remained much as it had been; in spite of the struggle over religion and the exacerbations caused by the different efforts toward realizing aspirations, the moral norms, though shaken, were preserved, and the common sentiments of the people remained strong. It is a short story of integration preserved against difficulties. One does not know that the community will remain integrated; the events of the next years may shake or break the wholeness.

Others have written accounts of the integration or disintegration of a little community. Per Gräslund, Swedish anthropologist, has written an account[8] of the recent changes in two villages on the east coast of Sweden. The changes were brought about by new technology, by the development of commerce and most of all by the effects of a law requiring the redivision of agricultural land. This law brought together the tracts of cultivated land of each farmer, where they had come through partition and inheritance to be widely scattered. The law had for its purpose the increase of agricultural production. It was never put into effect in one of the two villages studied, Harstena, but was carried out in about 1880 in the other, Kråkmarö. Gräslund shows that the history of Kråkmarö since the land reform has been one of disintegration. The village became less of a whole. The communal life became much reduced; men came more and more to work separately, to own separately. Houses were moved out from a common settlement each to stand on the owner's separate homestead. The increase of farming reduced the hunting and fishing, and the farming was done separately. The old village association, which had regulated common affairs, the number and care of livestock, and the conduct of hunting and fishing, declined greatly in function and authority. The post of leader became a duty rather than an honor. As common work decreased, the common sentiments that held the people together declined. The new pattern of settlement in scattered farms removed much of the effectiveness of the old controls by talk and example. The authority of the old over the young grew less. People began to move away from the community. Some sold their houses to city dwellers for use as summer homes. Kråkmarö is a dying village. It dies because it has ceased to be a whole.

The history of a village in terms of its loss of wholeness has been written also by D. L. Hatch in his doctoral dissertation submitted at Harvard University in 1948.[9] The village Hatch describes is a New England "town"—a village and its geographically bounded rural hinterland. In size, this community, called by Hatch "Hilltown," is comparable with Kråkmarö, and the story of its disintegration is very similar. That it was a story of disintegration that Hatch was writing apparently became clear to Hatch only in the course of his study. He came to Hilltown to study the effects of the invasion of the New England community by Finns. He found that the coming of the Finns was not the important determining event, and came to describe his study as an account of the town as it was changing from a relatively integrated and self-sufficient rural community to one dependent on cosmopolitan society. The character of the study as a history of the loss of wholeness is made more fully explicit by the summary and analysis of Hatch's work given us by George C. Homans in his book *The Human Group*.[10]

Homans presents the case of Hilltown as illustrating a type of social change to be called social disintegration as contrasted with another type, social conflict. For us interest lies in the similarities of the histories of the loss of wholeness in Hilltown and Kråkmarö. Kråkmarö experienced no immigration of aliens, and Hilltown was not required by law to make over its pattern of land ownership. But Hilltown, like the Swedish village, once carried on much of its labors communally and lost these customs as the commerce and political organization of the larger world came to play greater parts in the villagers' lives. Both communities had in the old days an effective organization of the adult males—the Swedish village association and the New England town meeting—and in both cases these local institutions lost responsibility and authority.

Gräslund does not go into much detail as to the changes in the sentiments that bound the people together in Kråkmarö, but it is clear that there as also in Hilltown, as men and women worked and played less often together, the common sentiments that held them together declined. Gräslund tells us that those in the Swedish village who had in the old days participated in the common enterprises of the village association attested to the fact that there was happiness and festivity in work, and adds that nowadays the lonely homestead owner certainly often works harder on his own land than he did on the village land, but that happiness, when it comes, takes a different character, and joy about work is not so easy when one is alone. The Hilltowners did not move apart from one another as did the people of Kråkmarö; they are alone right in the village. On winter evenings, only one or two men sit in the general store. They sit there just for the wood fire. "It isn't a place to visit now. Folks just wait here to get a car to go to work in, that's all," says the proprietor. The norms of the community with respect to such matters as theft, sexual irregularity, and class position are weakened and have become unclear. People do not have strongly internalized values. The ethos is vague and the goals of life are clouded. Hillside, too, has lost its wholeness.

There is so much that is similar in the histories of these two communities, remote from one another, and so much in the stories that suggests the histories of the disintegration of other rural small communities, that one feels that there is here a change that deserves to be seen as generic—a natural history of disintegration of small rural communities in the course of the development of civilization. Homans includes in his analysis of the story of Hilltown an arresting sentence: "Civilization has fed on the rot of the village."

The considerations of this chapter began with the question: Can a holistic history be written of a little community? In pursuing the possibilities which the question suggests we have remained on the whole in the position of the outside viewer. We have thought only of the history of the little community as conceived by that historian who looks at the community from outside of it and writes that history as he has come to see it. It might be possible to say something about the history of a little community from the inside view. Such a history would be a people's own story as that people have come to conceive it. It would show how a group conceives its unity in relation to time. I think that Boas referred to the mythology of the Tsimshian Indians as the tribal "autobiography." Also in more advanced societies, with holy books and orthodoxy, legend and epic may be taken as literal historic truth. History written from the inside view is the temporal dimension of world view and is probably best considered with that concept.

From our own outside view at least three possible meanings have been discovered in this chapter for the phrase "holistic history." First, the question may refer to the literary unity of the resulting written work. A history in this sense would be holistic in that it satisfies aesthetic expectations. It offers a unity of subject matter of beginning and ending, of, perhaps, uncertainty of outcome and its resolution. If the histories of little communities are written holistically in this sense, the result will at the least provide us with agreeable reading. Furthermore, it may very well be that the aesthetic unity discovered in a pattern of events by an outside historian is itself a revelation of an aspect of the holistic reality.

Second, the history of a little community may be holistic in that its writer tries to see the community as a whole as he writes the story, and uses conceptions either explicitly or implicitly to refer to aspects of its whole nature. So, one might write a history of ethos or world view, as Von Martin in his little book called *The Sociology of the Renaissance*[11] has written a history of the transformation of the ethos of the Middle Ages. In so far as people come to write such histories of little communities, we will be helped to understand the generic holistic nature of little communities, as my thinking of Chan Kom as a history forced me even after writing the book to see new dimensions of the holistic nature of that little community and to find words—aspirations, policy, and mood—for those dimensions.

In the third place, a history of a little community may be holistic in so far as the wholeness of the little community is itself the subject of the history. We are likely to get histories of this kind written by social scientists rather than historians. Disintegration is a concept for social scientists and they are more likely to attend to it than are the professional historians.

We may also recognize the possibility of writing the history of cultural integration or re-integration. But this will be a harder thing to do because the integration of the little community takes place characteristically in isolation, and it is harder to witness an isolated situation. But if we could write what happened to the Indian communities of Paraguay after the Jesuits withdrew, if we write histories of the way in which heterogeneous people arrived on a frontier, say a new settlement in Alaska, come to form themselves into a community in which there is a greater degree of wholeness, we shall be writing something complementary to histories of disintegration: we shall be writing the history of a becoming whole.

VIII

... A COMMUNITY WITHIN
COMMUNITIES

This book began with the idea of a community as a small settlement of people self-contained and distinct from all other communities. Nevertheless we are well aware that no real community
is perfectly so. Unless the account of an early explorer of the Arctic
can be trusted to the effect that a band of Eskimo was encountered
whose members knew of no other living beings on earth, all people
everywhere, whether they live in city, town, village, or nomad band,
know that outside their own community lie other people and other
communities. Therefore, in the minds of all community-dwellers
there are at least two elements of thought to define the relations
between the people of one's own community and people outside
of it: the idea of distance and the idea of difference. The members
of the little community define themselves as a group partly by
contrast with less well-known people who are "out there," and who
are not quite like themselves.

Moreover, it is a familiar fact that the course of human history
has on the whole run in such a way as to reduce the distinctness
of the little community. At one time, before what V. Gordon Childe
has called "the food-producing revolution," people lived in very
small hunting and fishing bands; and in most parts of the world
the hunting and fishing produced so little food that a few people
required for their support a large territory. At that time all the
little communities were indeed little. And they were pretty much
isolated from one another; each was self-dependent. The course of
history, as we all know, has been such as to increase the numbers,
decrease the isolation and greatly increase the mutual interdependence of peoples.

Now we speak of the world economy, and know that events in
one part of the world can affect almost everybody in it. The little

community we are likely to study today is not plainly distinct, and is plainly inclosed within other communities with which its fortunes are bound. In the third chapter we considered the question whether in describing the social structure of the village of Maya peasants we should include the school, the local branch of the Socialist party, and the organization of shareholders in the communal lands—all organizations that had been brought about by agents of the Mexican national government. The Maya village I knew is not fully self-contained. To describe it completely we must reckon with parts of outside communities, or influences from communities that have their centers and their principal being elsewhere than in the village.

How, in describing the little community, are we to include the fact that it is a community within communities, a whole within other wholes? Is it possible to describe as a whole a community whose life is modified by bits of other communities in whose local life we find institutions and offices recently imported into it? What forms of thought are available to us for conceiving and describing a whole that is both inclosed within other wholes and is also in some part permeated by them?

In trying to understand the concept of social structure we began with that idea as put forth by Firth, and then as by Fortes, and only after we had begun to understand the concept as a considered idea to guide systematic study did we attempt to make use of it in connection with facts from Yucatán. But now in beginning to think about the sequence and interrelations of communities, let us reverse this procedure. Let us begin with the facts as we find them in the simplest and most nearly self-contained of the four little communities that have been chosen for special attention here, adding then ideas and concepts as they are suggested either by these facts or by the anthropologists or sociologists who have reported these and other communities to us.

The band of Siriono Indians is easily the most distinct and self-contained of the four. Holmberg, who lived with these Indians for more than six months, had great difficulty at first even in finding the band with which he later associated, so secluded and shy were these Indians; and when he had gained admission to their group he was completely dependent for all material support and all human association upon this little group of about sixty people.

This was such a little community as was all humanity could offer fifteen thousand years ago.

The Siriono band is composed of people all related to one another; it is made up of several matrilinear extended families, each embracing several nuclear families. The band camps together on high ground provided with trees with edible fruits during the rainy season. During the dry season the band breaks up into smaller familial groups. When settled at a camp, the band has a single house; the chief, an officer of very limited powers, occupies the center of this house.

We should find it difficult to write much about the social structure of the Siriono band; beyond the simple familial groups and relationships there is almost none. The people of the band occasionally combine into co-operative hunting parties. The band also provides wives and children. Furthermore, no doubt, it provides a certain amount of common defense against marauders, human or animal, and surely, even in this community where quarreling and indifference are common, a certain primary human warmth always acceptable to mankind.

Outside the band are other bands of Siriono Indians of the same culture and language. But relations with these other bands are very slight. Holmberg tells us that if an Indian wishes to visit such another band it may take him ten days to reach it. He is not sure where to look for it, because its location is frequently changed according to the necessities of the hunting and the weather. When members of two different bands do meet each other, relations are usually friendly, but there are no political or ceremonial institutions that bring the two bands together in any sort of even temporary common action.

Most marriages are made within the band; a man may find a wife in another band, but this occurs very rarely because of the distance between bands, the disposition of the men of a band to keep their women to themselves, and the rule of matrilocal residence which would compel a man if he married a woman from another band to move away from home. In short, there is very little concept of a tribe here, and no tribal institutions.

The Siriono recognize also the existence of other kinds of Indians, those with whom relations are unfriendly. The Siriono do not practice warfare, although they have occasionally killed white men and "missionized" Indians, either to get food or tools or in revenge for other killings. On the whole, the Siriono strive to avoid these other Indians. For the most part, they avoid also the white men of the mission stations and the Indians who have taken up life in connection with the mission.

This is a very simple arrangement of community within communities. Nothing inside the band represents the outside world at all. It is entirely self-contained, except as fears of hostile Indians or occasional thoughts about friendly bands of other Siriono may enter into the native's view of the world. A rare marauding expedition in which the band may be predator or prey slightly qualifies this self-containment of the community.

A simple diagram would represent the inclosure of this little community within others: a small circle, the circumference strongly marked, outside of which would be placed distant other circles, some perhaps colored green for "friendly" and some red for "hostile" with the faintest of lines of relationship between some of these and the band of our central interest.

The situation could be diagrammed differently. One could draw two large circles around the small circle denoting our band. The inner circle of these two would represent the less distant and more friendly outside world of other Siriono. The outside circle would represent the more distant and unfriendly world of other Indians and white men.

We have then two diagrams, one schematically cartographic, and the other diagrammatic, to represent this state of communities within communities as it appears most simply in the case of the Siriono. Let us take the system of concentric circles as our initial form of thought for taking account of the community within other communities. Let us see what becomes of it as we try to make use of it in describing little communities of greater complexity than the Siriono.

This is the form of thought employed by Evans-Pritchard in describing what he calls "structural distance" in the case of the Nuer of the Sudan. I present his diagram of thirteen concentric circles[1] in simplified form. His first four circles, representing nuclear family, homestead, and group of related families I combine into one circle: the village.

The nine circles, the nine successively outward communities

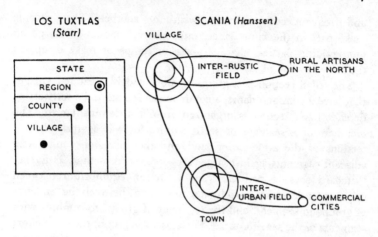

LOS TUXTLAS
(Starr)

STATE
REGION ◉
COUNTY ●
VILLAGE
●

SCANIA (Hanssen)
VILLAGE
INTER-RUSTIC FIELD
RURAL ARTISANS IN THE NORTH
INTER-URBAN FIELD
COMMERCIAL CITIES
TOWN

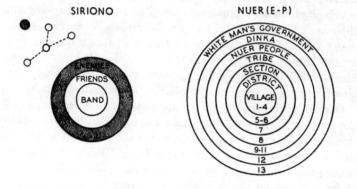

SIRIONO
ENEMIES
FRIENDS
BAND

NUER (E-P)
WHITE MAN'S GOVERNMENT
DINKA
NUER PEOPLE
TRIBE
SECTION
DISTRICT
VILLAGE 1-4
5-6
7
8
9-11
12
13

which Evans-Pritchard recognizes as inclosing the village, are in the simplified diagram reduced to six. The principal fact for us now is that the first four circles or communities of these six are constituted of people of the same language and culture as the Nuer of the village at the center. They are four progressively remote communities of people bound to one another by common institutions, sentiments, and sense of belonging together.

The district is composed of neighboring villages that have easy and frequent communication with one another. These people "take part in the same dance, inter-marry, conduct feuds, go on joint raiding parties, share dry-season camps or make camps in the same locality."[2]

The tribal section is a group of more widely separated villages that have a common name, a common sentiment, and a territory to defend. Each section is organized around a dominant clan. The members of a segment or section unite for war against adjacent sections of the same order, and on other occasions unite with adjacent segments against larger sections. There is thus, as Evans-Pritchard says, a political system "in an equilibrium between opposed tendencies toward fission and fusion, between the tendency of groups to segment, and the tendency of groups to combine with segments of the same order."[3] The closer the group, the more effort is made to compose a feud; between distant members of the same tribe disputes usually go unsettled or are reconciled by force.

Outside the section is the tribe. This community also has a common name, and a common territory, co-operates in warfare and is organized around a dominant clan. The tribe is the largest group the members of which act together for raiding or warfare. If one man kills another tribesman, blood-wealth is paid for the homicide. In the killing of a man of another tribe, though he is a Nuer, blood-wealth is not paid. The age-sets, the groups of young men classified according to their age-position, are organized tribally.

Outside of the tribe is the community of the Nuer people: all the people who speak that language and have that common tradition regard themselves as one unique community and look upon their common way of life as distinct and good. Besides the common language and customs, a man is known to be a Nuer by the evidence of his physical person: a Nuer's front teeth are knocked out at puberty, and six horizontal cuts are made across his brow. All the Nuer tribes occupy contiguous territory. When a Nuer meets another Nuer who is a stranger to him, friendly relations are established. If a Nuer meets a Dinka, the relations are hostile. While a man rarely marries outside his tribe, such marriages, when they do occur, are recognized on both sides. When Nuer fights Nuer, women and children are spared. But when Nuer fights Dinka, it is war to the uttermost.

With the community of the Nuer people, we have reached the

fifth circle of the simplified diagram. There are two more. The next to the last circle represents the community of the Dinka, a people similar to the Nuer in language and culture, yet different. They are the bitter enemies of the Nuer. To the Nuer, the Dinka exist in order to be their enemies. The Nuer raid the Dinka for cattle and slay them out of patriotism.

Finally, in the outermost circle, lies the white man's government. With this world the Nuer does not even share common understandings as to enmity. Evans-Pritchard does not tell us much about the relationships that Nuer have with this remote world. He refers to recently instituted government courts and to American church missions. If we were among the Nuer today, twenty or more years after Evans-Pritchard worked there, we should perhaps find more to say about the effects of this outermost circle upon the Nuer little community.

Let us review and simplify the inclosure of the Nuer village within outer communities. The village is inclosed first within a neighborhood of intimately known other villages. Outside this come two groups with political functions chiefly, the tribal section, organized around a leading clan, and the tribe, a more inclusive group and the largest unit that acts collectively. And outside this lie other tribes also of Nuer. Thus far, in these eleven concentric circles as Evans-Pritchard has them, or in five circles as I have simplified them, we recognize one moral world. At the borders of the Nuer territory the Nuer steps into a world of alien and hostile peoples, more hostile than alien in the case of the Dinka peoples, more alien than hostile in the case of the white man's government. Evans-Pritchard's first seven circles outside of the village correspond, in their essential nature, to the single band of the Siriono together with the friendly bands of other Siriono outside. In the case of the Nuer, the community of "my people" is subdivided into a whole series of communities inclosed within one another and characterized by a transition from intimate relations and functions and from domestic institutions to less intimate relations and functions and to political institutions.

With the Nuer as with the Siriono, there are two kinds of communities outside the larger community of "my people": traditional enemies and the relatively recent and almost completely alien interference of the white man and his civilization. The white man has no place within the Siriono band, and if he has in the Nuer village, we are not told about it in the book I quote.

In these two cases, the scheme of concentric circles seems almost adequate to represent the situation. As I have suggested, the diagram is most in need of some modification to indicate the important difference in quality between, on the one hand, all those concentric communities of the Nuer which share a common culture and some sense of belonging together, and, on the other hand, the hostile and alien people outside of Nuerland. There is perhaps a certain violence of transition between the community of Nuer and that of the Dinka that the scheme of circles does not fully express, and the transition must be even greater as one moves to the circle of the white man's government. Further I imagine that the peculiar kinds of relations of the Nuer with the white man's government and possibly the missions are not fully represented by a spatial scheme which simply puts the white man in the farthest circle beyond the Dinka. What if the white man, the alien government, puts its agents of influence directly into a little community with which we imagine ourselves to begin our work?

In describing the relations of the village of Chan Kom with other communities, in the book written in 1933, I, too, used a diagram of concentric circles,[4] except that I put the circles on a map, and so pulled them out of shape so that they might more or less correspond with the actual territories and settlements included within each area on the map. I recognized three communities concentric to Chan Kom. The first of these is a cluster of hamlets all within twenty kilometers of Chan Kom. This is that community of frequent personal contacts over which Chan Kom exercises economic, cultural, and political leadership. Next comes a wider community embracing villages of importance and influence similar to that exercised by Chan Kom. These villages are not economically or politically dependent upon Chan Kom. Relationships are frequently friendly within this zone. Wives are occasionally taken in a village that lies here. Visiting goes on, especially at times of festivals. The first zone is a political unit, but the second is not.

Outside of both, I recognized a third zone, perhaps a hundred kilometers in diameter, including many villages of similar culture and similar importance to Chan Kom. In this wider community intermarriage and visiting are much less common, and disputes between villages are not rare. Nevertheless, there is in this wider community, I wrote, "a larger polity, a consciousness of common interests that may, in emergencies, be fanned into flames of regional patriotism."[5] During the revolution of 1917, the villagers of this zone fought together. This third outer community corresponds in this part of Yucatán, if anything does, to the tribe of the Nuer. If I had thought of it, I might well have added a fourth zone to represent all Maya-speaking rural villagers, most of them very slightly known or quite unknown to the people of Chan Kom. Like the Nuer and like the Siriono, the Maya villager recognizes in another Maya language, custom, and manners like himself, even if he has never seen him before, one of his own kind.

This comparison of Chan Kom with the Nuer village leads us, however, in a direction of thought which has serious consequences for the use of the diagram of concentric circles to describe the relations of communities in peasant villages such as Chan Kom. Let us look more closely at the situation in Chan Kom as compared with the situation reported by Evans-Pritchard for the Nuer.

First, the political and military organization of the Nuer villages is more complex and more regularly hierarchical than it is with the Maya, and among the Nuer the role of kinship in uniting villages and districts and tribal segments is much greater. Kinship connections decrease and political functions and institutions increase as one goes outward until a peak of political activity is reached in the tribal section; political action then declines while consciousness of common culture persists until one comes to the territories of the Dinka.

Second, in the larger territory within which the Maya lives his life are to be found town, small city, and larger city. These constitute a progressive series of urbanized communities in this order increasingly exterior to the life of the village. These are apparently lacking in Nuerland. In the Maya villages, the political organization, and the economic, are in large part controlled by authority and decision from outside the world of common cultural consciousness: from the world of the European or Europeanized townsman and cityman. The relations that the Chan Kom people have with townsmen and citymen, with people who are not thought of as their own kind of people, are much more numerous, influential, institutionalized, and immediately present in the village itself, than in the case of the Nuer. On the other hand, the difference in culture between the native of Chan Kom and the man of town or city is much less than the corresponding difference in the case of the Nuer—remote from the Nuer as town and city may be.

Thus the folk community of regionally united Maya is an aspect or dimension of the total society of Yucatán, and indeed of Mexico. The city, the town, and the villages considered all together present themselves to us as a new kind of larger whole of considerable distinctness and integrity. Looking at this other large whole, one would not see a series of concentric circles around one village, but rather a complex aggregation of settlements to which any one village such as Chan Kom would be related in a number of kinds of relationships and functions. Even if we put aside the possibility of describing this larger whole—the state of Yucatán, let us say—how are we to describe such a single village in Yucatán as Chan Kom so as to take account of its relations with town, city, and national state?

Among those who have addressed themselves to this problem is Dr. Betty Starr, who has sought for a solution in connection with facts from a part of Mexico not far from Yucatán: the region of Los Tuxtlas, in southern Vera Cruz.[6] Like Evans-Pritchard, she begins with the family, and she recognizes certain other groupings, concentric to one another, within the village itself.[7] We will here consider her work as it relates to the communities that inclose our little community, the village.

Dr. Starr describes the Mexican villager as related not only to his village and its component subcommunities, but also to several communities outside of it at successive degrees of remove from it. One is the *municipio*; the word "county" roughly suggests the nature of this community. Next is the region, a group of counties. Within these two successive communities the villager still finds people of his own kind; he has a sense of in-group with respect to both county and region, but in lessening degree. Thus in this respect Dr. Starr's region corresponds to Evans-Pritchard's Nuerland and to my third zone, or perhaps to my missing fourth zone, for the Maya. Outside of the region, as Starr describes it, are other regions with which the villager feels little affinity.

How does Dr. Starr think of these successive societal entities? She thinks of them as a series of communities each of which is characterized by a nuclear center with a depending surrounding rural area. The nuclear center of the *municipio* or county is the head town *cabeçera*), that of the region is the capital city.[8] She finds this kind of structure also in Japan, and in rural Georgia, U.S.A. In a later and unpublished work[9] she makes it plain that this kind of rural-urban structure requires for its realization certain factors including rural settlement in villages rather than in scattered farms, the sort of compact and nucleated town-planning of Spanish America and elsewhere, a uniform habitat, and an even spread of communication. More generally, I would add that its realization requires the presence of urban centers of influence: towns and cities exercising widespread influence over the economies and governments of the people round about.

Here, I think, the most interesting aspect of Dr. Starr's analysis lies in her recognition of the important and regular qualitative differences in the kinds of relationships that really prevail between the villager, on the one hand, and the people and institutions of the next outer or wider community, the county or the region, on the other. For Dr. Starr does not regard this ordered series of inclosing entities *simply* as a series of areas, one within another. It is significant that she does not often use the word "community" to denote them; she calls them "levels." Moreover, she does not use a diagram of concentric circles. When she makes a diagram,[10] it is a series of squares arranged so that the eye, moving from the village to the symbols representing county and region begins in the lower lefthand corner and moves up as well as out. The word "levels" suggests a series of steps. The communities or levels of integration are different in kind of relationship, and these changing kinds of relationship depend in part on the fact that the townsmen and citymen have institutions, moral life, and view of the world different from those of the villager, while at the same time the villager's life is in long-established adjustment to controls and influences coming from these more urban communities. Dr. Starr brings this out when she tells us that as one moves up the levels, social relations become more impersonal and come to be affected by the principle of superordination and subordination. This is to say that as one moves out of one's village, if one is an Indian of this part of Mexico, one enters into relationships which draw upon only one interest one has, or one role—as a buyer in a market or a litigant in a law court perhaps; and into relationships which express the class or other status differences that prevail in that part of the world between Indian and non-Indian, city person and rustic, laborer and white collar official, and so forth, distinctions which may not be apparent in observing only the day-to-day life of the village itself.

This is a form of thought, expressed in words and in diagram, which can take account not only of the relations of these Indian peasant villagers to one another within their own village, but also of their relations to townspeople and city people who have a life that is only in part shared with them. The series of steps suggests, better than would a simple scheme of concentric circles, the change in the qualities of relationships, the movement into a world wider and more complex than is a single local community with one common set of conventional understandings. The drawing I made of three ovals inclosed within one another, for Chan Kom and its hinterland, is inadequate for the facts I myself reported in the text of the book. Dr. Starr's eccentric series of squares better suggests the viewpoint of the Mexican villager who looks outward from his village and also upward to urban ways of life that are centered in the Spanish-built town and then city which he knows about and occasionally visits.

We seem to need a recognition of a series or range of kinds of communities according to their degree of independence from city, manor, national state, or other center of a different or more developed mode of living. Dr. Starr recognizes this. There are societies without towns and cities "organized primarily upon the principle of extended kinship."[11] We think of the Nuer. Here almost all the relationships of the individual tend to be personal and many-sided. Here we think of the community within communities as a series of concentric circles. At the other extreme are the fully urbanized people who live in the city, or who live in the mind of the city while dwelling in the country or in the farther countryside. These people are in large part organized in terms of relationships, many of them impersonal, with distant people and institutions. Here no diagram of circles and no diagram of regular steps would help us very much. In between these two extremes are the societies in which rural people with long-established local cultures live in partly self-contained little communities; but these little communities are also involved with, and dependent upon, the town and the city. These are the societies of peasantry or of rural people yet distinct from townspeople. In societies of this middle type the form of thought represented by the concentric circles is insufficient to stand for the relations of communities within communities. The form of thought to be used must be one that will take account of the different qualities of relationships that prevail on the one hand as the villager looks inward toward his village, his neighborhood, his family, and, on the other hand, as he relates himself to those aspects of town and city or manor which he must use to sell his grain or his services, buy his hoe or his gun, pay his taxes, or try his lawsuit.

It is, I think, just to Dr. Starr's helpful analysis to say that it represents the system of communities from the point of view of the villager, and that it does not fully take into account the lines and patterns of persisting interaction between villager and townsman, townsman and villager. The diagram in the form of steps leading upward to higher levels of relationship does not quite represent the systems of relationships, economic, cultural, and personal, that compose the larger society of both town and country, and in that it fails to show the situation as it would appear to one viewing town and countryside equally from a point of view above and fair to both. It should be possible to look at a society of the middle kind—at a rural-urban society in which the economic and social relationships are still distinct and fairly stable—from a point of view inclosing equally both village and town, or manor and countryside, and to recognize the relationships and activities of the villager as one of the two reciprocal halves of a relationship and an activity of which the resident in the town or in the manor is the other half.

It seems to me that Dr. Börje Hanssen has done just this in one part of his recent study of rural-urban life in Scania at the end of the eighteenth century.[12] Dr. Hanssen's principal concept is the "activity-field." This is both an area and a pattern of acts and relationships. The activity-field is represented spatially, on a map or diagram, for Dr. Hanssen approaches his materials in the first instance ecologically—"ecologically" in the modified sense usual in urban sociology, meaning the spatial and temporal expression of human relationships.

When Dr. Hanssen represents the activity-fields of the villager they appear as concentric circles. His conception of fields inclosed within one another—household and family, friendly adjacent villages, and outer fields characterized by stranger-relations—is substantially that which is conceived by Evans-Pritchard for the Nuer. But the great advantage of Dr. Hanssen's activity-field for describing a rural community of peasant and townsman lies in the fact that it enables him to recognize differentiation of activities and relationships within a village or town, and to represent the different kinds of relationships and activities that certain groups within the village have with people outside of it. Dr. Hanssen puts this point in the following words:

When investigating a certain town ..., it would appear more realistic to regard each specific group as a separate behaviour-field, than to let the whole community in question represent one field. That goes for highly differentiated urban communities generally, but naturally not for relatively undifferentiated village communities. [The present investigation] shows how the result can be faulty if it is not remembered that groups distinct economically and in respect of social class comprise different fields, and if it is assumed instead that such juridical and administrative concepts as "towns" comprise a whole. Certain groups in the town of this area had much more intimate connections with the population of the surrounding countryside than with each other.[13]

The villages Dr. Hanssen studied in Scania were, however, differentiated. This sociologist was able to take account of the difference between the way of life of property-owning peasants in the village, on the one hand, and the unpropertied cotters on the other. The cotters took employment in parsonages and in manors as the landed peasantry did not often do. Further, Dr. Hanssen was able to recognize the trading activities between town and countryside, between one village and another, and between town and commercial city. The description of the rural-urban region is thus made from a viewpoint that is just to both town and country, and that sees the whole as interrelated activity-fields. Some of these fields are, for the villager, inclosed within one another; but even here the cotter and servant has a system of fields different from that of the land-owning farmer, and this consequence of the town and manor on the village is taken into account. Finally, the diagram Dr. Hanssen produces (which is given here considerably simplified) allows us to study the persisting patterned relationships of townsman and villager, manor dweller, and servant of the cotter class. Dr. Hanssen has given us a tool offering fresh advantages to students of communities in which town and country have interpenetrated one another.

We are not, of course, to lean too heavily upon any diagram in our effort to describe and analyze community life. No diagram tells us what words can. Each is a framework for thought, a plan of the possible significant relationships, to be tried and then qualified or perhaps rejected. Perhaps the series of diagrammatic forms considered in this chapter does show us again how it is that the concepts, verbal or diagrammatic, that we use in description and analysis undergo modification and development as the subject matter to be described and analyzed changes—in this case, changes from the almost isolated primitive community to the rural village in a national state.

In these pages too little attention has been given to the relationships that in many cases exist between the people of one band or village and those of another. Small communities are such convenient units for study and analysis that the eye of the anthropologist is not often enough lifted to view the larger community composed of a few or many bands or settlements linked in more or less stable relationships. The case of the Siriono, where each band is truly an isolate, is exceptional today. In many parts of even the uncivilized world the band or settlement is a part of a regional network of relationships. The band may be for the most part distinct and independent, but with latent relationships through kinship with many other similar groups; in parts of aboriginal Australia connections of people are open to extension through recognition of kinship connection between one man and another: the local society can expand outward almost indefinitely to provide for the occasional traveler. In West Africa there are peoples, like the Tiv of Nigeria, "who number well over half a million, and all of whom regard themselves as descended from an ultimate ancestor, Tiv. Every local settlement is, through its main body of male kinsmen, linked by ever widening, if weakening, ties of kinship and is ultimately associated with all the others."[14] Such ties make it possible for people to move safely over a wide area, "and there is a sense of unity among the whole population."

There is, then, even in societies without the added dimension of gentry, town, or city, a kind of community much wider than the little community. We may study more closely than has yet been done these far-flung networks of social relations. They have their structure too. And where the small community does form a part of a national state, the rural networks include not only town or manor, but also the relations of village to village. Dr. Hanssen's study takes some account of these. Those who have recently been studying rural India tell us that in parts of that country the village is plainly an insufficient unit of study; it is no isolate but rather a focus for understanding wide and complex communities. One village may have traditional relationships through marriage and caste with scores of or even with several hundred other villages. There the village is a unit in some senses; in others the unit is the rural network or lattice. As work proceeds, we shall come to study these, and perhaps to distinguish types of rural lattices. In western Guatemala the rural lattices are composed chiefly of relationships of primitive commerce, with travel to attend festivals or to visit shrines constituting a secondary basis of connection among settlements. In India the castes and exogamous marriages make for rural networks based on more personal, intimate, and hereditary kinds of connections.

In the case of civilized societies and national states, this review of some attempts to˜ develop forms of thought for describing communities that are not isolates exposes a problem with a double aspect. The problem is how to understand a community that is not only a simple band or village but is perhaps many villages in important relationships with manors, towns and cities. Because no one village is really independent, but is a part of a much larger and more complicated system, our interest is drawn toward the description of the more complicated system. Detaching one's self, so to speak, from the village, one moves to consider the whole region or even the whole national state as the entity to be studied and understood. And how shall one study so large and complex an entity? On the other hand, in so far as one remains within the village or other local community and retains a determination to study just that village, one is required to find ways to describe what I have just called the penetration of manor or town into the village. There are now people in the village who have worked in the town or manor and have been thereby changed. And all the villagers are more or less affected by, perhaps, the school, the visiting trader, the missionary, and the more distant but perhaps significant example and suggestion manifest by the townsman or gentry-person known to them. And how shall we describe this interpenetration?

Among anthropologists, Professor Julian H. Steward has given great attention to the problems of describing a national state.[15] He makes the important distinction between two features of national state societies: those that function and must be studied on the national level; second, those that pertain to sociocultural segments or subgroups of the population. To understand the national state we must take account of national institutions such as schools, banking, and influences of the fully literate and the elite; the local differences among little communities; the effects of education and propaganda on villager and on townsman; and the relationships among all these things. The difficulties are great but not unsurmountable. Professor Steward has attempted to surmount them in the study he and his associates have made of Puerto Rico.

I turn away from the task of describing a national state and come back to the problem of describing a village community into which the manor or the town or the city has penetrated. The point of difficulty here is the fact that right there in the village things go on, acts are performed, thoughts are entertained, by the villager, which cannot be accounted for merely by referring to the several concentric spheres of activity of the local community and its traditional ways of life. These acts and thoughts of the villager have to be described as part of the changed village life and as qualitatively different from the acts and thoughts characteristic of the local tradition.

I recall the presence in Chan Kom of a school established for the people through decisions and policies with which the people had little to do. I recall the organization of villagers, brought about by townsmen, expected to vote the straight Revolutionary party ticket. I still wonder how to express, in words or perhaps in a diagram, the criminal hearing I observed in the village on an occasion when certain Indians were charged with killing cattle that had broken into their cornfields. Local people conducted the hearing, but a messenger had been sent off to tell the authorities of the city of the event, and while the investigation was taking place in the village the local officers who conducted it kept discussing among themselves what would be the attitude and action of the official from the city on the matters that they were at that moment concerned with. I cannot forget the long efforts of the Chan Kom villagers to persuade the national government to give them formal title to their communal lands, or the endless discussions over the merits of the school or about the trustworthiness of those strange people, the American archeologists, who were doing something mysterious in the ruined stone buildings of the ancients. All these things are a part of the life of such a little community. They happen right in the village, yet they are somehow outside of it. How shall we deal with the relative outsideness of these things that happen in the village?

Here, I think, we can return to Professor Steward's distinction between elements in the national state that represent the local and traditional way of life that was worked out there by those people out of the circumstances that immediately surrounded them; and, on the other hand, the elements that come from and represent the national state, state-wide or nation-wide, and that, to be understood fully, would have to be studied on the national level and studied largely in terms of explicit rules and deliberately created forms. We can consider the village of Chan Kom as a complex of folkways and stateways.

This complex of stateways and folkways is a needed dimension of the reality of such little communities as fall in the middle group of Starr's three groups along a range of difference that she imagines, a range on which the Siriono would occupy one terminus and the "Gold Coast and the Slum," or the people between Philadelphia and Wilmington, the other. We may come to conceive folkways and stateways more abstractly than does, I think, Professor Steward; we may conceive them as generalized qualities. To describe the whole within the wholes, we may use a form of thought which conceives of two kinds of organized human life as interpenetrating one another, right within the little community itself. The interpenetration is observable in certain frontiers between the two as these frontiers appear in the life of the village. When the villager adjusts himself to the visit of the tax collector or political organizer, when the village fathers discuss the newly introduced school, when the villager thinks of himself as a poor, hard-working peasant so regarded by the townsman to whom he goes or who comes to him—in all these moments and situations there is this frontier, the margin of adjustment between folkways and city ways. Some of these adjustments are old and stable, like the relationships of status between peasant and townsman. Some are new and ill defined, as those that appear when a court or school or mission is first introduced by the national state into the little community.

So, in thinking about peasant communities or about partly urbanized rural communities, we begin to shape a form of thought that will conceive of primitive, folk, or peasant life as a general and abstract kind of living, as an imagined total structure, qualitatively different from the kind of living that comes to characterize towns and cities. We could perhaps see in the village two kinds of abstractly distinguishable kinds of life and kinds of communities, and see these, right in the village, in relationship to each other. The interpenetration of town and country can be conceived not only as a system of differentiated activity-fields but also, as Dr. Hanssen too has noticed, as an intermingling of two styles of life. This interpenetration, this intermingling, occurs within the village, within, indeed, the individual villager himself.

IX

... A COMBINATION OF OPPOSITES

As the attention in these chapters moved from ecological system to social structure to type of person to world view, in each case there was conceived a new arrangement of parts within a whole. From looking centrally at the relations between the working activities of the people to the land on which they live, we came, in the consideration of world view, to the experiences of the people of the community with regard to the entire universe about them and to the groupings of these experiences in their own thinking and feeling. This book is about alternative mental forms for conceiving little communities as wholes.

In attending to any one of these forms we have not stopped to ask the question, "What is the content which fills the form chosen to describe this particular little community?" We did not ask if Evans-Pritchard correctly described the ecological system of the Nuer. Maybe another student also interested in ecological system would find a different such system if he studied the Nuer. I wrote with admiration of Professor Fortes' description of Tallensi social structure. Is it certain that Professor Fortes has rightly described Tallensi social structure? Do we accept the descriptions by Professor Kluckhohn of the ethos and world view of the Navaho, or is it possible that if another man studied the Navaho for many years he would present something about them still in terms of ethos and world view but of a notably different ethos and world view?

In this chapter I take it to be possible that two quite contrasting accounts of a community may result from two different studies of that community. But I entertain a possibility that lies beyond that easy expectation; that a means to better understanding of a little community might be found in the deliberate construction of alternate and complementary descriptions of it. I turn in this chapter to those who have indeed employed such contrasting conceptions, within the same kind of mental form for their descriptions, in enlarging our understanding of social and cultural wholes. Beginning with contrasting descriptions made by two different students, I pass to the devising and the using by one man of mentally constructed contrasting conceptions.

The question now is addressed particularly to the possibility that this one community before us may be described not as having just "this" content but as having also "that" content—that it may be two things of the same kind: two views of the world, two types of personality, two sets of emphasized values, two kinds of social relationships. I ask if this may be true in some little communities or perhaps in all of them. I ask further if this possibility can be made the basis of another deliberate instrument of understanding and description of band or village. The community may have more than one face; it may, within the guidance of any descriptive concept, be understood not simply as just "this" but as also "that."

Maybe one can conceive rather deliberately and explicitly both the "this" and the "that" and use these alternative and perhaps complementary mental constructions to help toward understanding of the one community before us. Like the green and red lenses with which certain photographs are viewed to enable the eye to see the colors of reality, so we might construct alternative lenses which, used together, would give us an improved view of the village before us.

As I look at the experiences of ethnologists, including my own, it seems to me that some communities have in fact been studied by alternative and contrasting views of the same reality. From one such experience I have learned a great deal as to the effects of the investigator's preconceptions and personal preferences in shaping the description he writes of a little community.

When I was a young man, beginning the study of anthropology, I wrote a book about a large village in Mexico. Seventeen years later Dr. Oscar Lewis, who is now at the University of Illinois, wrote another book about the same village. Looking back on my earlier and much slighter work, Dr. Lewis in his book sums up the contrast between impressions given of the village in the two books in the following words:

The impression given by Redfield's study of Tepoztlán is that of a relatively homogeneous, isolated, smoothly functioning and well-integrated society made up of a contented and well adjusted people. His picture of the village has a Rousseauan quality which glosses lightly over evidence of violence, disruption, cruelty, disease, suffering and maladjustment. We are told little of poverty, economic problems, or political schisms. Throughout his study we find an emphasis upon the cooperative and unifying factors in Tepoztecan society.

And he sums up the impression he thinks given the reader of his own book in the following words:

Our findings, on the other hand, would emphasize the underlying individualism of Tepoztecan institutions and character, the lack of cooperation, the tensions between villages within the municipio, the schisms within the village, and the pervading quality of fear, envy and distrust.[1]

These summary characterizations of the effects of the two books seem to me, on the whole, just. The two accounts of the same community do give these contrasting impressions: the one of harmony and a good life; the other of a life burdened with suffering and torn with dissension and corroding passion.

Moreover, Lewis established the objective truth of certain of the unpleasant features of Tepoztecan life. He has shown that more than half of the villagers did not own land at the time that he studied the community; that many were in serious want; that stealing, quarreling, and physical violence are not rare in Tepoztlán; that politics in the village leads to the use of brute force; that differences between rich and poor lead to serious dislikes and distrusts; and especially that within many families there are many kinds of frustrations, suspicions, and sufferings. It is true that the two books describe what might almost seem to be two different peoples occupying the same town.

How is this great difference to be explained? Could it be that, in the seventeen years that intervened between my study and Lewis', the character of the people changed that much? Lewis does not think this can have been the case; nor do I. The formal social and economic conditions did change significantly, and I think it likely that some of the difference represented in these two accounts represents a real declining sense of security of the Tepoztecans, brought about by the increase of contact and communication with the ways of the town and the city. I do think that the greater part of the explanation for the difference between the two reports on this matter of Tepoztecan life and character is to be found in differences between the two investigators.

Lewis thinks so, too. He recognizes what he calls "the personal factor,"[2] and he recognizes the very different kinds and degrees of preparations for work in Tepoztlán which he and I experienced, each of us coming to the task at notably different points in the development of anthropological method and interest.

Lewis here emphasizes, as the principal explanation for what I suppose he would think of as an unfortunate emphasis I gave to my description, the interest I had in the change of a society from a folk society to one more urban. The criticism of the folk-urban conception which Lewis introduces at this point in his book cannot be closely relevant, however, to the problem of explaining the difference between the two published views of Tepoztecan man, because I did not have that conception in my mind when I studied Tepoztlán; it was developed afterward. I had at most in mind the simple thought that Tepoztlán was a kind of community intermediate between primitive tribal group and town or city, and that changes were occurring in Tepoztlán which moved it along a road of transition from the one to the other.

I think that it is simply true that without benefit of any well-considered scheme of theoretical idea at all, I looked at certain aspects of Tepoztecan life because they both interested me and pleased me. I saw the almost ritual meaningfulness to the Tepoztecan of his daily work; I saw the delight taken in preparations for the many festivals and the pleasure, solemn but deep, at their consummation; I saw the pride the people had in their little mountain-walled country, so long inhabited, so deeply grown into their thoughts and feelings. In writing my book I emphasized these things because they came to my particular interest and taste. In this sense, the book was written from a personal point of view.

I was aware of the incompleteness of the account I published. I think I knew I was saying, "Look! Here is an aspect of peasant life you people up there may not be thinking about." I had not studied the disease, the dissension, and the suffering. I suppose I did not think of my book as a rounded study. Indeed, I expressly disclaimed that it was; I thought of it as a statement of one phase of a complex truth.

But if a little community is to be known by phases of the complex truth that it is, we must have available accounts that report other and complementary phases. That is why, given my book, Lewis' book is so very valuable. It is valuable not only because it makes good use of the resources and procedures for research developed since 1926, but also for the reason that Lewis is especially interested in the problems of economic need and of personal disharmony and unhappiness, topics which I did not investigate.

The principal conclusion that I draw from this experience is that we are all better off with two descriptions of Tepoztlán than we would be with only one of them. More understanding results from the contrast and complementarity which the two together provide. In the cases of most primitive and exotic communities we have a one-eyed view. We can now look at Tepoztlán with a somewhat stereoscopic vision.

There is, I think, a second and related lesson to be learned from the experience. I think we must recognize that the personal interests and the personal and cultural values of the investigator influence the content of the description of the community. Whatever be the intellectual form chosen for description, or if no clear guiding conception is employed at all, the village or band will be described in a way in some significant degree determined by the choices made, perhaps quite unconsciously, by the student of the community.

There are hidden questions behind the two books that have been written about Tepoztlán. The hidden question behind my book is, "What do these people enjoy?" The hidden question behind Dr. Lewis' book is, "What do these people suffer from?"

An account of a little community is not something that is given one as out of a vending machine by putting in the appropriate coins of method and technique. There is no one ultimate and utterly objective account of a human whole. Each account, if it preserves the human quality at all, is a created product in which the human qualities of the creator—the outside viewer and describer—are one ingredient.

This truth has appeared in other cases in which scientists with different viewpoints on life studied the same community with contrasting results. One outstanding such case is that of the Pueblo Indians of the American Southwest. Their society has been described by certain well-trained anthropologists as highly integrated, and their typical personality as gentle, co-operative, modest, and tranquil. Other well-trained anthropologists have described the same people as marked by hidden tension, suspicion, anxiety, hostility, fear, and ambition. Now it seems to some of us that these different accounts result from the approval the first anthropologists gave to the moral unity of Pueblo life, and from the disapproval the second group of anthropologists gave to the authoritarianism and repression of Pueblo society.[3] It appears that both accounts are true.

It seems to me that with the recognition of the influence of personal choices on the resulting description we arrive at the possibility of combining two contrasting viewpoints into a combined viewpoint of the protean and unattainable absolute reality. I think we may well conceive of the process by which understanding of human wholes is advanced as a kind of dialectic of viewpoint, a dialogue of characterizations. "This," but on the other hand "that," is the orderly swing of the mind toward truth.

A viewer of a community may accomplish such a dialogue within himself. If not strongly bound by the self-denying ordinances of science, he may indeed consciously use his own values as the organizers of the two possible positions with regard to the community. He may in effect ask himself, as the organizing question for his work, "Do these people lead a good life or a bad one?" A question of value may be the evident central axis of his thought. And then he may provide an answer that is in two parts: he may say, "On the one hand, this community is good in 'this'; on the other, it is bad in 'that'." If the viewer and student is humanly perceptive, if he makes the moral criteria quite plain, and if he maintains a steady and self-critical judgment upon his own perceptions, he may present quite convincingly a community in terms of such a moral dialectic.

Such an account of a village is that given us by George Bourne in his book, *Change in the Village*,[4] published in 1912 about a Surrey village. This is a description of the conversion of an old peasant settlement into a suburban community. Bourne is able to see what is to be reported because of his sympathetic perception of the old values in the peasant, values lost in his son and grandson. And he judges some aspects of the old life as good, some as bad; he also judges some aspects of the new life as good and some as bad. In the old life he emphasizes as good: self-reliance, joy in work, the ritual quality of work-acts. He appreciates a certain quality of character which he calls "quietness of soul." He applauds the fitness of these peasants' understanding of the land and the respect one man accorded another when no one from town or city was close at hand to look down upon them; he sees the values that arose out of a variety of tasks well learned and out of the satisfaction of doing many things well. He did not like the mental apathy of the old state of affairs—the dullness of mind, the coarseness, the brutality or the drunkenness, nor did he like the emotional starvation, the meagerness of all aesthetic experience. Turning to the new life, he saw losses: the old sense of joy in work was gone, the sense of confidence and meaningful activity that arose out of the old adaptiveness to the land; the old self-reliance and much of the self-respect. There came a new insecurity, not merely a fear that a man might be dispossessed from his homestead by the new landowners, the city people, but also an insecurity as to what life was all about. Worse, there came with the introduction of the demands of the townsmen a new servility, a disposition to accept an inferiority now thrust upon the peasant.

On the other hand, Bourne saw advantages, growths toward the good. The church helped in this forward movement, not, interestingly enough, by making any significant contribution to religion that Bourne could see, but by improving manners and self-respect. The newspapers were a new good, for they stimulated the mind and produced the first significant intellectual discussions in the community. And, finally, political action—participation in the government of their country, not merely in the village itself—Bourne saw to be a new good.

Bourne does not offer his book as a work of science. Nevertheless it is a good book. It tells us much about the community described and about a general process of change in small communities. Its truth is accepted by the reader. Bourne's book suggests the possibility of formulating alternative viewpoints of the little community in such a way as to make the single viewer produce a combined viewpoint of the reality before him.

I go on now to say that it seems to me not necessary that the personal value choices of the investigator be made the basis of the two combined views. We might find a basis for a double scheme of thought in the communities themselves. We might see in the community two contrasting ways of life, each of which we might imagine fully as it might exist in a pure form, a sort of Platonic idea only imperfectly realized in the actual village itself.

So, looking at the Surrey village described by Bourne, we might see it in its time of transition as describable in terms, first of the old isolated peasant life, and, second, in terms of the more urban or suburban life it is coming to be. We could come to understand the actual situation in so far as the Surrey village represented the one imagined type of isolated and integrated society on the one hand, and in so far as it represented the new, more dependent community of individuated, distressed, and freshly inquiring people on the other hand.

Perhaps we could so define the two imaginary types of societies that the same types would serve to describe the changes that Hatch reported for the New England village. In short, we might develop a pair of mental forms that would be as free of our value-judgment as we could make them, and that would have a content derived from real societies and from the course of historic transformation of societies as that transformation actually occurs in history.

What if we could make ourselves two lenses for the understanding of any one little community, lenses to see the whole in relation to elements of human living that are present in varying combinations in all communities? Further, what if these contrasting conceptions expressed a course of change of human societies characteristic in the sense that on the whole throughout human history the course of change has been away from the one and toward the other? Such a pair of conceptions would provide a useful basis for comparing one little community with another, or a little community with one not so little, or an earlier period in a society with a later. Such a pair of conceptions would not require that two different investigators describe the same community but would provide for an increased understanding of the community through a description of the community, as it is and as it changes, as that description provides questions to be answered by the investigator from the facts in the community before him.

The questions would then be double: "In what respects is what is here, what was here, and what is coming to be, representative of the first type of community imagined, and in what respects representative of the second?" The same investigator would answer these and related questions as the facts in the community he was studying required him. One might expect that by the use of these mental forms, a "this" explicitly defined in contrast to an explicitly defined "that," both aspects of the little community, of human life, and of social process, might be understood that would not be so readily understood without these mental forms.

Such a pair of explicit conceptions should meet three qualifications: (1) the two must contrast with each other; (2) they must correspond with differences found to be really present in communities we study and present in the course of history; (3) they must be susceptible of objective use, of relatively value-free description in their own terms, of the particular little communities of our interest.

If anyone before Sir Henry Maine made important use of such a pair of conceptions, I do not know who it was. At least it is true that with Maine the use of polar ideal types for the understanding of societies became common. After the publication of his book *Ancient Law* in 1861,[5] there are dozens of writers to cite in this connection.

Maine's two central conceptions were "status" and "contract," a transformation of society from a kind of group united in terms of familially assigned rights and duties, to one in which individual and secular contractual connection came to be prominent. Maine discovered this pair of contrasting conceptions in the history of Roman law. He used his "this" and "that" to describe in generic, or as we might say now, in sociological terms, the history of Western society, especially the jural and political aspects of that society. He stated the contrast of this transformation, the two poles of the movement, in a variety of related ways. "Starting, as from one terminus of history, from a condition of society in which all the relations of Persons are summed up in the relations of Family, we seem to have steadily moved towards a phase of social order in which all these relations arise from the free agreement of Individuals."

In a lecture[6] Maine delivered in 1875 (after he had written his second important book on *Village Communities East and West*),[7] he contrasted the brotherhood within the primitive small community with the hostility its members show to outsiders and emphasized also that inside the primitive community economic competition has small part. He stated a point Max Weber soon afterward repeated: that with the course of history the spirit of brotherhood of the primitive group spreads outside of it in diluted form, while competition for exchange comes to penetrate into the primitive group; it becomes that "regulated private war" by which ancient or primitive society is "gradually broken up into indistinguishable atoms."

Much of the generalizing of Maine as to the transformations of ancient Greek and Roman society is supported by Fustel de Coulanges in his work, *La Cité Antique*,[8] written soon after Maine's book. The decline in the ancient priestly family and the separation of law from religion of which De Coulanges writes are more particularly historic descriptions of Maine's more abstractly stated transition from familial to individuated society, from personal and sacred law to law more impersonal and secular. One can read into the book by De Coulanges a contrast between two imagined types of society which the author himself does not explicitly state.

I do not know that the Frenchman was influenced in his thinking by Henry Maine, but I think that Maine's writings influenced an American and a German who wrote books in this same line of thought in the following two decades. Lewis H. Morgan's book, *Ancient Society* (1877),[9] uses the terms "societas" and "civitas" for two contrasting kinds of society, the one based on kinship, the other on territorial connection—the society of kindred versus the state society of citizens. Morgan developed this distinction—essentially the same as Maine's—into an elaborate series of intermediate transitional stages through which he would have had us believe all societies had passed or would naturally pass. In so far as this scheme assumed to describe an actual sequence of events invariable for all societies, it proved unacceptable, and Morgan's sequence of stages is not much approved today (except perhaps in Soviet Russia).

A more productive turn to the idea was given by Ferdinand Tönnies.[10] Instead of seeing the contrast as between two stages of history as one period in the development of human society followed by a later and different period, Tönnies conceived of two imaginably distinct and contrasting aspects of all societies. In effect he said: One may conceive of a society, the *Gemeinschaft*, characterized by absolute unity derived from the intimate contacts of communal personal association and participation in common values. Here the will of the individual is spontaneous and affective. On the other hand, one may conceive of a society, the *Gesellschaft*, in which the unity is highly individualizing and differentiating. In the *Gesellschaft* the parts of the whole are hardly more than physically juxtaposed, relations are impersonal, and the will of the individual is deliberate and rational. The *Gemeinschaft* is to be plainly seen in the family and predominates in primitive and peasant societies; the *Gesellschaft* is a development of civilization.

A similar turn of thought is represented by the pair of conceptions central to Emile Durkheim's *De la division du travail social* (1893).[11] There is the social segment, a community independent of all others, whose members grow up under conditions so uniform that their consciences, as Durkheim puts it, are concrete, uniform, and strong. In such an imagined society all generations are present sharing the same attitudes and values and no other set of attitudes and values is thought by anyone to be possible. The social segment is characterized by the sacred. Its solidarity Durkheim called "mechanical," meaning that it is integrated by a moral consensus, by the conformity of all the consciences of the individuals to a common type. Contrasting with the social segment is the social organ, a community dependent on other communities and on its own division of labor, which is complex and unfixed. In this imagined community there is a minimum of understandings holding together its members. Durkheim called its solidarity "organic," referring to an integration dependent on differences, interdependence, and reciprocal usefulness, like the relationship between two organs in a body or two parts in a machine. The social organ is characterized by secularity; in it there is no common conscience. As Tönnies saw the history of civilization as the extension of *Gesellschaft* at the expense of *Gemeinschaft*, Durkheim saw it as the extension of the social organ at the expense of the social segment.

Of course these few words about each of a half-dozen works in social science do injustice to them all. What each of these writers has to say on the few points I have in each case brought forward is complex and important. I merely point to these ideas to provide a basis for three observations: (1) the recognition of contrasting conceptions useful in understanding real societies has occurred so many times in the minds of many students of societies ancient, primitive, or modern, that the usefulness of this form of thought is strongly suggested; (2) the fact that the ideas, though so differently expressed, prove to be congruent, the facts from any one society being susceptible of description in any one set of terms, with much overlapping of reference, suggests that these ideas do correspond to a widespread and generally prevailing trend of human history; and (3) in view of all that was written in this framework in the nineteenth century, no very great claims to originality may be made by those of us who have made use of and developed these ideas in the twentieth.

We later Americans who have worked in this tradition of thought have tried to use these ideas in connection with the detailed and empirical community research of our day. At the University of North Carolina Howard W. Odum,[12] concerned with the characterization of geographic and cultural regions of the United States, developed pairs of contrasting conceptions in this tradition; folkways versus technicways or stateways, and culture versus civilization, and defined the "folk society as natural" in contrast to "civilization as technical." Robert E. Park, impressed by W. G. Sumner's concept and book, *Folkways*, poured creative ideas into his many students, including Howard Becker and myself. Becker began with the contrast between sacred and secular present in the dichotomies of Tönnies and of Durkheim and produced a complex and much differentiated typology of sacred and secular societies.[13]

My own efforts[14] went to develop an imagined or ideal-typical folk society in considerable detail of characterization and to make use of the conception in describing, in more general and abstract terms than is usual in studies of changing primitive society, some comparisons among tribal, peasant, and urban communities in Yucatán. More recently I have become interested in the characterization of the over-all transformations of human living from precivilized to modern times, as guided by the conception of the folk society and in the examination of the types of urban societies as they affect the folk societies and give rise to new forms of society,[15] and the notion of the folk society as a mental model with which to examine and to generate questions as to many a real community has been reconsidered and provided with modifications by several recent writers.[16]

There is today no lack of mental apparatus for examining any one real little community with regard to the presence in it of aspects on the one hand of a more primitive or folklike kind of society and on the other of the kind of human association that appears most plainly in cities and becomes prominent with civilization. One may choose from among a variety of models of this invention. Each manufacturer turns out a device somewhat different from the others on the market; but any of them will do some of the work.

The work these ideal or imagined systems of parts making up a whole will do is this: They will enable one to see aspects of the community that are in complementarity to each other and that further provide bases for comparing that community with others, or with itself at other times, in respect to the questions raised by the imaginary system.

One will take, for instance, the conception of a complete folk society, stated abstractly as a society small, homogeneous, impersonal, sacred, and so forth, and try it on the community that one is interested in understanding. One will try it on, not so much to see where the conception fits, but to see where it does not fit. No society can exactly fit, for the mental form we are now using is an invention, a construction of our own. The Siriono Indian band fulfils the description I have offered of a constructed type of folk society in almost all respects, but the reader of Holmberg's report will find evidence that even in that extremely isolated, homogeneous, and self-contained little community the consciences of men are not perfectly uniform and strong, as Durkheim has it. Indeed, the very harshness of their conditions of life brings it about that, as Holmberg says, "the social norms that prevail are elastic enough to allow for a considerable range of behavior." The moral rule is that food should be shared within the extended family; but, in fact, except in times of abundance, it rarely is. There is a good deal of individuated, self-serving and purely expediential behavior in this little community that runs against the writ of the typical folk society as I wrote it. The usefulness of the imagined construction lies in the fact that it enables us to see in the Siriono aspects of life that might not appear significant to us if we did not use the construction.

The conception of an abstract folk society creates new questions to answer. Now we ask, "What conditions of living prevent the development of uniform and strong consciences? What conditions permit and produce such development?" We begin to form more general propositions. We may say that among food-collecting peoples living in harsh natural conditions, certain of the characteristics of the folk society cannot be developed; such a society will be more individualistic, less communalistic than other societies; or that the moral norms of the society will be less altruistic than they will be in societies better provided with food, shelter, and physical security.

The most complete approximation of the imagined folk society will not be found among such peoples as the Siriono. The folk society, as I have described it, does not correspond to the first or earliest possible associations of humanity. It represents a more fully developed society existing in terms of one moral order.

The conception of a folk society, in detail of interrelated parts, is not matched in the literature by a corresponding and complementary description of an opposite type. The secular society, as described by Becker, the aspect of communities called "technicways" and "stateways" by Odum, and the brief general descriptions of modern city life given by Park[17] and Wirth,[18] in part provide the contrasting ideas needed. To identify the city with the opposite of the folk society is convenient by a simple negativing of the propositions that identify the folk society, but the kind of living, the kind of behaving we oppose to the folkways is present in many rural areas much affected by the city or characterized by communities of heterogeneous and secular-minded people. A military camp, a factory in the countryside, some frontier settlements, exhibit the phenomena that contrast with the life of the folk society.

When, on occasion, I read such a statement as "This society cannot possibly be a folk society," or "This large village is not a folk society," I find this form of words confusing. I find myself revising these statements to read: "In my judgment the elements of folk society are not very prominent in this community," or "As compared with a very isolated primitive band or tribe, this community is in these respects less folk-like." Such statements seem to me to make sense. And I want chiefly to know not how much or how little the community corresponds with an imagined model but in what ways it does represent the model and in what ways it does not. The double conception does not serve to assign societies, one by one, into classes bearing labels, "folk societies," "urban societies," or any other labels. The double conception serves me as one of many considered conceptions that give me understanding of particular societies. Also it serves me in asking questions about the changes that go on in particular societies and in describing those changes in more general terms—in terms of such processes as these conceptions cause us to recognize and to conceive generically.

I prefer to begin with this statement: "In every isolated little community there is civilization; in every city there is the folk society." If I turn the matter around in that way, I will use these pairs of imaginary contrasts to help my understanding of what is really there in that particular community and to ask the important questions that will set me to explaining how it is that just this combination of qualities is there.

It does seem possible fruitfully to add to the equipment of mental forms for understanding little communities some conception or pair of conceptions of imagined "pure" societal states. It appears useful to carry forward the effort of understanding by relating the community studied to a great trend of history and to see in each little community aspects of it that express an early and more primitive condition of mankind, and aspects that represent a later, more civilized, or urbanized aspect.

In studying the little communities that are neither very primitive nor very modern and urbanized but that lie somewhere between these extremes, the pair of conceptions, the two lenses for seeing a compound reality, will prove particularly useful. For in Chan Kom or Middletown, the early and primitive society and the secular, civilized, urbanized society that might be fully conceived or defined, are both present in important degree and in an interpenetration that demands analysis.

To use the mental forms, which I have in this chapter brought forward for the understanding of peasant and rural small communities, will help, I think, to deal with that difficult problem, "How shall we delimit the peasant village or the small town?" The distinctness of the isolated primitive band or settlement is apparent and easy to explain: We draw a line around the settlement or around the settlement and the lands over which the hunters wander or the primitive farmers till their fields, and we say, "Here are the limits of the community." But in Plainville and in Middletown the limits of the community cannot be adequately defined in spatial terms. They cannot because the people who live in Plainville or Middletown think about many things that exist outside of Plainville or Middletown, and the thoughts of other men and women in other communities in America or across the seas come into Plainville or Middletown and enter into the thinking and doing of the people there. Where there are travel, newspapers, radio, and television, the meaningful limits of the little community can have no territorial definition; there is no line to be drawn around the community to define where it is.

But if we think of Plainville or Middletown as an interpenetration of two opposite kinds of living, thinking, and feeling, as analyzable, as if we saw in Plainville or Middletown first an isolated, homogeneous, sacred, and personal community of kinsmen, and then as if we saw in it the heterogeneous, secular, and impersonal community that we find approximated in cities, we will find ourselves defining the community not in terms of space but in terms of a position relative to two kinds of human collective living, as just this local and particular arrangement of aspects of the one in relation to aspects of the other. The definition is with regard to types of institutions and states of mind, along a line not drawn on the ground but conceived in the orderly and schematic arrangement which our minds bring to the real community before us.

The development of imagined types of societies helps us, too, in making our descriptions of little communities more accessible to public confirmation or correction. To state the scheme of ideas formally, and to state it in terms that do not imply too much of a judgment of value as to the kinds of societies imagined, is to reduce the effect of personal influences that may otherwise enter into the description. It is to set outside of me, in a language abstract and impersonal, as becomes the language of science, a characterization whose fitness to the particular data brought from the real community may be publicly assessed.

When I went to Tepoztlán I did not have "the concept of the folk-culture and folk-urban continuum," as Lewis suggests. I began to develop the concept as I wrote the book about Tepoztlán, but the concept was not really apparent to me until several years later. It seems to me that, as I developed the concept, the more personal and valuational quality of my work decreased. I do not see in the use of the concept my scientific damnation; I see in its use the beginning of my salvation. It seems to me a staff with which I may go safely forward.

To the little community, as to anything that is studied, the investigator's mind always brings some preconceptions as to the orderly and schematic arrangement of things. The description and the explanation are not a photograph made upon a mind's sensitized plate. They are creations, made of what is there as in part guided by the ideas the investigator brings to that community. The formation of the preconceptions is no doubt a complex matter. Into it many things probably enter: concerns with matters of practical action in that community; preferences for historical or for more generalizing inquiry; personal valuations upon this or that kind of life or kind of person; the convenience or the habit of studying this aspect of the community rather than that; the experience or advice given as to the use of particular technical methods of getting knowledge about people. These preconceptions act upon what we find in the community, and are in turn influenced by what we find there. While we describe the community, we often try also to systematize and to justify the revised preconceptions into what we may call a theory or, more modestly, a point of view. Each of the resulting statements of program and method is two things: a contribution toward the common effort to shape instruments of understanding; and a rationalization of personal inclinations and experiences.

None of us can truly say that his way of work is necessarily the best way or that it either should or will prevail over all others. All advance in knowledge is a dialectic, a conversation. To hear the relative truth of what one is one's self saying one must listen to what the other worker says about what one's self has described otherwise. The point I have striven to make in this chapter is that, among the many and varied mental instruments for the understanding of little communities, is to be included a controlled conversation, a dialectic of opposites, carried on within one's self.

X

...WHOLE AND PARTS

Most simply and immediately we can ask of any community study: What does this account tell us about just this community? In reading Holmberg's monograph on the Siriono we may become interested in how these Indians grow dog-tired in pursuit of food and are made thereby snarling or indifferent. We may read Evans-Pritchard's description of the Nuer community and so understand and appreciate humanly the close involvement of those Sudanese with their cattle; or we may come to comprehend the relations of sense of kinship and sense of common lifeway together with the adjustments to rain and drought in bringing about the social structure of the community. In reading James West's *Plainville* it may be the conflict between the old ways and the new that interests us: the influence of the plow, the automobile, and scientific agriculture in changing the life of the people and in bringing them into relationships with a wider world. Whether or not any study of a little community carries our minds outside of that community, it may in itself have interest for us. Intrinsic interest is no small thing.

But of course these accounts do usually carry our minds outside of the community that is described. Plainville may suggest the story of the reader's own home town. Reading of the adjustment made by the Nuer to their land and their cattle, one who happens to know the Lapps may begin to make comparisons with that people, so different from, and yet so similar to, the Nuer in their dependence on their herds and in the migratory movements depending on the change in the seasons and on the needs of the herds. Every study of a community has at least by implication a comparative aspect. The study of the community is forever bursting the bounds of time and place under the impact of general questions.

The general questions are in part read into the account by its reader and in part they are put there by its author. The author may not fully declare his interests and purposes. In my second book about Chan Kom I did not fully declare my interest in the microcosmic aspect of the changes that took place in that village, but rather introduced the theme to the notice of the reader without prior and candid declaration of intentions. On the other hand, Per Gräslund announced almost on the first page of his monograph what his purpose was in trying to find out what happened to certain Swedish communities as a result of the application of the law requiring a redistribution of the land.

It is fair to remark that the ends of the reader of a study of a community may not coincide with those of the writer. A clear instance is provided by the use made in these chapters of four principal descriptions of little communities. I have used them to help me to think about, among other things, outlook on life and the relation of the inside view to the outside view. Clearly these purposes were not among the principal intentions of the writers of the four descriptions or perhaps were not within their intentions at all.

Whatever a community study may have in it for purposes which we, as readers and as students, do not share with the author of the study, to understand the study we are required to take the author's position with regard to it. A written account of a community is something like the community itself: to understand it one needs to take the inside view of it. Of the published study, the inside view is the author's view. With what ends in mind did he make the study?

I will here ignore the private ends, the personal motives with which the field worker and author did the work. I attend only to those of his purposes which he shares with some community of people. Commonly this community is that from which comes the investigator: his fellow citizens, or his fellow scholars and scientists. Occasionally, however, the study is shaped at least in part by the purposes of the community that is studied. In the "social survey" of the sociologist,[1] the ends in view may be shared by the investigator and by the people he studies: both are interested in social problems of the community and their solution. Dr. Sol Tax has defined a kind of anthropological study he calls "action anthropology."[2] His students, who come from outside of the Indian community to be studied, organize their investigation around the questions and problems that the Indians of that community themselves find to be important to them. In many studies, however, the interests of the investigator in accomplishing practical action are not fully shared by the members of the community he studies, and the theoretical scientific interests of the investigator are shared by them not at all.

The ends of the study are in part announced by the explicit questions asked by the author of the facts from the community and by the terms and categories which he uses in presenting it to us. So we find ourselves asking not only, Why was this study made? but also, How was it made? To know, to judge, and to make use of it we need also to consider the means taken by the investigator to reach understanding of the community and to arrive at formulations about it.

It is convenient to divide the means used to reach understanding into two. There are on the one hand the more immediate procedures closely related to special operations in the field or in the library or workroom. We may call these the technical aspects of method. These we may set against another aspect of method: the concepts, or what I have called here the "forms of thought" for guiding the investigator's choice and arrangement of facts. Both concepts and technical methods or procedures are always present, in varying forms and degrees of distinctness. Recognizing, then, both aspects of method, we divide the question as to the investigator's methods into two: In what mental forms did the investigator of the community conceive and analyze it? And: With what particular technical procedures did he study it?

In these pages no considerable attention has been given to technical method. The subject of interest has been the forms of thought used in conceiving a community, and this choice of subject involves the assumption that concepts are prior to technical methods. Without demonstration, it is here supposed that the concept asks the more general question about the community and so declares the public purpose of the investigation; the technical method is then chosen or devised to meet the needs created by the question and its purpose. If this assumption is sound, then the technical methods used in a study cannot be evaluated apart from the concepts used and the questions asked with reference to the community studies: then there is no universal technical method; one uses the techniques called for by the forms of thought and inquiry with which one begins in that instance of research.

The questions as to technical method are many. We may ask whether the community chosen is fairly representative of the class or region which it has been chosen to represent. We may ask whether the investigator told the people of the community that he was investigating them, and how intimately he participated in their common life while he was studying them. We may become interested in the use of particular procedures: the making of censuses; the collection of genealogies; the recording of biographies; the use of particular tests; and the many useful devices of the statistician. In all such matters of technical method we may attempt to judge whether the most suitable procedures were chosen and whether they were well used. The question raised earlier in these lectures as to whether the Rorschach tests may be used in exotic communities, and the question whether a sample of people so tested is large enough and is properly chosen, illustrate the large group of special questions as to technical method.

By the concept or mental form for conceiving the community we may include all the prearrangement of facts which the investigator brings to the village or other small society that he studies. There is always some prearrangement of the facts before the actual investigation. Even that student of the small community who says that he is going there to make "a rounded study" has made a precommitment to look in several previously identified directions. He will look at the technology, the economy, the social structure, the religion, and so forth, and he knows that unless he has found out something about each of these and of other aspects of the life, the study he makes will not be sufficiently "rounded."

The mental forms for conceiving a community are generic names for that community or some parts or aspects of it. Each such name sets a something emphasized against a field or in a context correspondingly subordinated. Each carries within it at least the question, What particular fact here before me corresponds to the general idea identified by the name? If I study the economy of the community, the functions of ritual kinship, or the primary institutions affecting personality, I have at least asked what there is, just here, that is to be spoken of as "economy," "ritual kinship," or "primary institution." And when at least two named things are so identified in the prearrangement, and when further some connection between the two is supposed, then I have posed a question of a relationship: then the prearrangement, the initial mental form, includes something often called a "hypothesis"—a foreseen connection or relationship stated in such a way as to facilitate its proof or disproof.

But these remarks about how we think in relation to how we work do poor justice to the complexity and subtlety of the actual happenings in our researching minds. Especially needs it be admitted that there is rarely an undisturbed relationship between the prearrangement and the particular observations made in the community. No, if my experience is like that of others, the prearrangement is frequently disturbed, remade, or even supplanted by other conceptions as the work proceeds. One sees possibilities at the beginning; but other possibilities, that modify or take the place of the first, come into the mind. I suppose this happens too in the ordered experiments with rats in mazes; it happens oftener in the study of so relatively unpredictable and complicated a thing as a human community.

The prearrangement that the student brings to the community may be defined by a practical problem of action in that community. The investigator may have asked, Why is this community not developing economically? Or he may ask, What is the consequence in this community of the law as to redistribution of the land? While no one of the four studies of which I have made principal use in these chapters was made to assist practical action in the community studied, such studies are common. The Society for Applied Anthropology and the quarterly *Human Organization*[3] have reported many recent studies of the kind.

The interest in action, as contrasted with understanding without necessary result in action, has developed very far among some of the many who have concerned themselves with communities. The small community, the village, the ideal city of Plato, so small it is not easily to be distinguished from a village, these have come to mean, for one thinker or another, the desirable and ideal form of human association and the center of effort to realize the good society and the good life. In this direction of thought about the community, the prearrangement of the facts, the forms of thought for conceiving it, are not the value-free concepts of descriptive and analytic science; the concepts are those of centrally important values chosen and declared. The little community is seen as something to be made good, and as something through which to make the great society good. Among those who have so conceived the community in recent times are Arthur E. Morgan,[4] Baker Brownell,[5] and Martin Buber.[6] Very recently Phillips Ruopp[7] has reviewed some of the thought about small communities that runs along the lines of value-choice, planning, and social and economic development. In the history of utopias and of social reform, the small community has long held a significant place.

This has not been the line of thought followed in these chapters. Here the interest has been in the thinking about communities without important reference to practical action in that community or outside of it. The interest here has been in understanding of the community, and of other things as they may be understood through the study of the community, for its own sake. We have followed the path of understanding marked "theoretical" or "scientific" or "scholarly."

But there are many kinds of searches for understanding without necessary reference to action, and here we have been chiefly interested in just one kind. In these last pages I attempt to show the place of this chosen kind of "nonpractical" understanding of communities in relation to some other kinds. For, in the published studies and in the current studies of communities several distinguishable kinds appear. Little communities are studied by people with different interests, training, and varieties of academic attachment. To compare and to judge what one investigator does with that which another does, the first question that we ask ourselves and make ourselves answer is the double question which begins and underlies this chapter: Toward what understanding, and with what forms of thought, does this investigator study this community?

The investigator may be interested in understanding the history of that *kind* of community in that part of the world. In this case the study is not made with reference to one particular village or other settlement, but with regard to all villages, all settlements, in that country or area. For the English village as a type, the studies reported in the books of Harold Peake[8] and of Professor Seebohm[9] are good illustrations. For Swedish villages, Professor Sigurd Erixon[10] has written a very impressive study. All these books describe the typical history and the typical nature of villages in that part of the world without, of necessity, identifying any one. In such studies the central questions are historical and ethnographical. The student is concerned with the forms of early settlement, with the influences of geography and the migrations of peoples on the form of settlement; he attends to the early institutions and their later modifications and is usually much interested in the changes which modern life has brought about.

In this kind of study of communities concentrated field work is only one element. The student may make use of many historical documents, and he moves about rather freely from one place or one element of community life to another. He does not stay in one village only.

A second purpose with which one may study a small community is to understand a complex nation or region not so much historically as in its contemporary condition. One wants to comprehend Sweden, or the American Southeast, and makes a study of one or more communities there to that end. Among American anthropologists, the phrase "community study" has come to refer to studies made with this purpose;[11] thus an anthropologist who studies an African village in order to learn something about the general nature of kinship systems is not making a "community study" in this limited sense; but West's *Plainville* or Allwood's *Medelby* are community studies, so understood. The purpose to learn about the whole nation through a study of one or a few communities is present, I suppose, in studies with mixed purposes. One learns something about Sweden through reading *Medelby* or Per Gräslund's study while one also learns something about more theoretical matters.

One may, however, make use of a community as a convenient place in which to study a special problem of general scientific interest. One may study a little community, not to find out all about it, but with reference only to a limited problem stated in advance. What are the characteristic consequences, for social structure or for group personality, of a migratory and pastoral mode of life? What are the generic features of that process by which a remote people of simple technology enter into relations with an invading people of more advanced technology? What are the consequences for capital formation of the introduction of a money-crop into a community theretofore producing only for local subsistence? One may study special problems in the context of the whole.

It is this "context of the whole" that is the characteristic of method often claimed by anthropologists who have studied so many communities, and have so often in each instance taken responsibility for finding out about all aspects of the life of the community. As Professor Raymond Firth puts it, "The ... characteristic feature of the social anthropologist's enquiry is that it is holistic in implication. Any particular item selected for examination is always considered with some regard to its place in the total phenomena in the life of the human group concerned."[12] And Professor Julian Steward, who has thought very much about community studies, writes that the first distinctive methodological aspect of the study of communities is that "it is ethnographic; the culture of a tribe, band or village is studied in its totality, all forms of behavior being seen as functionally interdependent parts in the context of the whole."[13]

That investigator who is interested in a limited problem of general relationships, a problem of some human uniformity, finds in the small community a place to study that general question in its full context of social reality. The community stands there always ready to serve the student of the mechanisms of learning, of the workings of simple economics, of the natural history of social movements. It stands there repeating to such students of the general relations of particular parts of the whole to one another that none of these things takes place except in the context of the total human situation. And it offers so many kinds of contexts, so many little communities! It offers the investigator opportunity to see how, in a multitude of variously composed arrangements for taking care of all that people require and much of what they desire, the generic relationships really occur. One can at least change the community, as one studies a special problem. The self-contained community is a poor but useful substitute for experiment. One hears it called "a veritable laboratory."

Again I have mentioned a kind of interest in understanding communities that is not quite that emphasized in these pages. I have not chosen any limited scientific problem to be studied as it appears in this or that society. My interest has not been to detach my mind from the community chosen for study at once to make comparisons of some one of its aspects with a corresponding aspect in another community. My interest has not been to attend only to some limited part of the community—its kinship terminology, its economy, its playgroups or its house-types. Nor have I asked of the community any one of the thousand questions asked by social scientists as to the relationship of some element of social life to some other element. The viewpoint I have induced you temporarily to share with me is a view of the community that does not atomize it, or choose from it some one fact or problem to study. This viewpoint has been as holistic as I have been able to make it. I have stayed throughout with the community conceived as one thing.

For, as was said at the beginning of the first chapter, the little community is one of a few prominent human wholes. Known directly, and even without much effort to analyze or classify, it provides that kind of understanding which is provided by coming to know a person, a history of a people, or a literature. Like a person, it is one of those integrated arrangements of all that that kind of whole requires to be that kind of a whole. Of all the conspicuous enduring forms in which humanity occurs, the self-contained community is the most nearly self-sufficient and the most nearly comprehensible in itself alone. Not even the personality is an exception to this, for no person can be understood by himself alone: he is part of his culture and his community. But the community holds those personalities within itself, and is small enough to submit itself to our effort toward total comprehension—although more and more, as civilization advances, it cannot be understood alone.

It is the generic nature of this whole that has given purpose to these chapters. The purpose here, in reviewing some community studies made by myself or by other people, has been understanding, but the understanding sought has been of a different kind from those I mentioned a few minutes ago. I have asked: How may we think of the community as a whole? What language about this whole conveys what kind of understanding about it? What movements of the mind, empirically guided, help to increase, on the one hand, understanding of just that one community, as a unique reality, and on the other, the generic and abstract nature of all communities, of all such human wholes?

This being the purpose, I am committed beyond description to analysis. I am not satisfied with taking a community, apprehended but unanalyzed, into my understanding. It is not enough to say to one's self that now one feels at home in Chan Kom or in some

Swedish village. One seeks to understand the relationships of some of the parts to one another within that whole. One seeks to understand the relation of parts to parts within a whole. One is interested in the small community as an analyzed system. It is true that the analysis has not here been pushed very far. These pages report something of a beginning made to form concepts for description of the whole; and in some cases one begins to see relationships, perhaps to be understood as causal, perhaps not, among the parts of the complex entity described by that concept.

This choice of purpose establishes the position here taken in relation to the purposes, viewpoints, and methods of others who look at communities from other points of view. Very near to this position are those who study the community as one aspect of more inclusive wholes: regions, nations, or areas. These students must be concerned with the relations of parts, of which our little community is one, in their larger wholes; and these relationships we have been helped to think about by the work of Starr and Steward and Hanssen. Close at hand and yet drawing ever farther away from us are all those who come to the community or find in it some special problem as to the relationship of some This to some That, some problem in economics, or some question having to do with the development of personality, or the causes of delinquency, or the relations of frustration to aggression, or the general nature of learning.

On this side of the position I have perhaps induced the reader to share with me, we look even beyond those who study small communities with reference to limited general problems to those who do not study communities at all in any way that retains the whole nature of the community. Still farther from where we just now stand are those who study the relations of parts to parts, of elements abstracted out from the whole in strict and limited relationship to each other, generally described. Those workers over there are those whose first aim is precision, both of definition and of operation, and whose hope is the compendency of abstract general propositions. What is now called "the behavioral sciences" includes, I think, the research of these workers. They are those who make a science from chosen parts of human wholes, placed in relation to other such parts, but not in relation to all the parts of the original whole.

If now, standing where we stand in the self-contained community, we turn our gaze in the opposite direction, we see a different kind of thinker and student, a different way of looking upon our community. Over there, on that other side, are all those who strive to present the concrete reality of each human whole as each, in itself, is. They are a various group. Included are novelists, philosophers, historians, philosophers of history, literary people, critics of literature and of art, historians of art, and writers of personal reminiscence. These people describe human wholes—personalities, civilizations, epochs, literatures, local cultures—each in its uniqueness. They share with us the interest in the community as a whole.

Many of these present the human wholes without the benefits and the limitations that science provides; they present each one directly, often personally; they draw from the reality such parts as, rearranged and transformed by their art, communicate that whole to us. They are often immensely convincing, and in many cases they convince most where their methods are most obscure and most personal. From such writers we learn about the human wholes almost as personal experiences of our own help us to learn about them.

There is a certain tension between the interest in the analysis of the community as a whole and the interest in the general uniformities of human behavior and institution. The empirical knowledge of concrete reality—what Max Weber called *Wirklichkeitswissenschaft*—requires us to preserve the wholeness of that whole. The more behavioral scientists out on the one side of our position will provide us with precise and explicit understanding of certain parts of our whole, but in doing so they will depart from the whole. Nor will they, in their own terms, restore it to us. When they get far along with their development of compendent, precise, abstract, and general propositions, I shall join in the general rejoicing. But I do not think it will be possible to get back to the human wholes from those propositions. As Weber said, concrete reality cannot "be deduced from 'laws' and 'factors'." "The analysis of reality," he wrote, "is concerned with the *configuration* into which these (hypothetical) 'factors' are arranged to form the cultural phenomenon which is historically significant to us."[14]

The purpose that defines the position I have suggested that my reader assume requires that we remain attendant to the configuration. But it requires also that we strive to make explicit the arrangement of the parts within the configuration. We seek to know the whole through identifying the parts of the whole and describing the interconnections among these and their relations to the whole. The community seen as an analyzed whole keeps the whole in the center of attention, makes explicit the perceptions of its nature (whether the perceptions are those of the inside viewer adopted by one who is outside, or whether they originate in my outside view), and relates parts to parts and to the whole by recognized and named kinds of relationships.

Such an analyzed whole is a form of understanding that lies intermediate between analytic denotative assertions of relationships of parts (cultural or personal), on the one hand, and unanalyzed literary or personal representations on the other. On one side are the propositions of learning theory or the systematic theories of not a few sociologists. On the other are Mrs. Gaskell's account of Cranford or W. Reymont's fictional description of a Polish village. In between are many structural and functional descriptions of small communities achieved by anthropologists. As a single example of a partly analyzed almost-whole, think of Malinowski's books about the Trobriand Islands.

The analyzed whole appears in the study of human wholes other than the little community. In a foregoing chapter I quoted from a writing by Dr. Margaret Mead in which she claimed as her method for the study of national character the recognition of a circular system including institutions and typical personality as combined and interrelated conditions of one another. The analyzed whole appears also in certain studies of the personalities of individuals. In these, no analysis is made in terms of the relationship of some particular stimulus to a particular response, or in terms of any simple mechanism. The personality is instead seen as an analyzed system of multiple interrelations of many parts within a whole. Rorschach tests and Thematic Apperception Tests are now used, not as the reading of a needle on a dial would be read, the inference automatically to follow the verbal signal given by the person tested. Instead, each item in the interpretation of the test is seen "more holistically and clinically ... in relation to the identified individual and to all other 'items' in his responses."[15]

Let us now in conclusion review the position taken here for the study of the community as a whole. Let us look once more at some of the concepts we have considered for the description and analysis of that whole.

The very general question of this book is: What language about the community (or other human whole) conveys what kind of understanding about it? Suppose we remain in the middle position already chosen, with works of fiction and personal impressions on one side of us and analyses of parts of our whole, in the manner of behavioral sciences, on the other side. We look now at a range of descriptions, in many kinds of books and reports, about communities. The analyses of causal and other relations between certain isolated parts lose the community as a whole. We see such analyses "out there" but we do not consider them now. Also, we see statistical propositions about our community. These do say things about the whole community. It is not difficult to identify the characterizations of statistical aggregates. They are achieved by making the assumption that every element in the whole is the equivalent of every other. This assumed, the nature of that particular community (or other whole) is communicated usually in the form of frequency distributions and measures of central tendency. The bell-curve, and all the other curves that appear, are the statistician's profiles of human wholes. The various measures of central tendency are his characterizations of the uniqueness of that whole. What the statistician tells us about a human whole is precise in great degree, but that which, of all that that whole is, he is able to tell us is not much.

The characterizations of the artist and of the sensitive reporter are of course not precise at all; but very much of the whole is communicated to us. We might call them all portraits. They communicate the nature of the whole by attending to the uniqueness of each part, by choosing from among the parts certain of them for emphasis, and by modifying them and rearranging them in ways that satisfy the "feeling" of the portrayer. Writers of novels, describers without scientific claims or training of the life of exotic peoples, do a sort of verbal portraiture of the little community.

There is also, in my opinion, a great deal of portraiture in the professional ethnologist's or sociologist's account of the community. What the more scientific describer of a community does is to arrange parts of the whole in ways that satisfy his feelings as to how they should go and in ways that are not fully connected with recognized rules or concepts. On the other hand, the ethnographer's portrait receives other validation from the documentation he can provide to his assertions, and from the many disciplines he has learned for his reporting and its later presentation.

In the portraitures accomplished by art, exaggerations, distortions, and substitutions of one sort or another play important parts. Caricature and satire are special forms of portraiture. Each describes the whole by overemphasizing something felt to be significantly true of the whole. Metaphor and analogy offer different and parallel images for understanding the whole, as does the parable: a narrative standing for a human something other than itself. And in the more nearly scientific portraiture of communities metaphors and analogies play a useful part. No one expects Professor Fortes to produce the tangible warp and woof of Tallensi social structure; the words bring forward a metaphor which helps us to understand Tallensi life, and, indeed, the concept of social structure itself.

Some of the more scientific concepts grow out of portraiture. I remember Ruth Benedict's first announcement that "culture is personality writ large."[16] She was, I think, speaking metaphorically. But the metaphor became a persisting intellectual structure for the understanding of cultures and personalities as the conception of basic personality and of primary and secondary institutions developed. The clarification, by Dubois, of modal personality, a statistical characterization of the human whole, completes the history to date of these ideas: portraiture, analyzed whole, statistical characterization.

Without being a caricaturist or a satirist, one may strive, by more controlled and public methods, to economize on the characterization of the little community to the point where one finds within it some fundamental and all-pervasive qualities that identify and distinguish it. In recent American anthropology there is considerable effort to reach summary characterizations of cultures by undertakings that follow explicit rules and defined conceptions. Such more orderly analysis is made so as to reach some essential dominating quality of character: "cultural focus" (Herskovits), "unconscious canons of choice" (Benedict), "culture themes" (Opler), "enthymemes" (Kluckhohn).[17] To us who read a summary characterization of a culture or community in terms of one of these concepts, each is connotative in so far as it leaves our minds free to range around in our experiences and find some connection of thought that will give added meaning to the characterization. It is denotative to the extent that the summary characterization restricts our minds to certain thoughts and indeed to limited operations upon limited facts.

Portraiture of human wholes is very connotative, especially the metaphorical varieties. Statistical characterization identifies the aggregate with almost perfect denotation. Ruth Benedict's characterization of the Kwakiutl as megalomaniac is connotative, and becomes somewhat more denotative as she demonstrates the applicability of the term to many aspects of Kwakiutl customary life. Her characterization of Southwestern Indian culture as Apollonian and that of the Plains Indians as Dionysian remains connotative even after reading *Patterns of Culture* carefully. The meaning depends in large part on whether one has read Dilthey, Spengler, and Nietzsche and on what one remembers about Apollo and Dionysius.

It is the community analyzed in terms of the intellectual forms comprehensive of the whole and susceptible of denotative development that centrally interests us here. We have found some of these intellectual forms, as world view, more nearly comprehensive than others, as ecological system. We have found some of these conceptions, as social structure, fairly denotative, and others, as world view, much less so. The study of human wholes lies today in a borderland between science and art. While the study of social structure is highly developed toward denotation and compendency, its conceptions have as yet been shown applicable to a rather limited universe of communities, and the power of the conception to include all aspects of the community life is as yet not quite demonstrated. The study of group personality struggles to find its dependable conceptions; comprehensive intellectual forms have been brought forward but are as yet little tested and only imperfectly thought out. And such a conception as world view, so little examined and so little related to limited fact, has as yet little denotative power. In using any of these conceptions a considerable amount of portraiture is to be accepted, especially in such a conception as national character or world view.

As we read the books and articles about villages and primitive bands and settlements, we rarely find any one ordering conception predominant in the description. The intellectual forms for describing communities hover over the writer of many an ethnographic account, influencing him strongly in one chapter and very little in the next. One who describes a community may employ one ordering conception in part of his work and another conception in another part. These ordering conceptions appear, here and there, modifying the portraiture in the direction of science.

It is, I think, the lodestone of the natural sciences—or, rather, of some idealized part of the natural sciences—that draws the effort to find intellectual forms of denotative power and potential compendency in one general direction: toward conceptions of functional or causal relationships of parts within the whole. Very predominately, the more developed conceptions for describing human wholes approximate the model of the machine or the organism. Less prominent, and yet significantly present, is the characterization of the whole as a system of logically connected propositions. Let us test these assertions with the descriptions of little communities with which we have been most concerned.

Holmberg's description of the Siriono band moves toward answering the question, What are the consequences for a little community of deprivation of food? As he describes the community he is guided by a conception, derived from anthropological and psychological teaching, of causal-functional relations between innate and acquired universal human "drives," and conduct and institution. Frustration in the effort to satisfy hunger thus explains Siriono social life and character.

Evans-Pritchard's account of the Nuer employs two mechanical causal-functional conceptions: ecological system and social structure. My earlier descriptions of Chan Kom are mostly portraiture, but here and there the same conception of causal and functional relationships within a machine-like or organism-like structure appears. But the chapter on the villager's view of life in *The Folk Culture of Yucatán* presents, very briefly, a comprehensive whole that suggests a dramatic form or a system of logically related propositions rather than a machine or a living body.

West's description of Plainville directs attention especially to the distinctions of status in the community and to the process by which persons are made into Plainvillers, but brings forward no single explicit ordering conception comprehensive of the whole community.

The possibility of developing certain intellectual forms for describing the community as a whole into more denotative and compendent systems of conceptions causes us to entertain this thought: that there might be a comparative science of human wholes. Whether it will ever happen or not, one can imagine a developing preciseness and compendency among such conceptions as social structure, group personality, and world view.

Whatever one may hope about this, I think it necessary to say that the characterization of communities as analyzed stable systems, by such concepts as I have first brought forward, is to be supplemented by other forms of thought for understanding them. We may, as I later said, characterize a little community as a history. The histories of villages and of small towns contribute to our understanding of their more generic or scientifically understood natures, but they do not fully combine themselves with the logico-functional-causal systems of much social science. Also, in the ninth chapter, we considered the use of imagined constructions of "pure" types as contributing to our understanding of communities. Such constructed types, as given particular content in that chapter, raise fresh questions as to the relations of our community to a major difference and a major historical change; by the use of such conceptions, one "prearranges" ideas as to the course and process of transformation of little communities; they thus create classes and hypotheses for a developing science.

Is the analysis of human wholes a kind of intellectual operation as to particular fact that leads into social science on the model of the natural sciences? Is the interest expressed in these pages to seek out and to clarify concepts for characterizing and perhaps analyzing small communities more or less as wholes a preliminary step in the development of a "behavioral" science made up of compendent general propositions as to precise relationships of defined units of something? Or does it lead toward science in a different way: by the refinement of the holistic characterization and the construction of typologies of wholes: a science of modal personalities or of world views? Or is the work of the mind in characterizing a human whole so different in kind from the work of the mind in making a natural science of human behavior or social relations that the former cannot lead to the latter?

In a long paper on world view,[18] Karl Mannheim adopts the position expressed in the sentence I have written just before this one. He asserts that the study of wholes is quite different in kind from behavioral science, and that it has its own methods. For him, the concepts with which we understand human wholes are "widely heterogeneous" from those of natural science. He thinks that the central concept for understanding a world view or other human whole may be something he calls "documentary meaning"— the underlying character or global orientation of acts and objects as understood by the viewer. So, for him, the movements of the mind in reaching this totality of meaning in a work of art or culture or in a world view are quite different in kind from what the mind does in forming generalizations as to the common properties of instances in forming classes, or in characterizing a totality statistically. Further, he thinks that the assertions we make about human wholes are not assertions as to the members of the group, on the average (as I suppose we usually understand our assertions about little communities to be), but are rather assertions with reference to collective subjects "which are pure constructs ... whose cognitive values consist merely in the fact that they serve as the subjective counterpart of the characterological units suggested by the documentary interpretation."[19]

A writer should not leave his readers on the last pages with unanswered questions, and I am doing worse than that: I confess I cannot answer them. I can at least say that I do not understand the absoluteness of the difference which Mannheim sees between characterizing a work of culture and stating a natural law. They seem to me very different, but not unrelated. And it seems to me that any mind, curious about human life, is free to move about, to change, a little or much, the way of thinking about some part of it that interests. I rather see a continuum of effort and ways of work between the novelist and the statistical experimenter. No one piece of work can very well take more than a small part of this continuum, but within it are many frontiers of near relationship. If I attempt to communicate to readers the world view or the "total community" of Chan Kom, there will be portraiture in my effort; therefore the work of historians and indeed of novelists will not be entirely irrelevant to me. The nature of portraiture may some day be made more explicit. Perhaps that is what Mannheim wrote about. He was concerned, paradoxically, with the rules for reaching intuited wholes! If I seek to express Chan Kom as a story of a resolution made by a people and its outcome, the work of the historians and even the novelists is yet more relevant. If I should try to represent Chan Kom as a few dominant purposes or forms of thought characterizing its people, I may read with profit what Professor Northrop has written from his philosophical position, or attend to the work of Whorf and others who have found an expression of such dominant forms of thought in the forms of the language spoken in the community. If I strive to make clearer the interrelations of customs and institutions and kind of personality, I may choose out a small number of these entities in order to show that the whole can be understood as these relatively few things in interconnectedness. Now the descriptions of mechanical systems or of the ecological or geographical systems of the descriptive natural scientist may help me. And if I fix my attention on the particular relationship, causal or functional, between some quite restricted part of the community to some other, I may find my work joining with that of those who define precise hypotheses and make experiments or strictly limited observations.

Wherever I work, whatever guides to my thought and method affect me, the product I turn out will meet different interests in the community of its readers, will serve different human ends. The communication of the nature of a culture, a community, or a work of art, is part of the business and the joy of human living, and needs to be carried on whether or not there is a strictly behavioral science. So, if the characterization of a community stops at some place between imaginative portraiture on the one hand, and a statement of a proved hypothesis as to part relations on the other, it may serve, although perhaps only a little, several of these needs and purposes. It may be a piece of humane education; a contribution to the understanding of just this analyzed system on which, perhaps, we can now more effectively act; a context of reality within which to examine or test some hypothesis as to a special problem; a tiny brick in some future wall of compendent general propositions as to the kinds and transformations of human communities; and a seed-bed or generator of possible propositions for a human behavioral science.

In the long time between now and some possible clarification of all method for all purposes, we who try to describe such a human whole as a little community need not be too much worried about the relation of what we do to that current halfgod, natural science, or its avatar in the world of the social, the behavioral sciences. For understanding is increased and the needs of mankind are met by any and all honest descriptions, responsible to the facts and intellectually defensible. To see what is there with the perceptions that our own humanity allows; to render our report so as to preserve the significance of these perceptions while submitting them to the questions and the tests of our fellows—that is our common duty, whatever the particular means we take to realize it. Understanding, and her apotheosis, wisdom, are the true gods within the temple; science is not; she is only a handmaiden, and serves with many others.

NOTES

NOTES TO CHAPTER I

1. A. L. Kroeber, *Anthropology* (New York: Harcourt, Brace & Co., new edition, 1948), pp. 316–31; "The Delimitation of Civilizations," *Journal of the History of Ideas*, XIL, No. 2 (April, 1953), 264–75.

2. Sigurd Erixon, *Svenskt Folkliv* (Uppsala: J. A. Lindblads Förlag, 1938).

3. Newell L. Sims, *The Rural Community, Ancient and Modern* (New York: Scribner's & Co., 1921), pp. 120–21.

4. A. de Tocqueville, *Democracy in America*, ed. by H. S. Commager (Oxford: Oxford University Press, 1946), p. 56.

5. Arthur E. Morgan, *The Small Community* (New York: Harper & Bros., 1942), p. 5.

6. Howard Cline, "Mexican Community Studies, Lewis: *Life in a Mexican Village, Tepoztlán Restudied,*" *The Hispanic American Historical Review*, XXXII (May, 1952), 212–42.

7. Morton H. Fried, "Community Studies in China," *The Far Eastern Quarterly* (forthcoming).

8. Richard K. Beardsley, "Community Studies in Japan," *The Far Eastern Quarterly* (forthcoming).

9. Reviewed in a very preliminary way in a seminar at the University of Chicago held in the spring of 1954.

10. Margaret Mead, "Character Formation and Diachronic Theory," in *Social Structure: Studies Presented to A. R. Radcliffe-Brown*, ed. by M. Fortes (Oxford: Oxford University Press, 1949).

11. Allan R. Holmberg, *Nomads of the Long Bow, The Siriono of Eastern Bolivia*, Smithsonian Institution, Institute of Social Anthropology, Pub. No. 10 (Washington, 1950).

12. Karl Nickul, *The Skolt Lapp Community Suenselsijd during the Year 1938*, Nordiska Museet: Acta Lapponica, V (Stockholm: Hugo Gebers Förlag, 1948).

13. E. E. Evans-Pritchard, *The Nuer* (Oxford: Clarendon Press, 1940; later editions, 1947, 1950).

14. Robert Redfield and Alfonso Villa Rojas, *Chan Kom, a Maya Village* (Washington: Carnegie Institution of Washington, Pub. No. 448, 1934); Robert Redfield, *The Folk Culture of Yucatán* (Chicago: University of Chicago Press, 1941); *A Village That Chose Progress* (Chicago: University of Chicago Press, 1950).

15. James West, *Plainville, U.S.A.* (New York: Columbia University Press, 1945).

16. Martin S. Allwood and Inga-Britt Ranemark, *Medelby* (Stockholm: Albert Bonniers Förlag, 1943).

17. Erixon, *op. cit.*

18. Alwyn D. Rees, *Life in a Welsh Countryside* (Cardiff: University of Wales Press, 1950), p. 100.

19. Mandel Sherman and Thomas R. Henry, *Hollow Folk* (New York: Thomas H. Crowell Co., 1933).

20. Ruth Bunzel, *Chichicastenango, A Guatemalan Village*, Publications of the American Ethnological Society, XXII (New York: J. J. Augustin, 1952). "The Quiche Indian is not a town dweller. He lives habitually in his *monte*, his homestead on his ancestral land. But although he does not live in the town he is very much of it" (p. 5).

21. Wendell C. Bennett and Robert M. Zingg, *The Tarahumara* (Chicago: University of Chicago Press, 1935).

22. Ernst Manker, "Introduction," in Karl Nickul, *The Skolt Lapp Community Suenselsijd*, p. 9.

23. Erland Nordenskiöld, *Modifications in Indian Culture through Inventions and Loans* (Göteborg: Elanders boktryckeri aktiebolag, 1930).

24. Franz Boas, "Decorative Designs of Alaskan Needlecases: A Study in the History of Conventional Designs Based on Materials in the U. S. National Museum" (1908), in *Race, Language and Culture* (New York: The Macmillan Co., 1940), pp. 564–92.

25. N. S. B. Gras, *The Economic and Social History of an English Village* (Crawley, Hampshire), (Cambridge: Harvard University Press, 1930).

26. Sigurd Erixon, *Kila. En östgötsk skogsby.* En byundersökning 1912–13. Etnologiska källskrifter utg. av S. Erixon och H. Nelson. III. Lund, 1946.

NOTES TO CHAPTER II

1. E. E. Evans-Pritchard, *The Nuer* (Oxford: Clarendon Press, 1940), p. 89.

2. J. H. Steward, *Basin-Plateau Aboriginal Sociopolitical Groups*, Smithsonian Institution, Bureau of American Ethnology, Bull. 120 (Washington, 1938). And even in peasant and other rural communities of modern states, the nature of the predominating crop may strongly influence characteristics of the community. Robert Manners and Julian H. Steward, "The Cultural Study of Contemporary Societies: Puerto Rico," *The American Journal of Sociology*, LIX, No. 2 (September, 1953), 123–30.

3. Robert H. Park, *Human Communities. The City and Human Ecology* (Glencoe, Ill.: The Free Press, 1952), p. 66.

NOTES TO CHAPTER III

1. Raymond Firth, *Elements of Social Organization* (London: Watts & Co., 1951), p. 42.

2. *Ibid.*, p. 31.

3. *Ibid.*, p. 32.

4. *Ibid.*, p. 30.

5. *Ibid.*, p. 30. And Meyer Fortes, "The Structure of Unilineal Descent Groups," *American Anthropologist*, LV, No. 1 (January–March, 1953), 22, gives as his reason for choosing the phrase "social structure" rather than "social organization" that it "draws attention to the interconnection and interdependence, within a single system, of all the different relations found within a given society."

6. M. Fortes, *The Dynamics of Clanship among the Tallensi* (London: Oxford University Press, 1945); *The Web of Kinship among the Tallensi* (London: Oxford University Press, 1949).

7. Here "individual" is used in the common sense meaning "a single human being," and not in the sense—in which I think it is used in some discussions of social structure—as "that, in a person, which is special, idiosyncratic, to that person."

8. M. Fortes, *The Web of Kinship among the Tallensi*, p. 12. In another paper (footnote 3, chap. iv) he writes of the "tissue" of social life abstracted from the "skein" of behavior.

9. As is, apparently, clearly true in the case of factional groups in certain villages of India: Oscar Lewis, "Group Dynamics in a North-Indian Village, A Study of Factions" (manuscript).

10. *Ibid.*. pp. 211–12.

11. Firth, *op. cit.*, pp. 35–40.

12. K. N. Llewellyn and E. Adamson Hoebel, *The Cheyenne Way: Conflict and Case Law in Primitive Jurisprudence* (Norman, Okla.: University of Oklahoma Press, 1941).

13. B. Malinowski, *Crime and Custom in Savage Society* (New York: Harcourt, Brace & Co., Inc., 1926), p. 105. Also: "Ashanti discuss the subject [the conflict between the ties of matrilineal kinship and those of marriage and parenthood] interminably, stressing especially the inevitability of conflicting loyalties." Meyer Fortes, "Time and Social Structure, An Ashanti Case Study," in *Social Structure: Studies Presented to A. R. Radcliffe-Brown* (Oxford: Clarendon Press, 1949), p. 75. This important paper relates to at least two of the matters lightly raised in this third chapter of the present book. By an elementary statistical analysis Professor Fortes shows how the differences in the compositions of real households in a community may be seen as variations around a mode brought about by the interaction of certain limited factors of expectation or ethical demand, especially between the ties of matrilineal kinship and those of marriage and parenthood. Further, his paper relates to social change, for by comparing two Ashanti communities, differentially affected by circumstance, he shows a shift in the mode of household composition (and in other matters) corresponding to this differential influence. It will be noted, however, that this approach to social change provides for examination of changes in the traditional structure and institutions; it does not at once deal with the introduction of institutions entirely extraneous to the community into its changing social structure.

14. Firth, *op. cit.*, p. 236.

15. Meyer Fortes, "The Structure of Unilineal Descent Groups," *American Anthropologist*, LV, No. 1 (January–March, 1953), 21.

NOTES TO CHAPTER IV

1. E. E. Evans-Pritchard, *The Nuer* (Oxford: The Clarendon Press, 1940), p. 262.

2. Morris Opler, *An Apache Life-Way* (Chicago: University of Chicago Press, 1941).

3. As this book goes to press, there is published *Truk: Man in Paradise* by Thomas Gladwin and Seymour V. Sarason ("Viking Fund Publications in Anthropology," No. 20, New York: Wenner-Gren Foundation for Anthropological Research, Inc., 1953)—an important work of the kind here referred to.

4. "When we describe structure we are already dealing with general principles far removed from the complicated skein of behaviour, feelings, beliefs, &c., that constitute the tissue of actual social life. We are, as it were, in the realm of grammar and syntax, not of the spoken word." Meyer Fortes, "Time and Social Structure, An Ashanti Case Study," in *Social Structure: Studies Presented to A. R. Radcliffe-Brown* (Oxford: Clarendon Press, 1949), p. 56.

5. Margaret Mead, "National Character," in *Anthropology Today* (Chicago: University of Chicago Press, 1953), p. 643.

NOTES TO CHAPTER V

1. A. L. Kroeber, *Anthropology* (New York: Harcourt, Brace and Co., 1948), p. 321.

2. *Ibid.*, p. 321.

3. *Ibid.*, p. 294.

4. Robert Redfield, *A Village That Chose Progress* (Chicago: University of Chicago Press, 1950), p. 157.

5. *Ibid.*, p. 159.

6. Kroeber, *op. cit.*, p. 294.

7. Redfield, *op. cit.*, p. 160.

8. *Ibid.*, p. 161.

9. Sylvanus G. Morley, *The Ancient Maya* (Stanford: Stanford University Press, 1946).

10. Jules Henry and Melford E. Spiro, "Psychological Techniques: Projective Tests in Field Work," in *Anthropology Today* (Chicago: University of Chicago Press, 1953), p. 418.

11. Morris Steggerda, *Maya Indians of Yucatán* (Washington, D.C.: Carnegie Institution of Washington, 1946).

12. Margaret Mead, "National Character," in *Anthropology Today* (Chicago: University of Chicago Press, 1953), pp. 642–67.

13. Henry and Spiro, *op. cit.*, p. 419.

14. Ruth Benedict, "Configurations of Culture in North America," *American Anthropologist*, XXXIV, No. 1 (January–March, 1932), 24.

15. Ruth Benedict, *Patterns of Culture* (Pelican Books, New York: Penguin Books, Inc., 1946), p. 44.

16. But a recent interest in testing isolated causal connections between specific child-training practices and specific customs relating to illness appears in John W. M. Whiting and Irvin L. Child, *Child Training and Personality: A Crosscultural Study* (New Haven: Yale University Press, 1953).

17. Abram Kardiner (with the collaboration of Ralph Linton, Cora Du Bois, and James West), *The Psychological Frontiers of Society* (New York: Columbia University Press, 1945).

18. Milton Singer, "Basic and Modal Personality," manuscript.

19. Margaret Mead, "The Study of National Character," in *The Policy Sciences, Recent Developments in Scope and Method*, ed. by Daniel Lerner and Harold D. Lasswell (Stanford: Stanford University Press, 1951), p. 74.

NOTES TO CHAPTER VI

1. E. E. Evans-Pritchard, *The Nuer* (Oxford: The Clarendon Press, 1940), p. 51.

2. *Ibid.*, p. 37.

3. Gerhart Piers and Milton B. Singer, *Shame and Guilt, A Psychoanalytic and Cultural Study* (Springfield, Ill.: Charles C. Thomas, Publisher, 1953).

4. Allan R. Holmberg, *Nomads of the Long Bow, The Siriono of Eastern Bolivia* (Smithsonian Institution, Institute of Social Anthropology, Pub. No. 10, Washington: U. S. Government Printing Office, 1950), p. 46.

5. Clyde Kluckhohn, "The Philosophy of the Navaho Indians," in *Ideological Differences and World Order*, ed. by F. S. C. Northrop (New Haven: Yale University Press, 1949), pp. 356–84.

6. Paul Radin, *Primitive Man as Philosopher* (New York: D. Appleton and Co., 1927); Radin, *The World of Primitive Man* (New York: H. Schuman, 1953).

7. Johan Olafsson Turi, *Turi's Book of Lapland* (London: J. Cape, 1931).

8. *Ibid.*, p. 20.

9. Marcel Griaule, *Dieu d'Eau* [Paris: Editions du Chêne (no date)].

10. B. L. Whorf, "An American Indian Model of the Universe," *International Journal of American Linguistics*, XVI (1950), 67–72; "Language and Logic," *The Technology Review*, XLIII (1941), 250–55; "The Relation of Habitual Thought and Behavior to Language," *Language, Culture and Personality: Essays in Memory of Edward Sapir* (Menasha, Wis.: Sapir Memorial Publication Fund, 1941), pp. 75–93; "Linguistics as an Exact Science," *The Technology Review*, XLIII (1940), 3–8; "Science and Linguistics," *The Technology Review*, XLIII (1940), 229–31, 247–48; "Some Verbal Categories of Hopi," *Language*, XIV (1938), 275–86.

11. F. S. C. Northrop, *The Meeting of East and West* (New York: The Macmillan Co., 1946); Northrop, *The Taming of the Nations* (New York: The Macmillan Co., 1952).

12. Ruth Bunzel, "An Introduction to Zuni Ceremonialism," in *47th Annual Report of the Bureau of American Ethnology* (Washington, 1932), p. 486.

13. Robert Redfield, "The Primitive World View," *Proceedings of the American Philosophical Society*, XCVI, No. 1 (February, 1952), 30–36.

14. F. Kluckhohn, "Dominant and Substitute Profiles of Cultural Orientations," *Social Forces*, XXVIII (1950); Clyde Kluckhohn, "Values and Value-Orientations in the Theory of Action: an Exploration in Definition and Classification," *Toward a Theory of Social Action*, ed. by Talcott Parsons and E. A. Shils (Cambridge: Harvard University Press, 1951); Evon Z. Vogt and Thomas F. O'Dea, "A Comparative Study of the Role of Values in Social Action in Two Southwestern Communities," *American Sociological Review*, XVIII, No. 6 (December, 1953), 645–54, and forthcoming monographs. See also Charles Morris, *Paths of Life* (New York: Harper & Bros., 1942).

NOTES TO CHAPTER VII

1. Louis Gottschalk, *Understanding History* (New York: Knopf, 1950), p. 136. The brief discussion of historical method and historiography in these pages on the whole follows Gottschalk.

2. As, for instance, was done by Oscar Lewis in his *Life in a Mexican Village, Tepoztlán Restudied* (Urbana: University of Illinois Press, 1951).

3. Robert Redfield, *The Folk Culture of Yucatán* (Chicago: University of Chicago Press, 1941), pp. 339–40.

4. Robert Redfield, *A Village That Chose Progress* (Chicago: University of Chicago Press, 1950).

5. M. M. Postan, *The Historical Method in Social Science* (Cambridge, England: The University Press, 1939), p. 36.

6. Lisa R. Peattie, "Value and Concept in Social Anthropology," manuscript.

7. Robert Redfield, "Does America Need a Hearing Aid?" *The Saturday Review*, XXXVI, No. 39 (September 26, 1953), 11.

8. Per Gräslund, "Harstena och Kråkmarö," *Liv och Folkkultur*, V (Samfundets för svensk folklivsforskning årsskrift, 1952), 68–109.

9. D. L. Hatch, *Changes in the Structure and Function of a Rural New England Community Since 1900*, Ph. D. thesis, Harvard University, 1948.

10. George C. Homans, *The Human Group* (New York: Harcourt, Brace & Co., 1950), chap. 13.

11. Alfred von Martin, *Sociology of the Renaissance* (London: K. Paul, Trench, Trubner & Co., Ltd., 1944).

NOTES TO CHAPTER VIII

1. E. E. Evans-Pritchard, *The Nuer* (Oxford: Clarendon Press, 1940), p. 114.

2. *Ibid.*, p. 116.

3. *Ibid.*, pp. 147–48.

4. Robert Redfield and Alfonso Villa Rojas, *Chan Kom, A Maya Village* (Washington, D.C.: Carnegie Institution of Washington, Pub. No. 448, 1934), p. 10.

5. *Ibid.*, p. 9.

6. Betty Starr, *Los Tuxtlas: A Study of Levels of Communal Relations*, Ph. D. thesis, University of Chicago, 1951.

7. *Ibid.*, pp. 14–18.

8. *Ibid.*, pp. 85 ff., 100 ff.

9. Starr, "Levels of Communal Relations," manuscript.

10. Starr, thesis, p. 11.

11. Starr, "Levels of Communal Relations."

12. Börje Hanssen, *Österlen* (Stockholm: LT:s Förlag, 1952); Hanssen, "Fields of Social Activity and Their Dynamics," *Translations of the Westermarck Society*, II (Copenhagen: Ejnar Munksgaard, 1953), 99–133.

13. Börje Hanssen, "Fields of Social Activity and Their Dynamics," p. 110.

14. Daryll Forde, "The Conditions of Social Development in West Africa, Retrospect and Prospect," *Civilisations, Revue Trimestrielle*, III, No. 4 (1953), 473.

15. Julian H. Steward, *Area Research: Theory and Practice*, Social Science Research Council, Bull. 63 (New York, 1950); "Levels of Sociocultural Integration," *Southwestern Journal of Anthropology*, VII, No. 4 (Winter, 1951), 374–90; Robert Manners and Julian H. Steward, "The Cultural Study of Contemporary Societies: Puerto Rico," *The American Journal of Sociology*, LIX, No. 2 (September, 1953), 123–30.

With regard to the description of peasant communities within states or civilizations: R. Redfield, *Peasant Society and Culture*, manuscript.

NOTES TO CHAPTER IX

1. Oscar Lewis, *Life in a Mexican Village, Tepoztlán Restudied* (Urbana, Ill.: University of Illinois Press, 1951), pp. 428–29.

2. *Ibid.*, p. 431.

3. John H. Bennett, "The Integration of Pueblo Culture: A Question of Values," *Southwestern Journal of Anthropology*, II, No. 4 (Winter, 1946), 361–74.

4. George Bourne, *Change in the Village* (New York: George H. Doran & Co., 1912).

5. Henry Maine, *Ancient Law* (1st American ed. from 2d London ed., New York: Scribner, 1864).

6. Henry Maine, Rede Lecture for 1875, quoted in Benjamin Nelson *The Idea of Usury* (Princeton, N.J.: Princeton University Press, 1949), pp. 137–38.

7. Henry Maine, *Village Communities East and West* (New York: H. Holt & Co., 1889; 1st edition, 1871).

8. Fustel de Coulanges, *La Cité Antique* (Paris: Hachette et Cie, 1905).

9. Lewis H. Morgan, *Ancient Society* (New York: H. Holt & Co., 1878. First pub. 1877).

10. Ferdinand Tönnies, *Gemeinschaft und Gesellschaft*, 8. verb. Aufl. (Leipzig: H. Buske, 1935).

11. Emile Durkheim, *De la division de la travail social*, 1893. Translated by George Simpson and published as *The Division of Labor in Society* (Glencoe, Ill.: The Free Press, 1947).

12. Howard W. Odum, "Folk Sociology as a Subject Field for the Historical Study of Total Human Society and the Empirical Study of Group Behavior," *Social Forces*, XXXI, No. 3 (March, 1953), 193–223.

13. Howard Becker, "Sacred and Secular Societies Considered with Reference to Folk-State and Similar Classifications," *Social Forces*, XXVIII, No. 4 (May, 1950), 361–76.

14. Robert Redfield, "The Folk Society," *The American Journal of Sociology*, LII, No. 4 (January, 1947), 293–308; "The Natural History of the Folk Society," *Social Forces*, XXXI, No. 3 (March, 1953), 224–28.

15. Robert Redfield, *The Primitive World and Its Transformations* (Ithaca, N.Y.: Cornell University Press, 1953).

16. Gideon Sjoberg, "Folk and 'Feudal' Societies," *The American Journal of Sociology*, LVIII, No. 3 (Nov., 1952), 231–39; Alvin Boskoff, "Structure, Function, and Folk Society," *American Sociological Review*, XIV (1949), 749–58; George M. Foster, "What is Folk Culture?" *American Anthropologist*, LV, No. 2, Part I (April–June, 1953), 159–73; Sidney W. Mintz, "The Folk-Urban Continuum and the Rural Proletarian Community," *The American Journal of Sociology*, LIX, No. 2 (September, 1953), 136–43; Mintz, "On Redfield and Foster" (Brief Communications), *American Anthropologist*, LVI, No. 1, (February, 1954), 87–92.

17. Robert E. Park, *Human Communities, The City and Human Ecology* (Glencoe, Ill.: The Free Press, 1952).

18. Louis Wirth, "Urbanism as a Way of Life," *The American Journal of Sociology*, XLIV, No. 1 (July, 1938), 1–24.

NOTES TO CHAPTER X

1. Niles Carpenter, "Social Surveys," *Encyclopedia of the Social Sciences*, Vol. VII.

2. Sol Tax, "Action Anthropology," *América Indígena*, XII, No. 2 (April, 1952), 103–9.

3. *Human Organization* (New York, quarterly).

4. Arthur E. Morgan, *The Small Community* (New York: Harper & Bros., 1942).

5. Baker Brownell, *The Human Community* (New York: Harper & Bros., 1950).

6. Martin Buber, *Paths in Utopia* (New York: The Macmillan Co., 1950).

7. Phillips Ruopp, "Approaches to Community Development," in *Approaches to Community Development*, ed. by Phillips Ruopp (The Hague: W. van Hoeve Lts., 1953), pp. 1–20.

8. Harold Peake, *The English Village. The Origin and Decay of its Community. An Anthropological Interpretation* (London: Benn Bros., 1922).

9. Frederic Seebohm, *The English Village* (London: Longmans, Green, & Co., 1883).

10. Sigurd Erixon, *Svenskt Folkliv* (Uppsala: J. A. Lindblads Förlag, 1938).

11. Julian H. Steward, *Area Research: Theory and Practice*, Social Science Research Council, Bull. 63 (New York, 1950).

12. Raymond Firth, *Elements of Social Organization* (London: Watts & Co., 1951), p. 18.

13. Steward, *op. cit.*, p. 21.

14. *Max Weber on the Methodology of the Social Sciences*, tr. and ed. by E. A. Shils and H. A. Finch (Glencoe, Ill.: The Free Press, 1949), pp. 74–75.

15. Lawrence K. Frank and others, *Personality Development in Adolescent Girls* (Society for Research in Child Development Monographs, Vol. XVI, Serial No. 53, 1951), p. 26.

16. Ruth Benedict, "Configurations of Culture in North America," *American Anthropologist*, XXXIV, No. 1 (January–March, 1932).

17. These conceptions are briefly reviewed by Clyde Kluckhohn in "The Study of Culture," in *The Policy Sciences*, ed. by Daniel Lerner and Harold D. Lasswell (Stanford: Stanford University Press, 1951) pp. 86–101.

18. Karl Mannheim, *Essays on the Sociology of Knowledge* (New York: Oxford University Press, 1952), chap. ii, "On the Interpretation of 'Weltanschauung'," pp. 33–83.

19. *Ibid.*, p. 61.

INDEX

Peasant Society and Culture

ACKNOWLEDGMENTS

To Swarthmore College and the William J. Cooper Foundation I am grateful for the invitation to give these lectures and for the pleasant period of residence at the College in March, 1955. I thank especially Professors Richard B. Brandt, Laurence D. Lafore, and Fredric Klees, who administered the Foundation while arrangements for my visit were being made and who showed me many kindnesses when I came.

The debt I owe to Professor F. G. Friedmann for the stimulations of a discussion he led about peasant peoples is more specially acknowledged in chapter iv. I thank Professors Pedro Armillas, Donald S. Pitkin, and Irwin T. Sanders for permission to refer to their unpublished manuscripts or remarks. J. A. Barnes, McKim Marriott, and Milton Singer read parts or all of the manuscript and made very helpful suggestions; I thank them. Miss Rosemary Witko has again done much in preparing the manuscript for publication.

Some pages of chapter iii have already appeared in the *Far Eastern Quarterly*, Volume XV, No. 1 (November, 1955). Permission to republish these is gratefully acknowledged.

The pages that follow may be read as something of a postscript to *The Little Community* (Chicago: University of Chicago Press, 1955). In that book (with the exception of one chapter) I thought of small communities as independent of things outside of them. In the present chapters there is a very preliminary exploration of one kind of dependent community, that of peasants, as a describable type.

I

ANTHROPOLOGY AND THE
PRIMITIVE COMMUNITY

Sudden growth is often awkward, and this is true of the academic disciplines as it is of human beings. Just as the young person who was a charming child does not quite seem to know what to do with arms and legs, so my own science, anthropology, as it develops, seems a little clumsy and unsure as to what to do with itself. I have chosen to present anthropology in these chapters in an aspect of growth, and the reader may find the spectacle just a little distressing. But I hope to get him to see the growth and thus to gain his sympathy for the awkwardness.

I should like to begin with the observation that the sciences of man tend to form around some abstract image of the very thing that they happen to be studying. This image is never more than an approximation to the manifold reality. It exaggerates and enhances the qualities of that part of the human and social scene to which that discipline is giving special attention. We might say that these images, while they ignore the many particular ways in which the reality departs therefrom, are yet truer than the reality—truer internally, so to speak, truer to the Platonic idea of the reality.

In some of the social sciences the image is very abstract indeed and far from the particular realities. The economist has attended especially to markets and has developed subtle conceptions of mentally constructed markets and of behavior in such markets; the usefulness of these abstractions depends upon the fact that they leave out very much of what goes on in human life. In other sciences no one image dominates; there are many vague images. Thinking of American sociology, I recall the importance of the city as a constellation of social problems and of the immigrant community as two of the kinds of social reality which tended to give rise to abstract statements as to the nature of things in that science. In psychology there may also be such influential recurrent realities from which abstractions have arisen: the experimental animal in the test situation; in Freudian psychology, the troubled urban patient in the medical interviewer's office.

In social anthropology it is, I think, quite plain what has been the recurrent reality which the science has tended to conceive abstractly. It is the primitive band or tribe, the small and self-contained human settlement. My science rests upon the kinds of experiences of a single anthropologist living with some few remote people whose common life is for the most part bounded by the valley, hunting range, or island of their ancient habitation. To go to some distant place, to find there a community of people all much alike and living quite according to tradition, to be responsible, alone, for finding out all about the life of that people, to need to look no farther than that little community for what is relevant to finding it out—this has been the typical expectation of the young anthropologist; and in most cases he has more or less realized it.

In the nineteenth century when anthropology was beginning this expectation did not generally prevail. For the most part the anthropologists of that time studied culture not cultures, all society but no particular society. E. B. Tylor, our founder, our Adam Smith, wrote about religion and gesture language and many other general topics and about culture in general. You cannot find out how any particular people lived, altogether and as a whole, from his books or from those of Frazer or McLennan or many others of that time. At the turn of the century anthropology, or ethnology as it was often called, was added to the list of interests to be represented in expeditions to explore the natural history of unfamiliar parts of the world. A. C. Haddon, a zoölogist, turned into an anthropologist between his 1888 and 1898 expeditions to the Torres Straits in Melanesia. On the second expedition he took along W. H. R. Rivers to "do" the natives; Rivers gave them tests of their sensory capacities and noted their customs. Though his development of the field method of recording genealogies led the way to the impressive understanding of kinship systems achieved in anthropology today, Rivers' and others' accounts of the natives observed on the Torres Straits expedition were published in a series of short papers each on some one topic; the reader sees no native life clearly as a whole.

Within this early prevailing concern with custom and culture in general or in topical pieces, one can discern, however, nineteenth-century beginnings of the study of primitive groups as self-contained integrated wholes. The beginnings were made by the missionaries who lived for long periods with exotic peoples before anthropology ever came into existence. But in 1851 Lewis H. Morgan on his way to becoming an anthropologist published a part-study of the Iroquois Indians. In 1888 appeared a scientific study of the Central Eskimo by Franz Boas: a round of life is there suggested, although there is little explicit analysis of the way the parts of the culture make up a whole. Before 1900 Boas helped to organize the Jesup expedition which resulted in accounts of certain American Indian and Siberian peoples in which the cultures are presented more or less completely.

Haddon, Rivers, and Boas had their trainings respectively in zoöl-ogy, psychology, and physiological optics and became anthropologists in the course of doing anthropology. They were the teachers of those first anthropologists who became such in universities. Two of these, A. R. Radcliffe-Brown and B. Malinowski, published books in 1922: *The Argonauts of the Western Pacific* and *The Andaman Islanders*. Each anthropologist had gone alone to a remote place, lived in a small and self-contained community, and come back to report a culture as a whole, and as a whole that could be understood as a system of functionally interrelated parts. (Malinowski's account was continued in a long series of publications about the Trobriands.) Attracting increasing notice as time passed, these books established clearly the model of research in social anthropology. This was what anthropologists conceived themselves as setting out to do. Each is a report, by a single investigator, of a whole that can be understood as providing for all of life's needs in some orderly way that makes sense to the people who live under it. Each is an account by a single investigator of a culture and community that stands alone, inde-pendent of others. Even the trading expeditions of the Trobrianders are part of the system that is Trobriand culture. In reading Radcliffe-Brown on the Andamanese one finds no important account of any-thing outside of the little communities he describes. And, indeed, it was true that these primitive communities could in fact be regarded without reference to anything much outside of them; they could be understood, more or less, by one man working alone. Nor need that man be a historian, for among these non-literates there was no history to learn.

In consequence of such a characteristic experience with isolated and self-contained little communities, the social anthropologist developed his methods and came to conceive of his universe of comparisons. From the fact of his sole responsibility to report a remote and unfamiliar way of life the anthropologist became the jack of all social science trades, learning something of the economy, family life, government, and religion of the people he studied. From this fact too, and from the convenient smallness and consistency of the primitive community, developed the disposition to present everything about a way of life. Where the student of civilized societies found himself studying some sliver of a great whole—a city slum, delinquency, settlement patterns, or a rural market—the anthropologist was giving us all of some very small whole. These small wholes showed themselves as tightly interrelated parts; they were of such a kind that, taking hold of one at any point, one found one's self compelled also to give account of a great deal of the rest. Conceived as a culture, the primitive community was seen as customs and institutions in a unique design of life. Conceived as a society, the social relations described were all, with small exception, to be found right there in that little body of people. Thus arose the concepts of "a culture," "the social structure," "basic pattern," and anthropological holism generally.

The primitive isolate, the community that is a whole all by itself, now something of an abstraction derived from many experiences approximate to the abstraction, became the model of research and the typical entity for comparisons and generalizations. Social anthropology came to be a natural history of equivalent and distinct social organisms. Wrote Kroeber recently: "So the anthropologist came to conceive of his universe of comparisons as made up of so many cultures or societies or social systems each conceivable as something distinct from all others."[1] The discovery of these natural wholes provided the natural entity, the organism or life-form, for that branch of natural history concerned with human beings. Haddon was justified. Around the world lay varieties of natural wholes:

animal species, cultures, or little isolate societies. The investigator collected and noted each and then, so to speak, spread them out on the laboratory table, comparing them one with another to learn the laws of their structure, function, and process.

Of course reality is not like this. Human living is not composed of mutually isolated small primitive groups, and, in so far as it was once so composed before the rise of civilization, it had long ceased to be arranged that way when anthropology took hold of the reality at that corner of it where the primitive isolate still existed. It is curious to note that just at the time when the primitive isolate as a model of study was being established in anthropology, Graham Wallas was writing a book that called attention to the fact that all the world was becoming one great society.[2] The primitive isolate became connected with the great society while the anthropologist was looking at it; indeed, the anthropologist himself was one of the instruments of this transformation. More and more, anthropologists came to study communities in many and complex relationships with other peoples and with histories known or knowable.

Anthropology barely hesitated before it redefined itself as a study of all kinds of people in all kinds of social and cultural situations. In 1923 Radcliffe-Brown, in a presidential address, defined social anthropology and ethnology as studies of the non-civilized peoples and confirmed this limitation on its subject matter by offering the practical value of these studies to "save us from many gross blunders in our dealings with native races."[3] In 1944 he said that social anthropology "has for its field all human societies."[4] Evans-Pritchard's position as stated in 1951[5] that social anthropology is "theoretically" the study of all human societies, a branch of sociological studies which chiefly devotes itself to primitive societies, would be accepted by many anthropologists, except, I think, by some who would not like even the *de facto* limitation to primitive societies. As early as 1939 W. Lloyd Warner[6] claimed all kinds of human societies, primitive or civilized, simple or complex, as anthropological subject matter and proved his view by studying the extremely primitive and the extremely civilized. American anthropologists have moved very rapidly to accept a part of the responsibility for studying civilized people, national states, and such world-wide events as industrialization and urbanization. In a presidential address twenty-eight years after that of Radcliffe-Brown, Ralph Beals[7] asked, in the name of anthropology in linkage with sociology, for a "common theory" to bring together studies of Asiatic cities, acculturation, and sociological urbanism. Today anthropology, especially American anthropology, studies just about everything human.

Today it is usual for an anthropologist to study a community connected with or forming part of a civilization or national state. There are recent books by anthropologists about communities in Malaya,[8] Burma,[9] Paraguay,[10] China,[11] French Canada,[12] Belgium,[13] and Missouri, U.S.A.[14] Evans-Pritchard published a book on the history of a Moslem sect under colonialism.[15] Ruth Benedict wrote a famous book about Japan.[16] Professor Lowie has a book about Germany.[17] A French anthropologist compares a French village with one in Utah.[18] A group of American anthropologists undertakes a study of the whole of Puerto Rico.[19] Another group studies industrial organization in Japan.[20] More and more often the anthropologist shares the work of the study with other kinds of scientists. There is an economist at his elbow when he studies a village in India, and when he sails for the South Seas, psychologists prepared to give projective tests may be among the party. The anthropologist no longer studies a primitive isolate, no longer sees only communities that form natural self-contained systems, and no longer works alone. His habits of work are undergoing profound change because of the sudden and wide expansion of his universe of subject matter.

Nevertheless, habits of work do not at once conform to a newly enlarged subject matter. The anthropologist moves into his widened world still guided by his primary conception, the abstract primitive isolate. So when he seeks his first experience and finds that really primitive people are nowadays far away and costly to reach, then, as Kroeber says, he takes the subway and studies a community of Boston Armenians.[21] It is as near as he can get to the primitive isolate —and it is cheap. And when he thinks about the urban Armenians, Japan, or the Missouri town, he tries out the conceptions he formed in working with real almost primitive isolates. That conception gave him understanding when he studied the Andamanese; now, maybe, it will still give him understanding when he studies Puerto Rico or Japan. It may give him understanding by showing him where his new kind of society is not like the isolate, and thus it may force his recognition of new conceptions and new ways of work. Margaret Mead has led in the study of modern national states by way of the group-personality or character of such peoples. She studies national character even from a distance, as in the case of Russia. It is a very different way of work from that once followed in the Trobriands and in the Andaman Islands. Nevertheless, in enumerating the contributions made by anthropology to the study of contemporary cultures, she puts forward the provision which the anthropological approach makes "for the disciplined use of the primitive small society as a conceptual model."[22] The isolated, self-contained community remains the abstract image around which social anthropology has formed itself.

In various publications[23] I have attempted to describe the conceptual model of the primitive small society for which Margaret Mead finds use even in the study of something that is very different from it: the group-characters of modern national states. I tried to make explicit the abstract and general qualities of that society and culture that can be imagined to be more isolated, more self-contained, than is even the Andamanese band. Once this description was on paper, other students of particular real societies forming parts of civilizations and national states made the indicated comparisons between this model and the peasant communities in which they worked. What they noticed was, of course, the differences. The Mexican or Brazilian village was not, in many ways, like the abstract model. In not a few cases these students drew the conclusion that the model was wrong. I would rather say that the abstraction, being, as Mead says, a "conceptual model," cannot be wrong. It does not describe any particular real society. It is there to point the way to the study of that which its use brings to notice. It can suggest the creation of other models. But whether one says that the concept of the folk society must be changed, or whether one simply says that the peasant village in which one works is different, in noted respects, from the model, is not a very important matter. What is important is that the minds of anthropologists are directed to the study of societies that depart from the model for the reason that those societies are bound with towns and cities, because national institutions are present in them, because the townsman and the more rustic person dwell in the same community but carry on somewhat different lives.

The fact is that anthropologists have come to see their real small communities as parts of larger and compound societal and cultural wholes. This concern with larger and more complex societies developed, to a degree, in the study of those parts of the non-European world where tribal societies had grown, outside of the great world civilizations, into native states. In recent years two of the leading students of the native civilization of ancient Middle America have recognized the fact of development, before the coming of the Spaniard, of townspeople and countrypeople among the Indians themselves. "The fundamental characteristic of Mesoamerica was that it was a stratified society, one like ours or that of China, based on the axis of city and countryside," writes Kirchhoff,[24] and Armillas sees in the ancient Maya society separation between the sophisticated aristocracy of the shrine-cities and the much more primitive rural people.[25] But these beginnings of the development of an aboriginal Indian, urban-rural difference and relationship are, of course, beyond our observation. A recent review of aboriginal peoples of South and Central America groups those peoples according to the scope and complexity of their political development; distinguished are homogeneous tribes, segmented tribes, politically organized chiefdoms, feudal states, city states, and theocratic empires.[26]

The students of African native societies soon found their subject matter bursting the bounds of the primitive isolate community. In African studies the developments away from that small isolate are of several contrasting kinds. West Africa provides examples of "large, dispersed tribes."[27] The Tiv of Central Nigeria are such a tribe. Here, scattered over a territory, live a population numbering about a million who know themselves to be one people, indeed, one body of kindred. In such a large yet homogeneous community the anthropologist may keep his methods of direct observation, for the "unit of personal observation"[28] may be assumed to represent the very large tribe. The investigator can study only a few people, but he studies a piece of that network of relationships, bounded ultimately only by the limits of the population of a million Tiv, which connects one individual, familial group, or small settlement with others. The whole society is not a structure of ruler and ruled, city people and countrypeople, but of kinsmen and neighbors.[29] Where people live in distinct camps or villages, as among the Nuer of the

Sudan, this expandable network of relationships of kinship and friendliness (or in the more distant connections, of hostility) may be conceived as concentric to formed small communities.[30]

In contrast are the primitive states of native Africa. In these there is centralized political power affecting the local resident from centers of authority outside of the small community. The Lozi of Central Africa presented Gluckman with small communities to be described, not solely in terms of relationships between people within those small communities, but also in terms of relationships these villagers had with many centers of power, complexly related, that lay outside of the little communities. So Gluckman, while he studied small local groups in the way traditional in anthropology, found himself responsible for studying the entire native state. He found people of different local communities united, as are people in the local communities of modern nations, by the fact of their similar interaction with state-wide centers of authority and influence.[31]

Indeed, the African societies lead the anthropologist away from the self-contained primitive community in a variety of respects too numerous to even mention here. I am thinking of the large markets, systems of production and distribution including thousands of people from widespread and, in cases, culturally different origins. Apparently no anthropologist has yet studied such a market system completely. I am thinking of the presence, within the primitive African state, of ethnically distinct subsocieties. Among the Lozi, for instance, and among the Lovedu of Rhodesia,[32] the anthropologist is faced with a plurality of distinguishable cultural groups united in one political organization. Tribes and parts of tribes may be united by allegiance to a religious ruler. And in West Africa the development of native states went along with the growth of towns and cities to the degree that Herskovits states the contrast in Dahomey between urban people and rural people: he finds that the people of the city of Abomey show an arrogant manner toward the villager, while the "villagers show all the typical reactions of European peasants toward city-dwellers—they are suspicious, evasive, non-responsive."[33] In short, West Africa was developing its own civilization and its own peasantry. In recent years, on top of this native civilization, or almost civilization, has rapidly come into being a great complex of new institutions resulting from the contacts with European life. The anthropologists who work in Africa in the future will be required, more and more, to study such new supertribal institutions as political councils representing a large region of many peoples, co-operatives and other marketing organizations, mutual aid societies of immigrants to towns, craft and trade associations, churches, social clubs, and political parties. Africa is being transformed into new kinds of large and heterogeneous communities, the forerunners of national states yet to emerge.[34]

American anthropologists have undertaken the study of national states and urbanized peoples in several ways. There are those, notably Warner and his associates, who have studied modern American towns and cities. There are students of national character, or group-personality, already mentioned. These students take leaps from primitive isolates to complex and heterogeneous societies and cultures. And there are the anthropologists who study small communities in Asia, the Middle East, Europe, and Latin America. It is through these last mentioned studies that anthropology has come to deal with the subject matter of these chapters: peasant societies and cultures.

Until recently the peasantry of the Old World were the business, not of anthropology, but of other disciplines. European and Asiatic peasantry interested economists, sociologists, and historians concerned with the origins of particular peasant institutions, especially agrarian institutions.[35] To these students the relations of peasantry to forms of landholding and to feudalism were topics of central interest. Folklore and the study of folk life (peasant life) were distinguished from the anthropologist's or ethnologist's study of primitive life (*Volkskunde versus Völkerkunde*). The student of peasant life characteristically did not make holistic community studies. He collected, and he made maps of distributions of customs and artifacts. The problems were historical; the methods led to lists of elements, to schedules and questionnaires, to comparisons of parts of cultures rather than of cultures and communities as wholes. The student of *Volkskunde* was not guided by the "disciplined use of the primitive society as a conceptual model." On the other hand, professors of anthropology or ethnology in France, Germany, and Great Britain were on the whole unconcerned with the study of the peasant villages of their own or other countries. Only recently the British anthropologists, for example, turned to the study of rural societies in England or Wales and began to send their students to Norway or to rural British Guiana.

It was by moving out of aboriginal North America into the study of contemporary village life in Middle and South America that the American anthropologists came first and in largest numbers to undertake the study of peasants. The move brought about a half-perceived transformation in the way in which the entities studied are arranged in the minds of American anthropologists. As already pointed out, when the idea of "a culture" became established, all cultures, primitive and isolated as those studied at that time were, came to be conceived as separate and equivalent entities spread out on a table for comparison. The tribes of California or of the Plains constituted a growing collection of recorded species comprising the North American part of the natural history of mankind. Only problems of diffusion, of the borrowing by one tribe of elements of culture from another, complicated this basis of comparison. Those early comparisons were side-by-side comparisons of societies unaffected by cities and civilization. When American anthropologists were concerned chiefly with North American Indians, the connections those tribes had with modern cities and civilizations could be and largely were ignored until they became a matter for study under the heading "acculturation"—the modifications of the indigenous life under influences from the white man's world.

But when the North Americans came to Latin America to do field work they found that the side-by-side ordering of societies as equivalent separate specimens was inadequate. They rapidly developed a different kind of ordering of their material. In Latin America, Indian life and Spanish-Portuguese life had had a long history of mutual influence. There the anthropologists quickly found something different from the distinct tribes or subtribes of aboriginal North America. They found in Latin America many kinds of peoples in many kinds and degrees of connection with town and city life. Almost with a sense of indignation, as if their abstract conceptual model had betrayed them, they rose to their new responsibilities and began to provide the very different kind of ordering of their materials which the Latin-American materials demanded.

Now the monographs about Latin-American life take considerable account of the trade with towns, of the participation of the villagers

in national institutions, and of the differences between the more
rustic inhabitants of the country and those whose way of life represents the town and the gentry class. Now cultures and communities
of Latin America are grouped not only according to their aboriginal
culture areas but also according to their "level" or typical place in
the whole civilization and culture of the state and civilization of
which they are components. The regional differences are of course
not to be ignored. But the differences between Brazil and Mexico are
not to be allowed to obscure the resemblances between certain rural
communities in Brazil and certain ones in Mexico.

One recent classification[36] recognizes primitive Indians, modern
Indians, peasant-type and town-type cultures. In this classification
the rural agriculturalists of Brazil, Peru, Haiti, Mexico, and Puerto
Rico find themselves in the same category. In content of culture the
peoples so grouped show many differences. They would not have
been put together by such ordering of cultures as was developed in
studying the Indians of the Plains or of the Southwest. They are put
together now as peasant-type peoples by Wagley and Harris because
in their cultures archaic European patterns prevail and because they
are rustics who nevertheless consider themselves part of a national
life. Thus, as a type, a type without localization (in America) and
with many cultural differences among themselves, they are distinguished by these later students from modern Indians, a contrasting
yet logically adjacent category, peoples in whose cultures the predominant elements are generically Indian, peoples who do not think
of themselves as part of a national life. This is a classification from
the bottom to the top, so to speak; it ranges societies from the most
isolated to the most urbanized. It involves the anthropologist in
studying the local community as a part of a much larger society and
compels him to recognize kinds of social and cultural relationships
for which his earlier experience did not quite prepare him: the relationships of the more and the less educated, of the townsman and
the countryman, of the national institution and the local and traditional institution.

In 1929 one of these rural Latin-American communities impressed
me as representing a type of society "intermediate between the tribe
and the modern city,"[37] like the peasant societies in Europe; and the
possibility of clarifying the typical characteristics of peasantry oc-

curred to me when Horace Miner published his account of a French-Canadian parish.[38] Since then the anthropological students of Latin America have more and more come to realize that the Latin-American small community is to be understood as a part of the state and the civilization in which it lies. Gillin studies the transformation of Indian culture into Creole culture, a supranational civilized dimension of Latin life.[39] Beals studies industrialization and urbanization as a form of acculturation.[40] Foster defines the intermediate type of society in Latin America.[41] Steward attacks head-on the national state and provides conceptions and methods for describing Puerto Rico both as local communities and cultures and as nationwide institutions.[42] And Eric Wolf,[43] Charles Wagley and Marvin Harris[44] are developing in some detail typologies of Latin-American cultures or of the peasant subcategory of such cultures. In Latin America anthropology has moved from tribe to peasantry.

Anthropologists have also come to study peasants in China, in the Middle East, and, especially in very recent years, in India. In each case the investigator sees a small society that is not an isolate, that is not complete in itself, that bears not only a side-by-side relation but also an up-and-down relation to more primitive tribal peoples, on the one hand, and to towns and cities, on the other. In some places the two-way relationship is both logical and actual: in parts of Latin America and India the peasant has real relations with townsmen, on the one hand, and with more primitive not-quite-peasant people, on the other. In every case the logical relationship, the intermediacy in the up-and-down relationship of the peasant, is recognizable, and sometimes the anthropologist recognizes it. Peasant society and culture has something generic about it. It is a kind of arrangement of humanity with some similarities all over the world. The remaining chapters will be concerned with some of these similarities. And an attempt will be made to see some of the aspects of culture and society that come into prominence as the anthropologist widens his ideas in his attempts to report justly some characteristics of the peasant.

In making these last assertions I am implying a definition of peasant society as a type. In the following exposition what class of peoples shall I have in mind in speaking of peasants?

It will be a type or class loosely defined, a focus of attention rather than a box with a lid. I do not think that any one definition of peas-

ant society arises inevitably from the facts. The difficulties of a definition are admitted.[45] Peasantry as a type are not as distinct as birds
are from mammals or colloids from crystals. Many a definition is
defensible; each is a fixing of attention on some characteristics chosen
by the definer as important; and whatever definition we choose, we
shall find other societies similar to, but not quite the same as, those
that are brought together by the definition we have chosen. We may
conceive those societies and cultures in which we are interested as
lying scattered about an imaginary field of real societies that differ
from and resemble one another in many different ways. The reader
might choose one cluster of neighboring real societies within the
field; I might choose another.

One may turn one's attention first to the systems of production
and to the economies of the little societies scattered about the imaginary field. One may then, as does Firth,[46] use the word "peasant"
for any society of small producers for their own consumption. Beginning thus, one has a very large cluster: included are such tribal
peoples as the Hopi Indians; indeed, this choice allows us to call
"peasants" such fishermen as the coastal Malay and even such col-
lectors and hunters as the Sioux Indians.[47] Among the many societies
and cultures that fall into this very inclusive category one may
perhaps find some significant resemblances, some "characteristic
shape to life," as Firth puts it.[48]

I, however, shall exclude the hunters, fishers, and herders from
these lectures. The pastoral people who have long-standing relationships to townspeople, as in parts of the Middle East and in Afghan-
istan, are in some respects like agricultural peasantry. To include
them in a series of comparisons would help us to understand what
tends to follow from a rural-town relationship rather than from the
agricultural peasant's attachment to his land. But one cannot do
everything at once. I also set aside the pastoral peoples. Let us look
at people who make a living and have a way of life through cultivation of the land.

As I now think of it, those peoples are to be included in the cluster
I shall call peasants who have, at the least, this in common: their
agriculture is a livelihood and a way of life, not a business for profit.
We might say that those agriculturalists who carry on agriculture
for reinvestment and business, looking on the land as capital and

commodity, are not peasants but farmers. This is the way Eric Wolf puts it in a recent paper,[49] and I follow him.

From this point of beginning, one sees a peasant as a man who is in effective control of a piece of land to which he has long been attached by ties of tradition and sentiment. The land and he are parts of one thing, one old-established body of relationships. This way of thinking does not require of the peasant that he own the land or that he have any particular form of tenure or any particular form of institutional relationship to the gentry or the townsman. I want to include in the focus of attention the Kwangtung peasant and the Bulgarian peasant who sell directly to city markets. Landlords are not needed to establish the fact of peasantry as I now think of it. A peasant community may be composed in part, or perhaps altogether, of tenants or even squatters on the land, if they have such control of the land as allows them to carry on a common and traditional way of life into which their agriculture intimately enters, but not as a business investment for profit.

It is, of course, quite possible to begin a consideration of peasantry with the historic association of rural Europeans with that peculiar complex of institutions known as feudalism. If one starts from feudalism, one does not first define the peasant; one defines a kind of economic, political, and social system in which peasantry are but one part. This is also a useful way of thinking about it. Sjoberg has recently in helpful detail described the feudal society sociologically.[50] In that kind of society there is "a small minority (an elite) supported by and 'exploiting' a large subservient populace which passively accepts its role. The upper class is differentiated in terms of its monopoly of power and authority, the 'correct' kinship groupings, and the highly valued achievements." Sjoberg points to the fact, important also in my view, that the elite include literati who "are official carriers of the classical written tradition which provides the social system with a sophisticated and elaborate justification for its existence and continued survival."[51] This guidance of the peasant from above "in the moral sphere," in the manor or the city, is also for me an aspect of peasant life which is interesting and worth some examination.

I shall follow Wolf's conception of peasantry as agricultural producers following a way of life on land the peasant controls. I shall add to this conception that emphasis on the relationship of peasant to an elite of the manor, town, or city which Sjoberg's presentation gives. I want to think about peasants as the rural dimension of old civilizations. Kroeber puts it simply: "Peasants are definitely rural— yet live in relation to market towns; they form a class segment of a larger population which usually contains urban centers, sometimes metropolitan capitals. They constitute part-societies with part-cultures."[52] But I am not inclined to limit the group of real peasant societies, within our view here, to those that form parts of admitted feudal societies. I want to include in our consideration the peasants of India, China, Japan, and the Moslem world, and I once attended a conference of historians and social scientists who could not reach any firm agreement as to whether feudalism, as it is known from Europe, is or was present in any of those other parts of the world.[53] So I shall not require that our peasants have any particular kind of economic and political relationship to their elite. The relationships of status between the peasant and the elite above him seem to me to be persistently important and similar in many parts of the world, and I shall try to say something about them.

It is, of course, important to learn what difference it makes that the relationship to the gentry is a feudal relationship. The peasant of feudal England and the peasant of late nineteenth-century England[54] have much in common. What are their differences, beyond those that have to do with their legal and customary relationship to lords? The Swedish countryman has much of the peasant in him still, though I am told that he may never have been in a feudal system and today is an educated participant in the national life.[55]

Our cluster of real little societies is now sufficiently well determined. We are looking at rural people in old civilizations, those rural people who control and cultivate their land for subsistence and as a part of a traditional way of life and who look to and are influenced by gentry or townspeople whose way of life is like theirs but in a more civilized form. Our cluster has on its edges other little societies in some respects like those that are in the center of our cluster but in other respects unlike them. We have mentioned the pastoral peoples in relation to towns. Herders of ancient Judea bore this relation to Jerusalem. In another direction from the center of the cluster are those peoples who settle on frontiers, carrying some tradition of peasant ways into a hinterland with open resources. Elman and Helen Service use the word "peasant" for the rural people of Paraguay.[56] These Paraguayans are peasants in their relations to townsmen and in many of their attitudes or values. On the other hand, they do not live in compact communities with closed agricultural resources as is true of so many peasants of Europe and Asia. They live in an underdevleoped country where land (though not good land) can be had for the effort of working for it; and they live in scattered farms, not villages. It may become important to examine the consequences of semi-frontier conditions in affecting the lives of these Paraguayans in directions away from what may prove to be true of the village-dwelling peasants with very limited land. And, in the opposite direction from such peoples as the Paraguayans and farther away from the center of our cluster of peasantry, the more remote frontiersmen call for attention. Such are the *caboclo* of the Brazilian Amazon and coastal selva. These rural dwellers are more solitary, individualistic, and independent of the city than are peasantry. In rural Brazil there seems to be a series of peoples more or less peasant-like, more or less frontiersmen.[57] And the gaucho is hardly a peasant.

The contrast between Latin America, on the one hand, and Asia and the older Europe, on the other, directs us to another way in which peoples may approach but not fully realize the qualities of peasantry as they appear in our central cluster. The rural people of Latin America, very generally speaking, are of one or two kinds: they are either transplanted European peasantry, or they are Indian peoples in an incompletely developed relationship to their urban elites. The peasantry of the old indigenous civilizations are fully what Kroeber calls them: "part-societies with part-cultures." They are the rural dimension of the common civilized life. But the Paraguayan or the rural Guatemalan *ladino* is less intimately and anciently related to his land and his habitat than is his Indian neighbor, while his Indian neighbor (in Guatemala) does not quite qualify as a peasant in so far as his tradition is a different tradition from that of the townsman with whom he forms a single society. There are, in his case, important cultural differences between the rural and urban parts of the Guatemalan or the Peruvian society. In Latin America, we find peasantry on the make: the people of Tepoztlán[58] are more like peasantry than are the Indians of the western highlands of Guatemala.[59] The same difference between rural people more fully peasantry and rural people with incomplete cultural relationships with their elite appears in the history of Europe and Asia. The people of Latium, out of whom Rome grew, became more fully peasants than were the rural dwellers of Syria in their relations to the Hellenic cities founded among them or than were the rural Britons to those Romans who built their towns in England.

We have come a long way from the realization of the primitive isolated community. The conceptual model of such an isolate may still serve us, forcing an examination of peasant societies in important ways different from the model. But now we can look at the peasant peoples in their own generic reality. What are their common characteristics? What aspects of social relations and of moral life are we to study; what aspects of human living that anthropologists neglected when they studied tribes and primitive bands shall we turn to now? The relations with outsiders to the small community will surely make new matters of interest for us. Kroeber remarks[60] that anthropologists used to study organisms, societies by themselves, but now they study organs, societies that are parts of larger societies. How are we to think about and study the small community as an organ and to study the larger organism of which it is a part? These questions can also be asked, in terms of culture, of the systems of traditional ideas and purposes. Chapter ii will have something to say about these questions in terms of social relations, chapter iii in terms of culture or tradition.

II

PEASANTRY: PART-SOCIETIES

In the course of their studies of small and self-sufficient primitive societies, anthropologists came to think of each such community as a system of elements in relationship to one another. Each was an analyzable whole. Each could be looked at by itself, without necessary reference to things outside of it, and could be understood as parts working together within a whole. Radcliffe-Brown showed how myth, ritual, and daily life worked together in the Andaman Islands. Malinowski made a name, "functionalism," out of his success in showing the many interrelations of custom, institution, and human need in Trobriand life. In *Patterns of Culture* Ruth Benedict showed us four primitive views of the good life as distinct and equivalent patterns—systems of another kind in which customs and institutions conform to implicit choices of basic values from the range of human possibilities.

Anthropologists have seen the primitive isolated community as several kinds of complete and self-contained systems.[1] It can be seen as a system of customs and institutions. It is sometimes seen, as in Benedict's book, as the fundamental ideas of good and bad which guide a people's life. And often, as in the important work of the British anthropologists in studying especially the native peoples of Africa, it is seen as a system of characteristic relationships between the kinds of people characteristic of that community. Although the phrase has several distinguishable meanings in anthropology,[2] let us here use "social structure" for the total system of persisting and important relationships that distinguish a community from others. Here we shall be concerned with social structure.

In studying a primitive society as social structure, the anthropologist looks at the kinds of roles, with attendant statuses, that tradition recognizes in that community. There are fathers and sons; perhaps it is important that mothers' brothers bear some special relationship to sisters' sons; there may be priests and laymen, chiefs and other people, buyers and sellers, and so on. These roles and statuses persist while the particular individuals who fill them enter them and leave tahem. The community is conceived as the arrangement of the more persistent and important of these roles and the conventional relationships between them. If the community is relatively compact and isolated, the investigator finds these roles and relationships within the band, settlement, or tribe that he studies. He does not have to go outside it.

Now I raise the question: Considering a peasant community as a system of social relations, as social structure, how shall we describe its relations with the world outside of that community? What are the modifications of concept and procedure that come about if we study a peasant village, thinking of it as a system of persisting important relationships among people? For peasantry, as the word was used in chapter i, are such by reason in part of their long-established interdependence with gentry and townspeople.

It may be that a peasant village, related as it is to people and institutions outside of it, is so incomplete a system that it cannot well be described as social structure. Perhaps we anthropologists shall come to describe not the peasant village but the larger and more nearly complete system: the feudal society, the complex region, the national state. Primitive states, complexly developed tribes, have been anthropologically described; Herskovits' *Dahomey* is one such account.[3] W. Lloyd Warner and his associates have made studies of American urban communities as representative of much in the national life. Margaret Mead and others, working very differently, have studied the national characters of modern peoples. Recently Julian Steward has proposed that any complex society might be regarded as composed of three kinds of parts. He distinguishes first such local groups as households, neighborhoods, and communities; these he calls "vertical divisions." Second, he sees the groups which are not local but which appear in many local communities and arise from some common qualities among the dispersed members, as occupation, class, caste, race, or special interest. These he calls "horizontal" divisions or segments. And third, he recognizes the formal institutions such as banking, trade, school systems, and official doctrine, which run through the whole large society affecting it at many points. This way of looking at a large complex society sees it as a kind of lattice in which the local units run in one direction and the groups that are not local run in the other direction, while the formal institutions of centralized authority and widespread influence, like the vines growing upon the lattice, perhaps, tie the whole together.[4]

Steward has used this set of conceptions in describing one modern state—Puerto Rico on its island.[5] The conceptions are not directed necessarily to societies with peasants in them. I suppose they could be used in describing Denmark or New Zealand. Their use puts anthropologists to work on complex societies in ways to which they are accustomed, for it breaks down these big wholes into two kinds of smaller groups each of which is thought to have something of a culture which the anthropologist can study. He can make studies of small local communities, of samples of the social classes, maybe, or of the religious groups. And the formal institutions—the law, the church, school or taxation systems—can still be studied from the center by the other kinds of social scientists who are used to that kind of thing; the anthropologist will, I suppose, attend especially to the local modifications of these national institutions.

The development of procedures appropriate to anthropology for studying large modern societies will go forward, and the very different ways of doing so provided by Julian Steward, Lloyd Warner, and Margaret Mead are evidences that the science puts forth its shoots on different sides of the growing tree. Here I look only at the growth outward from the local community study. I try to distinguish some of the kinds of social relations that one comes to describe if one begins with some local peasant community and tries to do justice to the fact that many of its relations are with outsiders.

In identifying three kinds of systems of social relations that we find it necessary to study if we leave the primitive isolate and attempt to describe a peasant society as social structure, I have been helped by a short publication of J. A. Barnes,[6] an anthropologist trained by British students of the social structures of primitive communities. Barnes, however, went to Norway and made a study of an island parish of that country. He found that he could not keep his attention solely on what happened within the parish: he had to follow the social relations of these rural Norwegians outside of their local community. Yet he saw that what he learned about the parish of Bremnes could "lead directly to knowledge of only a very small sector in the social life of the nation." Thus Barnes studied his little rural community not as a self-contained isolate (which it obviously is not) nor as a sample fully representative of the whole (as anthropologists study the Sudanese Nuer or the Tiv of Nigeria), nor yet as one element in a comprehensively planned study of a modern state (as did Steward). Rather, Barnes pushed outward from the local community, recognizing in the parish he studied kinds of systems of social relations in part new to the anthropologist of the primitive isolate, systems that connect the small community with other such communities, with the Norwegian nation, and with industrial systems wider than the nation.

The Norwegian parish is today probably not a peasant community. It is outside of but not very far away from the cluster of little communities to which I have here applied the word "peasant." Of every ten men in Bremnes three are fishermen, one is in the merchant marine, two are industrial workers, two are in other occupations or are retired, and only two are in agriculture. One might say that Bremnes is partly seafaring, partly agricultural, and partly a rural community in a modern nation. The people are educated and take a large part in their national life. Yet just because Bremnes is farther away from the primitive isolate community than are the rural communities of less modernized countries, what Barnes found there in the way of social relations will help us to learn what to look for in peasant societies of Asia or Latin America. We need a basis for comparison on the more modernized side of peasantry as well as on the more primitive side.

Barnes finds that these rural Norwegians are members of many kinds of social groups. The groups are so many and so variously related to one another that it might be difficult to arrange them very strictly according to Professor Steward's lattice.[7] Barnes collects them into what he calls "social fields" of three different kinds. Each social field is a conceived system of activities and social relations somewhat separable from the other two. Each has, I think, a lesson for us in our effort to push beyond the self-contained community to the understanding of the social structure of peasant societies.

First, "there is the territorially-based social field, with a large number of enduring administrative units, arranged hierarchically, one within the other."[8] This ascending series of local groups includes hamlets or neighborhoods, wards, and the parish itself, which is then a part of several larger ascending series of units with administrative, judicial, or ecclesiastical functions each including other parishes of Norway.

It is at the level of the parish that we can see a transition from local life to national life. Looked at from the point of view of one studying the nation, the parish of Bremnes is a unit of civil and ecclesiastical administration. There is, for instance, a grouping of parishes of that region which in turn belongs within an archdeaconry which is part of a diocese. These groupings are formal and serve very special functions and relationships. Within the parish, relationships are more personal and involve more of human life. Nevertheless, in modern Norway the separation between local life and national life has become obscured by education and the full articulation of local and national institutions. In societies in which the rural people are still clearly peasantry, the territorially based social field or system which Barnes describes for Bremnes unites local life and the life of the feudal system or the state; and in peasant societies the two parts are clearly distinguishable. At the bottom the series of units consists of people in personal and traditional relationship to one another; there kinship and neighborhood are the prevailing connections. At the top of the series are people in more impersonal and formal institutional relationship to one another. As a system of hierarchically arranged social relations, a peasant society is two connecting halves. We may be able to see a sort of link or hinge between the local life of a peasant community and the state or feudal system of which it is a part. In an Indian community of western Guatemala, where the local life and the national life are wide apart, the link or hinge is very obvious; it consists of the administrative officers sent down from the city to relate the Indian community, which is organized within itself, to the national life.[9] The parish priest and some shopkeepers may be other parts of the hinge. In the Andalusian town, a community of town-dwellers with peasant characteristics, the hinge is also present in a conspicuously different group of professional and wealthy people who live their mental lives in part away from the town where they dwell, in the city, and "who represent the government to the pueblo, and who represent the pueblo to the government."[10] In the old-fashioned Chinese peasant community one would find the hinge in the mandarin negotiating between the *yamen* of the imperial power and the village elders. In the Balkan village the line between the local life and the national life, between the two parts of the ascending territorial-political series, is held by the priest and the mayor.[11] Later something will be said here about the functions in the cultural life of the people who hold the hinge.

Even in Bremnes, though the people are for the most part no longer peasants, it is the territorially organized local life that gives the society stability. "The same fields are cultivated year after year, and new land comes into cultivation only slowly . . . for the most part people go on living in the same houses and cultivating the same land from year to year."[12] A century and a half ago, we may suppose, this was the social system of dominant importance; only the fishing, not yet industrialized, modified the peasant life of that time.

But fishing has now been industrialized in Norway to the degree that for the man of Bremnes parish it is an activity fairly independent of his life on the land. Fishing is highly competitive; "herring fishing is war," people say. Here loyalties to kinsmen operate to only a limited extent. "Any man can try to get himself included in a crew and each owner seeks to engage the crew that will catch most fish. During the herring season, men from Bremnes sail in vessels belonging to other parishes, and vessels registered in Bremnes sometimes have on board fishermen from as much as six hundred miles away. In effect, there is something like a free labour market."[13] The social field through which the Bremnes man moves in his role as fisherman is composed of unstable relations with many kinds of men in many different places—shipowners, skippers, net bosses, cooks, and others —with whom he has happened to become linked; and each man's social field for fishing intersects the vast, world-wide organized fishing industry.

This is the second lesson from Barnes's account. It is the market, in one form or another, that pulls out from the compact social relations of self-contained primitive communities some parts of men's doings and puts people into fields of economic activity that are increasingly independent of the rest of what goes on in the local life. The local traditional and moral world and the wider and more impersonal world of the market are in principle distinct, opposed to each other, as Weber[14] and others[15] have emphasized. In peasant society the two are maintained in some balance; the market is held at arm's length, so to speak. We may see the intermediacy of the peasant community in this respect also if we suggest a series of societies in which the separation of the world of the market is progressively greater. The Andamanese band approximates a self-contained isolate. But from time to time people of one band will take up some of their bows and baskets and go to visit another band. There they will make presents of what they have brought and receive from their hosts presents of some of their artifacts.[16] The economic life is not even distinguishable as such: it is a casual exchange between friendly persons on a basis of good will. In rural India, in a society with a great division of labor, much of the exchange of services is involved in hereditary status in the form of caste. There are also markets where trading is relatively free. In the Guatemalan American Indian community of Chichicastenango, a peasant society except for the cultural separation between the Indian and the urban elite, most of the men devote large parts of their lives to commercial travel; they walk about a wide circle of markets buying and selling.[17] But this commercial life is separate from the social and political life of the town and hamlet. Observers have been struck with the insulation of the Guatemalan trader from the influences of the many other local cultures through which he moves.[18] As a trader, this Indian semi-peasant leads a separate life; he enters a distinct "field of activity." The Bulgarian peasant buys from and sells to the city, but we are told that his weekly trips to town and city introduce few changes to the village.[19] In the city the peasant is an onlooker; he talks chiefly with other peasants. So in this case too peasant world and city world are kept apart, though in apparent contact. Inside a peasant village commercial life and agricultural life may fall into separate patterns of thought and action. In the intensely agricultural Yucatecan village, the Maya, more of a peasant than is the western Guatemalan Indian, carries on his agriculture as a mode of life, indeed, as religious activity, as does the Hopi or the Zuni. But he sells half his maize to market. Growing in the field or offered to the gods, maize is traditional, sacred, moral. But once made ready for sale, the people call it by a different name; and the commercial dealings with maize have a certain separateness from the local dealings with it.[20] And trade with hogs or cattle is a secular activity in which one joins with any buyer or seller one happens to meet.

Every peasant society offers for our study some field of economic activity which is to some degree separated out from that closely integrated union of all activities which characterizes the primitive isolate community. The economic field comes to have, as Barnes says, a different "analytical status." One has to make a special study of that field. In studying rural Swedish life of a century ago, B. Hanssen describes[21] the relations of those villagers, chiefly cotters, with those gentry of the manor with whom they took service, as a distinct field of activity. In that case the field was not wholly economic: the cotters entered into the domestic life of the manor; some of the peasants had for parts of their lives persisting relationships, of utility and also more or less cultural, with some of the gentry. A connection between the two halves of the double society, peasantry-gentry, was made by a field with separate analytical status, but a field in which, no doubt, the examples of custom and manners provided by gentry life were made to influence the peasantry. The fishing field of modern Norway is fully industrialized; the rural fisherman is largely separated off from the life on the land, and the fishing field is fluid, competitive, increasingly independent of the ties formed in the local life.

"Market" means both a state of mind and a place to trade. We can use both conceptions in studying peasant and rural life. Barnes refers to the industrialized fishing of the Norwegian as a "social field." The field is not spatially defined; it is a set of activities, attitudes, and relationships that belong together wherever and whenever the Norwegian enters industrialized fishing. Such a field we may study as a more or less coherent body of things done and thought. Also, of course, we may study those markets which do have geographical definition. McBryde has described one kind of market in western Guatemala: the people who come together in one town at one time to buy and sell.[22] One can also describe the people who move about the country from one market, in the former sense, to another town market. Taken together, these ambulatory merchants in all their relationships of trade are another kind of market with definition upon the land. Students of rural sociology and economics describe the regions in which goods of one kind or another are sold, and the regions from which are drawn the buyers who come to centers of sale and distribution. Arensberg and Kimball, anthropologists, have well described such markets, centering on crossroads, fairs, and shops, in rural Ireland.[23]

The third "social field" which Barnes recognizes in the Norwegian parish he calls a "network." All the relations of all kinds of the rural people with one another and with people elsewhere are thought of as a network in which people are the knots or points, and relationships, of whatever kind, are the threads or lines. Barnes, however, here thinks in particular of that part of the total network that is left if the relationships of the territorial and the industrial systems are removed. To distinguish this residual part of the network, and to give it a name suggestive of its presence in every society that is more than the imagined primitive isolate, let us call it "the country-wide network." The simple fact that creates this network is that every person, through kinship, friendship, acquaintance, or some common interest, "is in touch with a number of people, some of whom are directly in touch with each other and some of whom are not."[24] In Bremnes this kind of network of relationships not only knits together people of the parish but connects them with people of other parishes. There it has no boundaries; there is no way of defining a group with membership; "each person sees himself at the center of a collection of friends."[25] But sometimes defined groups are formed, fishing crews or committees, out of clusters of people in such boundless networks.

In every society, however primitive, some attention is paid to the connections of one kinsman to another or of one friend to another. People are nowhere organized only into lineages or other formed and bounded social groups. So there are always boundless networks in so far as genealogical kinship is extended outward or as mere acquaintance or other occasional personal association creates a relationship. In the primitive societies it is kinship that largely contributes to the qualities of such networks as there are. In some of them there is a kind of latency in the kinship which allows it to expand at the edges of the local community to include individuals newly encountered. One remembers the way in which in central Australia strangers to one another establish friendly relations through identification of some third individual to whom each applies a kinship term.[26]

If the tribe is large and dispersed, its people not settled in distinct villages, as is true of the Tiv of Nigeria, the whole tribe is one great country-wide network. But if we study the early Plains Indians, or the Indians of the Amazon, or the tribesmen of Luzon, we do not find ourselves much concerned with country-wide networks. The band, the camp, the village, or the tribe is a relatively discrete social system. Between it and other such systems there are no very impressive and persisting networks of relationship. One unit may join another or separate off, and one individual may be captured or otherwise become a part of a local society to which he was once a stranger. But the communities are compact, and relationships for the most part institutionalized in kinship or other kinds of groups. As to the compactness, Barnes puts the point well when he says that in primitive societies the mesh of the network is small, in civilized, urban, or mass societies the mesh is large. "By mesh," he writes, "I mean simply the distance round a hole in the network . . . in primitive society many of the possible paths leading away from any A lead back to A after a few links; in modern society a smaller proportion lead back again to A."[27] In Zuni the links go right back to the man with whom you started. In rural Norway the links carry one outside of the parish to distant communities. In peasant societies as in primitive, many links are those of kinship, but the mesh is wider and looser. In French Canada the peasant travels, but travel is to visit relatives. If there is no relative in the neighboring parish, the peasant does not go there, but he may make a pilgrimage to the shrine of St. Anne de Beaupré and make his stay with relatives in Quebec.[28]

This fact of the developed and widespread country-wide network in societies that are not primitive gives the anthropologist another kind of system of social relations to study. He cannot keep his attention solely on the peasant village or scattered rural community of neighboring farmers. He finds himself looking down on village tied to village, farm to distant relative, and town to countryside, in a web of social relations. The connections that people have with one another, apart from the system of relationships that begins in the family and the neighborhood and grows upward to the formal government of the state, are in peasant and in rural communities so significant as to demand description in their own right. Where the relations continue to have localization, and constitute a system of ties relating people to one another although they dwell apart, then they seem to emerge from the societal map to meet our scientific imaginations. Points and lines meet the concept-forming eye of the mind. We begin to wonder what will be the ideas by which we shall characterize that class of social systems, that aspect of social structure, that might be called country-wide networks.

Plainly the purpose or interest which relates people in the network is an important matter of similarity or difference. Oscar Lewis has compared Mexican and East Indian rural societies to stress a difference of this kind.[29] If we look down on the Mexican countryside we see village connected with village chiefly through trade, visiting at festivals, and, less, important, through performance of governmental duties and through pilgrimages to shrines. The local communities tend to be endogamous, each has a more or less homogeneous culture, and the sense of local community loyalty is strong. The people who go out from one local community to another, or to a town, on the whole do so as separate individuals or family parties carrying on perhaps similar but parallel and independent activities. The activities are incidental to a familial and cultural life lived within the village. We do not find whole groups with culture and social structure that have persisting relationships along the country-wide network with other such groups in other local communities.

This is what we do find in India. Should we look down on the countryside of India, we should see each local community connected with many other local communities through caste. The internal unity of the village is qualified or balanced by the unity that is felt by the villager with a fellow caste member of another village. In times of stress the fellow caste member of the other village will come to one's aid. In the cases of the higher castes this unity may be felt over wide areas, and it may be institutionalized by genealogists and caste historians.

Furthermore, the country-wide network of rural northern India is composed of widespread connections of marriage. The villages are exogamous. In the Punjab, for example, "each village is said to have a traditional set of villages to whom its girls regularly go in marriage and another set from which it regularly receives wives." Here there is a country-wide marital network. With reference to the Punjabi villages studied by Marian Smith "the marital community to be con-

sidered would start four miles away and have to include at least
those villages up to eight miles distant."[30] In Kishan Garhi, a village
southeast of Delhi, again there is no marriage within the village.
"Daughters of the village move out and wives of the village move in
at marriage, moving to and from more than three hundred other villages."[31] When Marriott studied this village, he found that fifty-
seven marriages then connected Kishan Garhi with sixteen towns and
cities. The connection a villager has with other villages than his own
remains very strong. In another village in northern India if a lower-
caste man gets into trouble with the upper-caste landowner he "may
still take refuge with his mother's, his wife's or his sister's relatives."
"Often a child spends two or three years with his mother on a long
visit to his mother's father's household in another village."[32]

In short, the principal elements of the country-wide networks of
India consist of familial and caste associations that persist through
generations. These associations connect one set of villages with another or some of the families in one village with families corresponding in culture and social status in other villages. It is as if the characteristic social structure of the primitive self-contained community
had been dissected out and its components spread about a wide area.
Rural India is a primitive or a tribal society rearranged to fit a civilization.

The closeness or openness of the mesh, the range or scope of the
network, the kinds of human interests served by the relationships
that make up the mesh, the stability of the relationships, whether occasional or permanent—these are all elements to be considered in understanding country-wide networks.

In these remarks I have perhaps extended and generalized the three
kinds of sets of social relations which Barnes notes in rural Norway
beyond his meaning and intention. I see in them exemplars for many
who will study societies that very plainly are more complex, more
interrelated with others, than are the primitive tribal communities. I
think we will find it helpful to look for the three kinds of systems or
"fields" which Barnes found in Bremnes: the hierarchy of territorially based groups; the more or less independent economic fields of
activity; and the country-wide networks of relationship. These three
kinds will not be found in peasant societies only. Their beginnings
occur also in primitive and non-European societies, and they occur

in modern states. One can think of them as three ways in which the primitive isolate is exceeded or in which it breaks down, is pulled apart and extended over the social landscape. Country-wide networks are notable within those African tribes that grow in size till they occupy a wide area with scattered houses and settlements. These are networks involving no peasantry. Such networks must have developed as between villages in the highlands of Mexico before the Spaniard came, and, in so far as the Aztec capital was an urban center with its elite, the networks were becoming truly rural. Wherever civilization has fully arisen we may speak of the networks as rural, for now there is an *urbs*. Yet local differences within the great civilizations in this respect are to be recognized: the networks of intimate peasant-elite relationships continued in England until very late to maintain something of the manorial form of medieval times, for the English gentry were countrymen themselves in contrast to their equivalents in France or Italy who lived the civilization of the city and kept farther apart from their peasantry.

The economic field is already present in the "silent market" of which German writers on primitive economy made much, and it grows in preliterate societies to the great markets of Abomey—we are told that ten thousand people might take part in such a market.[33] But it is industry outside of the indigenous local life, especially capitalistic and highly technological industry, that takes the Camar worker from his Indian village to work in the cotton or jute mills, the African tribesman to labor in the diamond mines, and the New Guinea tribesman to toil on the distant plantation. The distinct economic "fields" of the peasant are on the whole less distinct and less disruptive of the local life than are those that affect the tribesman. The more primitive man is the man likely to enter modern industry when it is established in his country; the landowning peasant, with a way of life already in stable adjustment to many aspects of civilization, is more resistant to industrialization.[34]

The political autonomy of the local community is much qualified in many non-European societies by chieftainship, councils, and other authorities affecting more than one band or settlement. In many an African society political and administrative authority is hierarchical, and there are non-territorially organized attachments to power, as instanced by the "sectors" and the loyalties to queens and storehouses among the Lozi: men of different settlements are united by the fact of a common tie to a center of power, itself subordinate to the king.[35] In the African kingdoms, such as Dahomey, units of the political system intermediate between kinship groups and the state are in part territorially defined, and so the "hierarchy of territorially based groups" that Barnes identifies for Norway is present. There is, however, one feature of this hierarchy that characterizes peasant societies. Indeed, it follows from the very basis of my choice in grouping as peasant societies those in which there are long-established relations with an elite whose culture is that of the peasant carried to another level of development. I have remarked on the two halves that compose the total society; there are two kinds of people, peasants and a more urban (or at least manorial) elite. The two kinds of people look at each other, at that joint or hinge in the total society, and have for each other attitudes that complement (but not always compliment) each other. The relationships between the two kinds of people define the relative status of one to the other. The lower kind of people recognize, in certain respects, the political authority of the other and also their "guidance in the moral sphere."[36]

The anthropologist who comes to peasant society through the study of the social structure of a peasant village will find that important parts of that structure are represented in the village by a few individuals or, perhaps, by people who are not in the village but somewhere else. In peasant communities remote from town, city, or manorial country estate, the elite may not be immediately present. In the Brazilian peasant village described by Pierson and his associates, there were none. The villagers managed their own local affairs. But they had relations with the elite when the villager went to the city or the officials came to them.[37] In the Yucatecan village that I studied the people were more or less peasantry; the relations they had with a more urban elite (*dzulob*, they called them) were many and frequent, but the schoolteacher was then the only resident from that upper and outer world. In many a European peasant village live a few people with urban manners and some learning who manage those affairs of the peasants which relate to the national state. To these administrative and cultural intermediaries between local life and wider life the word "intelligentsia" has long been applied. Sanders uses it to denote the small group in the Bulgarian village composed of the mayor, the doctor, and the schoolteachers. These people associated with one another, showed their separation from the peasantry, talked politics and perhaps literature, organized and led all the patriotic celebrations, and provided something for the peasants to recognize as better than themselves. Sanders writes: "The *intelligentsia* . . . had more importance than their village duties seemed to indicate. They were the channels through which the national state, the national church, and the national school system expressed themselves. . . . Their high status rested not only upon the influence they wielded as representatives of powerful institutions, but also upon the fact that they were educated."[38] Much the same is said by Miner of the curé and the senator in the peasant parish of French Canada. These two, and their relatives, "are so far removed from the society of the parish that they cannot carry on personal social contacts with the other parishioners. . . . Their position is due to contacts which they have with the world outside the parish, from which sphere they have received recognition far higher than anything the parish can give."[39] In early Norway most of the priests lived in the country and each parish had its bureaucrat; these persons were part of an urban elite.[40]

The Andalusian town of Alcalá recently described by Pitt-Rivers provides a striking instance of the two kinds of people, each representing one distinguishable half of a double society, and both dwelling in the same compact community.[41] As the agricultural people live in the town and identify themselves with it, and not a rural village or dispersed settlement, they are not typically peasants, although in many respects their manner of life and thought is like that of Bulgarian or Italian peasants. In the town lives also an educated class, called *señoritos* by those of the town who work the land or otherwise live the socially inferior kind of life. The *señoritos* are distinguished by superior manners, acceptance of responsibility to protect inferior dependents, a higher sense of honor, and the fact that they do not participate in the local customs. They provide the small ruling group; they serve as the intermediaries, administrative, and also cultural, between near-peasant and city. The *señoritos* identify themselves with the common people as against a rival pueblo or against a predatory bureaucracy from outside, but identify themselves with *señoritos* of other pueblos in the business of administration and commerce. Within the pueblo the investigator discerns two contrasting ways of life corresponding to the two social classes: ". . . one can see, in place of the sanctions of law, the sanctions of the pueblo's mockery; in place of the food-control, the clandestine mills and the black market . . . in place of the Civil Guard, the bandit and the smuggler. In place of the schools, the *maestros rurales;* in place of the doctor, vet and chemist, the *curanderos;* in place of the . . . trained nurse, the . . . country midwives. And for the purpose of invoking the powers of religion in such matters, in place of the priest, the *sabia.*"[42] Here we have the folk in the town, the urban elite in common habitation and in one social structure with a more folklike people.

The social structure of peasant and peasant-like societies includes, then, the relations of cultural influence and example between the elite half and the peasant half of the whole larger social system. It will not do to describe these relations only as relations of ruler and ruled or of exploiter and exploited, although these elements are likely to be present. The student will want also to describe the prestige or contempt, the feelings of superiority or inferiority, and the examples of excellence to be emulated or of baseness to be avoided that may be present in the relations between peasant and elite. The peasant is a rustic and he knows it. The educated man, whose life is in part in the local community and in part—at least mentally—in more urban circles, looks down on the peasant. "Oh what a rogue and peasant slave am I!" exclaimed Hamlet in one of his frequent moods of self-depreciation. All over the world the terms applied to rural people by urban people imply contempt, condescension, or—and this is the opposite face of the attitude—a certain admiration for the virtues of the simple, the primitive, and the hardy. On his side the peasant admits his relative inferiority as to culture and manners but naturally claims the virtues accorded him and sees the city man as idle, or false, or extravagant. He sees himself as low with regard to the common culture but nevertheless with a way of life morally superior to that of the townsman.

The isolated primitive community presents the student of social structure with a simpler and smaller system. There social relations are compact, congruent, and largely personal. With the growth and the spread of civilization social relations extend themselves out from the local community, lose much of their congruence (as in the development of industrial fields of activity), and develop many kinds of impersonal and formal varieties of connection. In peasant societies we see a relatively stable and very roughly typical adjustment between local and national or feudal life, a developed larger social system in which there are two cultures within one culture, one social system composed of upper and lower halves. The cultural relations between the two halves are to be emphasized. Sjoberg puts it well: ". . . the elite exhibits to the peasant the highly valued achievements . . . and provides the peasant's social system with a sophisticated justification for its existence and survival."[43] The priest and the senator in the French Canadian parish, the intelligentsia of the Bulgarian village and the *señoritos* of Andalusia, in East Indian peasant communities the pundits and the gurus, show by their examples and tell by their teaching of another and higher version of that same life which the ordinary peasant lives. We may think of peasant culture as a small circle overlapping with much larger and less clearly defined areas of culture, or we may think of the peasant life as a lower circle unwinding into the upward-spreading spirals of civilization. If the student of peasant society is to describe the systems of social relations of that society, he will study those social relations that communicate the higher dimension of the civilization to the lower or peasant dimension. Let us look into the matter in the next chapter.

III

THE SOCIAL ORGANIZATION
OF TRADITION

Out of that anthropology which rested on studies of isolated primitive or tribal peoples arose the concept, "a culture." The Andamanese had a culture, as did the Trobrianders, the Aranda of Australia, and the Zuni. Each culture came to be conceived as an independent and self-sufficient system. Recently words have been found to make clear this conception of an "autonomous cultural system." It is "one which is self-sustaining—that is, it does not need to be maintained by a complementary, reciprocal, subordinate, or other indispensable connection with a second system." Such units— such cultures as those of the Zuni or the Andamanese—"are systems because they have their own mutually adjusted and interdependent parts, and they are autonomous because they do not require another system for their continued functioning."[1] The anthropologist may see in such a system evidence of elements of culture communicated to that band or tribe from others, but he understands that the system as it now is keeps going by itself; and in describing its parts and their workings he need not go outside the little group itself. The exceptions, where the band or tribe relies on some other band or tribe for a commodity or service, are small and do not seriously modify the fact that that culture is maintained by the communication of a heritage through the generations of just those people who make up the local community.

The culture of a peasant community, on the other hand, is not autonomous. It is an aspect or dimension of the civilization of which it is a part. As the peasant society is a half-society, so the peasant culture is a half-culture. When we study such a culture we find two things to be true that are not true when we study in isolated primitive band or tribe. First, we discover that to maintain itself peasant culture requires continual communication to the local community of thought originating outside of it. The intellectual and often the religious and moral life of the peasant village is perpetually incomplete; the student needs also to know something of what goes on in the minds of remote teachers, priests, or philosophers whose thinking affects and perhaps is affected by the peasantry. Seen as a "synchronic" system, the peasant culture cannot be fully understood from what goes on in the minds of the villagers alone. Second, the peasant village invites us to attend to the long course of interaction between that community and centers of civilization. The peasant culture has an evident history; we are called upon to study that history; and the history is not local: it is a history of the civilization of which the village culture is one local expression. Both points, in recognition of both generic aspects of the peasant culture, were clearly made by George Foster when he reviewed recently his experiences in Latin-American communities and wrote that there the local culture "is continually replenished by contact with products of intellectual and scientific social strata."[2] He said also that "one of the most obvious distinctions between truly primitive societies and folk [peasant] societies is that the latter, over hundreds of years, have had constant contact with the centers of intellectual thought and development. . . ."[3]

This is a new experience for one whose ways of work were developed in studying such primitive isolates as Australian tribes, Andamanese, or Trobrianders. It calls for new thoughts and new procedures of investigation. For studies of villages, it requires attention to the relevance of research by historians and students of literature, religion, and philosophy. It makes anthropology much more difficult and very much more interesting.

How shall we begin to take mental hold of this compound culture that deserves a special word, "civilization"? Let us begin with a recognition, long present in discussions of civilizations, of the difference between a great tradition and a little tradition. (This pair of phrases is here chosen from among others, including "high culture" and "low culture," "folk and classic cultures," or "popular and learned traditions." I shall also use "hierarchic and lay culture.") In a civilization there is a great tradition of the reflective few, and there is a little tradition of the largely unreflective many. The great tradition is cultivated in schools or temples; the little tradition works itself out and keeps itself going in the lives of the unlettered in their village communities. The tradition of the philosopher, theologian, and literary man is a tradition consciously cultivated and handed down; that of the little people is for the most part taken for granted and not submitted to much scrutiny or considered refinement and improvement.

If we enter a village within a civilization we see at once that the culture there has been flowing into it from teachers and exemplars who never saw that village, who did their work in intellectual circles perhaps far away in space and time. When George Foster looked at Latin-American villages with civilization in mind, he saw chiefly what had come into those villages from preindustrial Europe: irrigation wheels, elements of the Catholic religion from "theological and philosophical reflections of many of the best minds of history over a period of centuries," church organization, religious dramas, political institutions, godparenthood, the humoral pathology of Hippocrates and Galen, and dances and bullfights that had worked their way downward from Spanish gentry to little Indian-mestizo farmers in Mexico or Peru.[4] In every peasant village we see corresponding things.

The two traditions[5] are interdependent. Great tradition and little tradition have long affected each other and continue to do so. The teachings of Galen about the four humors may have been suggested by ideas current in little communities of simple people becoming but not yet civilized; after development by reflective minds they may have been received by peasantry and reinterpreted in local terms. Great epics have arisen out of elements of traditional tale-telling by many people, and epics have returned again to the peasantry for modification and incorporation into local cultures. The ethics of the Old Testament arose out of tribal peoples and returned to peasant communities after they had been the subject of thought by philosophers and theologians. The Koran has the content it has because it arose among Arab not Chinese peoples, and the teachings of Confucius were not invented by him singlehanded; on the other hand, both teachings have been and continually are understood by peasants in ways not intended by the teachers. Great and little tradition can be thought of as two currents of thought and action, distinguishable, yet ever flowing into and out of each other. A picture of their relationships would be something like those "histomaps" we sometimes see, those diagrams of the rise and change through time of religions and civilizations.

The two traditions are not distinguishable in very isolated tribes or bands. In reading Radcliffe-Brown on the Andaman Islands we find nothing at all about any esoteric aspect of religion or thought. Apparently any older person will be as likely to know what there is to know as any other. This diffuse distribution throughout the population of knowledge and belief may be characteristic of very large primitive societies of much greater development of the arts of life than the Andamanese enjoyed. Thus, among the Tiv of Nigeria, a tribe including about a million agricultural people, "there is no technical vocabulary, because there are no professional classes, and little specialization beyond that which is the result of sex or age. Every aspect of tribal life is everybody's business."[6] This is a primitive society without a great tradition. Among the Maori, however, "two different aspects of all the superior class of myths were taught. One of these was that taught in the *tapu* school of learning, a version never disclosed to the bulk of the people but retained by the higher grade of *tohunga* (experts or priests) and by a few others. The other was that imported to the people at large, and this, as a rule, was of an inferior nature, more puerile and grotesque than the esoteric version."[7] And in West Africa, where aborigines had developed complex states, a distinction between what we might call a littler and a greater tradition appears in the control by certain priests of elements of worship, recognized by the people as recondite and esoteric. Initiates into these cults are secluded for seven months of instruction in secret. Also, there are differences as between layman and specialist in the understanding of the religion: the priests of the Skycult in Dahomey clearly see distinctions among deities and their characteristics about which laymen are very vague.[8] Among Sudanese peoples reported by Professor Griaule[9] there is extraordinary development of highly reflective and systematic specialized thought among certain individuals.

These instances suggest the separation of the two traditions in societies that do not represent the great world civilizations. The content of knowledge comes to be double, one content for the layman, another for the hierarchy. The activities and places of residence of the carriers of the great tradition may remain close to those of the layman, or the priests and primitive philosophers may come to reside and to work apart from the common people.

This series of non-European societies arranged according to the degree to which a distinguishable great tradition is or was present can be supplemented with some references to the ancient Mexican and Mayan societies. These fulfil the logical series, for there is little doubt that those Meso-American peoples had developed something that might well be called a civilization in so far as the growth of a great tradition is its sign. Adopting the words of a recent leading student of those civilizations, I identify the hierarchic culture of the Maya with the monumental stone architecture for temples and palaces, the highly sophisticated art, the hieroglyphic writing, complex arithmetic, astronomy and calendar, the deities not directly associated with the earth or the forces of nature, and the theocratic government. On the other hand, outside of the shrine-cities and in the little villages there was a lay culture of the subsistence activities, the crafts, the village, and related organization, and a religion based on the forces of nature. In the following words, I think Dr. Armillas somewhat exaggerates the separation of great and little traditions among the pre-Columbian Maya, but he does recognize just the conception that interests me: "a new concept of the classic Maya civilization . . . that it was formed by two cultural strata or subcultures corresponding to two social groups: the dominant aristocracy of the ceremonial centers and the hamlet-dwelling farmers. The dominant group was apparently of religious origin, although martial or commercial segments of it might have been developed later. The village communities seem to have preserved their folk culture little affected by the culture of the upper class. The pseudo-urban character of the ceremonial centers, if it is true that they had not a large resident population and that some of the functions of real cities were lacking, and strong class barriers might have been the factors preventing the cultural influence of the ceremonial centers from filtering down to the rural masses, transforming their folk culture into peasant culture. If this view is correct, the world outlook and moral order of the Maya sophisticated aristocracy and the rural people must have been sharply different. In this light the collapse of the classic Maya civilization was in fact the disintegration of the pan-Maya upper stratum of society, leaving practically intact the underlying local folk cultures. That this actually happened has been made very apparent by Longyear's report on Copan, and the hypothesis is not in contradiction with the scanty data we have on this collapse from other places."[10]

There is a growing conviction that the development of aboriginal American civilization passed through phases and developed cultural and societal relationships similar to those that appeared in the independent beginnings of the civilizations of the Old World.[11] Elements in the development of civilization which are common to both the Old and the New World origins of civilization are those characteristics which are generic to indigenous civilizations: the separation of culture into hierarchic and lay traditions, the appearance of an elite with secular and sacred power and including specialized cultivators of the intellectual life, and the conversion of tribal peoples into peasantry. Some part of the course of events in the Meso-American instance can be recovered. But, of course, it is beyond our immediate observation, and the record of its events is overlaid with the strong impress of another civilization that invaded America from abroad.

In the case of the peasant societies of Latin America it is this impress of an invading civilization, one not indigenous but entering the local community from abroad, that is likely to strike the student of culture. It impressed George Foster: he saw elements of culture that had worked their way from Spanish gentry downward to communities perhaps founded by American Indians. But the Mexican and Peruvian cases are hybrid civilizations. We might call them "secondary civilizations" in contrast to the primary civilizations of India and China where the civilization is indigenous, having developed out of the precivilized peoples of that very culture, converting them into the peasant half of that same culture-civilization. (India and China, it is sure, have been strongly influenced since their founding by other civilizations; nevertheless, continuity with their own native civilizaton has persisted; Chinese and Indian peasants remain connected with their own civilizations.)

Some of the Latin-American local cultures are incomplete aspects of both the great tradition of Spain and the great tradition of that part of aboriginal America. Had I studied the villages of Yucatan as aspects of civilization, I should have conceived the culture of the village as referring to the Spanish-Catholic great tradition and also as referring to a now vanished great tradition that was once maintained in the shrine-cities of Yucatan by native priest-astronomers. The shaman-priests of the villages I studied carried on rituals and recited prayers that would have their full explanation only if we knew what were the ritual and the related body of thought at Chichen Itza or Coba. Certain prayers recited in the present-day Maya village include phrases that I am sure would have been more understandable to the Maya priest of the early sixteenth century than they were to the Indian whose praying I heard. The secondary civilizations, especially where one great tradition has supplanted, but incompletely, another and native great tradition, provide situations that the anthropologist may regard as instances of acculturation still going on. So far as the "decapitation" (as Kidder called it) that Spanish conquest brought about four centuries ago, they are also instances of "deculturation"—removal of a great tradition.

In the comments that follow I shall be thinking for the most part of the primary civilizations of the Old World. In coming to study peasant villages of primary civilizations, the anthropologist enters fields of study that have long been cultivated by historians and other humanistic scholars. He slips in by the back entrance: through the villages, by way of the little tradition, and after the fact of centuries of interaction of peasant and philosopher, both indigenous and so representatives of local culture, and both the makers of that civilization. He looks about him, he finds a mode of life that records this long interaction, and he sees people and institutions—priests, teachers, sacred books and tales, temples and schools—that still carry it on. To describe this village life at all fully will take him far from the village and, as he pursues the interactions of the traditions in the past, into sources of information relatively new to him. He becomes aware of the numerous and impressive studies by historians and students of art, literature, and religion. Do these studies have a relevance for him who makes a field study of a peasant village?

In their principal and important work, the humanist and historian stand somewhat remote from studies of present-day peasant life. A recent collection of excellent papers on what is called "Chinese thought"[12] is concerned with the reflective ideas of Chinese philosophers, poets, and moralists. It includes hardly a reference to what went on, in periods covered by the book, in the minds of Chinese peasants. It is probably impossible to know. It is, however, possible to know something of what goes on in the minds of Chinese peasants today—political conditions permitting. The scholars of the great traditions of India are concerned first with the development of the Vedic philosophy among a small number of reflective thinkers, ancient and modern. A recent English translation of the Upanishads[13] is provided with a commentary in which matters understood by Indian philosophers, not by peasants, are discussed, although those teachings distantly, and after much diffraction and diffusion, are reflected in the lives of peasants. In this particular book we are not told about this distant reflection in peasant life. We are told about the interpretation of certain Vedic texts by Sankaracharya, a thinker of the eighth century, and we are instructed on such matters as the differences between the strands of thought called non-dualism, qualified non-dualism, and dualism.

Nevertheless, in other writings or, at least, in passages of other writings an occasional historian-humanist seems to be coming forward to meet the anthropologist who is at work in the village. A recent student of Chinese religion, impressed with the mixture of teachings that have made up that religion and by the great differences between the beliefs and practices of peasants and those of educated Chinese, states that "instead of dividing the religious life of the Chinese people into three compartments called Confucianism, Buddhism and Taoism, it is far more accurate to divide it into two levels, the level of the masses and the level of the enlightened."[14] Reading this, one asks, how then did the enlightened come to transform popular belief into their own kind of religion, and how was it that with the presence of educated teachers in China for many centuries the masses transformed these teachings into their kind of religion? One might become interested in the ways in which the high tradition is communicated to the common people and how it becomes a part of the little tradition.

Every great tradition has its teachers, and the humanistic scholar of that tradition is in a position to tell us something about who these teachers are and about how their teachings reach the common people. For India these matters have been interestingly described by V.

Raghavan.[15] He tells us something of the customs and institutions by which the Vedic lore and the religious and ethical instruction of the philosopher and religious thinker were and are communicated, by intention and organized effort, to the masses. He tells us of compositions, notably the epics and the Purāna, which were made expressly to broadcast Vedic lore to the people at large. The prefaces of these compositions "were recited to vast congregations of people gathered at sacrificial sessions . . . by a class of reciters called Sutapauranikas." Hindu culture was, he says, carried to Cambodia and other lands by endowments made by rulers for the recital, in temples they built, of Hindu epics. With regard to south India Raghavan traces an unbroken tradition of deliberate provision, by ruler and teacher, for recitation in the vernacular languages of the ancient Hindu epics, especially the *Ramayana*. Professor Raghavan, historically minded and familiar with the Sanskrit classics, follows their course through many centuries and languages and through modifications of institutionalized instruction. The stories were not only recited, they were also expressed in devotional hymns sung by traveling singer-saints. So this Sanskritist, pursuing the great tradition downward, comes into the villages of present-day India. He is thinking of peasant India when he writes that "hardly a day passes without some sweet-voiced, gifted expounder sitting in a temple, *mutt*, public hall or house-front and expounding to hundreds and thousands the story of the Dharma that Rama upheld and the Adharma by which Ravana fell."[16]

This same interest on the part of humanistic scholars in the relations between the hierarchic and the lay cultures is shown in a work about the relations between Islamic doctrine and the local cultures that became Islamized. In the introductory chapter Professor G. von Grunebaum considers different ways in which the conflict, coexistence, and interaction of the Islamic high culture and the local cultures can be described. Adopting the terms that are used in this book, he writes: "This is to say that one of the two patterns is recognized as the more advanced; it is assumed to make authority; it is almost exclusively represented in the writings as well as the public actions of the elite; social prestige is dependent on its adoption. In the *dâr al-Islâm* the Islamic pattern is in general in the position of the great tradition. In contrast, the little tradition is the catchment of the popular undercurrent; its effectiveness is still felt by the intelligentsia, but 'officially' it will be denied or deprecated. Where the hypotheses of the great tradition are considered beliefs, the hypotheses of the little tradition will be considered superstitions. In fact, the social position of a person may depend on which of the two traditions he determines to live by."[17]

Von Grunebaum distinguishes between two kinds of adjustment between these two patterns or traditions. They may become accommodated to each other, as when the Islamic teachers recognize the popular tradition as the religion of the ignorant or tolerate local practices which might have been considered heretical. Saladin sent a Christian cross to Baghdad; it was first despised but in the end was treated with reverence. In Turkey and Syria Muslims were or are permitted to resort to the invocation of Christian saints. The expounders of hierarchic Islam, says Von Grunebaum, may integrate the local belief or practice with orthodoxy by interpretations of doctrine that provide a sanction for it. "The Prophet himself set the precedent for this procedure by giving an Islamic meaning to the heathen pilgrimage rites which he welded into the Muslim ḥajj to Mecca. . . ." This integration or incorporation of the local culture is abundantly illustrated by "the justification within the framework of orthodoxy of the cult of the saints."[18] In spite of the apparently uncompromising monotheism of Islam, the saint "is interpreted as the possessor of gnostic knowledge" and so accepted, or Koranic evidence is found to prove the existence of familiars of the Lord, therefore of saints. Here the Islamist comes to meet the anthropologist. Professor von Grunebaum, discussing the interaction between local saint and Islamic orthodoxy, sees from the top, so to speak, the same interaction that Westermarck,[19] studying local saints in Morocco, saw from the bottom.

The Islamist can study a great tradition from its first origins, and the first interrelations of hierarchic and lay culture are relatively close to his own day and power of observation. Islam, a doctrine thrown up from local culture, itself became a secondary civilization as it moved into Persia and India. The Sanskritist and the Sinologist are concerned with much more ancient and complex interactions of great traditions, slowly developing from primitive thought and practice, themselves dividing and undergoing much modification and restatement, while influencing and being influenced by the thoughts and actions of millions of little people. All these scholars tell the story of the relationships between the two strands of culture in civilization from the point of view of the elite, of those who uphold the great tradition. Raghavan follows Vedic lore downward into the villages. Von Grunebaum reads the writings of Islamic thinkers and teachers and reports their struggles with the local and lay cultures. Both reach the village and the peasant in the course of their studies, and now they will find arrived there the anthropologist—a fellow ill prepared to report his villagers as terminal points in the long history of a great doctrine. Yet the anthropologist cannot ignore these connections with philosophy and with refined schools of thought. He sees their traces and their professional representatives in the villages. He may wish he had stayed with autonomous cultures, alone and undisturbed, in a community that is a world to itself and in which he, the anthropologist, is the sole student. But in considering peasantry, he has taken on something else.

He has taken on some part of the responsibility for the study of a composite cultural structure comprised of little and great traditions which have interacted in the past and which are still interacting to-day. He shares the responsibility with the historian and the humanist. Both can conceive of the civilization which they study as a persisting and characteristic but always changing interaction between little and great traditions. So conceived, the civilization is a content of thought with its expressions in action and symbol. The civilization is compound in that it has parts or levels, each present in some of the people who carry on that civilization more than in others. These people live similar but notably different lives, and they live them apart, some in villages, some in cities or shrine-centers, temples, or monasteries. These parts or levels are something other than local (regional) cultures; they are something different from the subcultures characterizing the occupational groups concerned with secular specialties. They are different because the learning of the great tradition is an outgrowth of the little tradition and is now an exemplar for the people who carry the little tradition. Great and little traditions are dimensions of one another; those people who carry on the lower layers and those who maintain the high alike recognize the same order of "highness" and "lowness."

Thought of as basic values, or as world view, the two layers or dimensions will be seen as similar and yet notably different. Even one who knows as little of India as I do may suppose that the world view of the little traditions of India is on the whole polytheistic, magical, and unphilosophical, while the different strands of the great Vedic tradition choose different intellectual and ethical emphases: the Vedas tend to be polytheistic and poetical, the Upanishads abstract, monistic, and not very theistic, while the important Vaishnavaism and Shaivism are theistic and ethical. Corresponding contrasts appear, to mention just one other great tradition, "when we compare Taoism as a philosophy . . . with Taoism as a popular organized religion. Thus in philosophical Taoism the emphasis is on the subordination of man to nature, whereas in religious Taoism the goal is in the acquisition of human immortality through magical means, in other words, the gaining by man of control over natural forces; likewise in philosophical Taoism any idea of divine causation is rigidly excluded, whereas in religious Taoism the universe is peopled by a vast host of anthropomorphic deities."[20]

As we proceed to understand civilizations thus composed, we shall need to improve the communication between humanist-historian and anthropologist. The former may come better to understand the relations of the reflective thought he studies to the total life of that civilization; the latter may be helped to describe his small community in so far as its ways of life affect and are affected by the teachings of the great traditions. The forms in which the two kinds of research enterprises are conceived and carried on differ notably, of course; but their relevance to each other can be clarified and cultivated. We need the textual studies of the historian and student of art and literature. The student of the hierarchic culture has for his subject matter a corpus of texts. These texts are not only verbal. The world view of Hindu thought is written in the architecture of its temples as well as in its philosophies.[21] The studies of the anthropologist are contextual:[22] they relate some element of the great tradition—sacred book, story-element, teacher, ceremony, or supernatural being—to the life of the ordinary people, in the context of daily life as the anthropologist sees it happen.

The textual and the contextual studies will easily be found to come into connection with one another where the content of the text has important place in the context of village life. The *Ramayana* is the ancient source widely influential in village India today. Derived from oral tales, it was fashioned into a Sanskrit epic by some poet—it is said, one Valmiki—and so became part of India's great tradition. From the ninth century to the sixteenth century it was translated into many of the Indian vernaculars and in these forms was taught and sung by those professionals of the cultural structure about whom Professor Raghavan has told us. In the sixteenth century Tulsi-Das made a Hindi version which became the script for many a village celebration. This writer, an exponent of high culture, made a kind of basic text. We are told that this version is perhaps better known among the common people of India than is the Bible among rural English people. But then, as time went on, the Hindi of the Tulsi-Das version became hard for the peasants to understand. They added to it accretions from their local popular usage. And now, in village India, this basic text requires interpretation to be intelligible to the villagers. This is how it is done in connection with the festival of Ram Lila. There are two kinds of participants in the dramatic representation of the stories of Ram and Sita and the struggle with Ravana. The pundit, on behalf of the greater tradition, steps on the stage and reads from the Hindi text of the sixteenth century—with later popular interpolations. It is necessary that this text be read, because it is holy. But it is hard to understand. So, while the pundit is yet reciting, the impersonator (who is an unlettered villager) "starts to enact the deed which the recitation mentions. The pundit pauses, and the actor, raising his voice, paraphrases in a speech in clear modern prose the verse which the audience has just heard."[23] So are the levels of the tradition linked in the actual arrangements for ceremonial moral instruction in the villages. So might we study Bible stories in the sermons of a rustic Western community or the actual communication and modification of Confucian teaching in Chinese villages.

When the anthropologist studies an isolated primitive community, the context is that community and its local and immediate culture. When he comes to study a peasant community and its culture, the context is widened to include the elements of the great tradition that are or have been in interaction with what is local and immediate. If he is interested in the transformations that take place through this interaction (diachronic studies), he will investigate the communication of little and great traditions with each other and the changes that may have resulted or come to result in one or both because of the communication. If he regards the peasant village as a persisting system, as synchronic studies (perhaps limiting his view of the lapse of time to the three generations that are sometimes said to constitute the period within which the recurrent changes that sustain the system take place), he will include in the analysis the persisting and expectable communications from the great tradition to the village as these are necessary to maintain the culture of the peasant. How is this to be done?

In some published accounts of peasant communities the reader does learn something of the ways in which local religious belief and ritual are like or unlike the belief and ritual of the hierarchic religious culture with which the villagers are in communication through their priests, teachers, or experiences in travel.[24] But procedures for the reporting and analysis of these communications and their effects, either in sustaining the local culture or in contributing to the history of its modifications and its effects on the great tradition, are yet to be developed. I suggest that it may be in the course of their work in India that anthropologists will come to develop them. It is in India that the great (Sanskritic) tradition is in constant, various, and conspicuous interaction with the life of the local communities. It is there that the teachings of reflective and civilized minds appear plainly in the festivals, rituals, and in the ideals of the peasantry. It is in India that a man's ascribed status, in the form of caste, is closely associated with the claim of that caste to participation in the rituals and ideals of life as inculcated in Sanskritic teaching. Professor Srinivas has given us an account[25] of the way that certain village people, the Coorgs, who had ways of life somewhat apart from the Sanskritic tradition, have been taking on, in part quite consciously, elements of Hindu culture. The Coorgs have come to think of themselves as Kshatriyas, people of the warrior *varna,* and have come under the influence of Hinduism to the point that four of their number have become *sanyasis,* dedicated holy men observing the teachings of the Indian high tradition. The Coorgs have taken a high place in the general Indian hierarchy of status; they have Hinduized their claims to status. So far does the great tradition reach and so much does it yet do in India to change the cultures of depressed or marginal peoples.

In very recent years Western anthropologists have come in considerable numbers to study the Indian peasant villages as they lie within Hindu, Moslem, or modern Western civilization. One such recent study begins to provide conceptions and ways of work for analyzing the mutual effect of hierarchic Hinduism and village culture on each other. This is a paper by McKim Marriott.[26] The viewpoint is "diachronic"; the subject is conceived not only in terms of social relations but also "culturally"—as customs and institutions in course of modification. In the village he studied, which he calls Kishan Garhi, in Uttar Pradesh, the religion consists of elements of local culture and elements of the high Sanskrit tradition in close adjustment and integration. He finds "evidences of accretion and of transmutation in form without apparent replacement and without rationalization of the accumulated and transformed elements." Fifteen of nineteen festivals celebrated in Kishan Garhi are sanctioned in universal Sanskrit texts. But some of the local festivals have no place in Sanskrit teaching; those that do are but a small part of the entire corpus of festivals sanctioned by Sanskrit literature; villagers confuse or choose between various classical meanings for their festivals; and even the most Sanskritic of the local festivals have obviously taken on elements of ritual that arose, not out of the great tradition, but out of the local peasant life.

This kind of syncretization is familiar to students of paganism and Christianity or to students of Islam in its relations to local cults in North Africa. Marriott proposes that the two-way interaction between little and great traditions be studied as two complementary processes to which he gives names. For one thing, the little traditions of the folk exercise their influence on the authors of the Hindu great tradition who take up some element of belief or practice and, by incorporating it in their reflective statement of Hindu orthodoxy, universalize that element for all who thereafter come under the influence of their teaching. Marriott cannot quite prove[27] that the following was indeed an instance of universalization, but he suggests that the goddess Laksmi of Hindu orthodoxy is derived from such deities as he saw represented in his village daubed on walls or fashioned in images of dung: the natures and meanings of the high goddess and the local godlings are similar, and some villagers identify the latter with Laksmi. Also, Marriott reports an annual festival in which wives go to visit their brothers in the villages of their origins and in which these women, leaving their brothers to return home, express their attachment to them by placing barley shoots on the brothers' heads and ears, the brothers reciprocating with gifts of small coins. One of the Purānas, a classic source of Sanskritic instruction, fixes the form for a Brahmanical ritual according to which, on the same day as that on which is held the village rite referred to, each village priest goes to his patron and ties upon his wrist a charm of many-colored thread, the patron then giving money to the Brahman. Did the local rite give rise to the ceremony fixed in the Purāna, or is it an application of what the Purāna teaches? Marriott inclines to the former explanation and thinks of this interaction between the two dimensions or layers of the religion as illustrating universalization.

The opposite process, which Marriott calls "parochialization," is that by which some Sanskritic element is learned about and then reformed by the villagers to become a part of their local cult. For example: a divine sage of the Sanskritic tradition, associated by the Brahman elders with the planet Venus, is represented by erection of a stone in the village. Brides are now taken here to worship with their husbands. But then the origins of the stone are forgotten; it comes to be regarded as the abode of the ancestral spirits of the Brahmans who put it there. Again, the Sanskritic tradition, as expressed in the great Indian myths, gives sanction to a festival celebrated in nine successive nights in honor of great goddesses of the pantheon of India's great tradition. In the village of Kishan Garhi the people include in the beings to be honored during the festival of Nine Nights a being they call Naurtha: each morning and evening during the nine days women and children worship this Naurtha by bathing, singing, and making figurines of mud. Naurtha has no place in the great tradition. Marriott is able to show that she has come into existence in the village through simple linguistic corruption—a misunderstanding of the phrase "Nava Ratra" which means "Nine Nights." So by mere linguistic confusion in the communication between the little tradition and the great tradition, a minor goddess has been created.

Marriott was able to learn something about the interaction of great and little traditions in bringing about the translation or substitution of meanings and connections of rite and belief because he has read some of the sources of Hindu orthodoxy and because in the village he studied he found some people much more than others in communication with those sources. The village includes the educated and the ignorant, and the villager himself is well aware of the difference. A more educated villager calls himself a *sanātanī*, a follower of the orthodox and traditional way; a Brahman domestic priest distinguishes "doers and knowers"; the ordinary villager says that a certain ritual is Nārāyan, a deity inseminating the mortar in which the family husks grain, but an educated man of the same village says that it is a symbol of the creation of the world.[28] Where there are such differences as between villagers, the connections the village has with the philosopher or theologian can be traced in part by the anthropologist in his community study. The analysis then moves outward and upward to meet such investigations of the downward movement of orthodoxy or philosophy as is studied by Von Grunebaum for Islam and by Raghavan for Hinduism.

One is encouraged to imagine the kinds of studies of the interaction of the two aspects of tradition that will develop in anthropology. Still thinking of India, where the material is abundant and interesting, I remark that the interaction may be conceived in a more cultural or in a more societal way. Marriott's study represents the former. Milton Singer, writing from India, is impressed with the importance of what he calls "the cutural media"—song, dance, drama, festival, ceremony, recitations and discourse, prayers with offerings —in expressing Indian culture. He is struck by the ways in which these forms constantly merge with one another and suggests that Indians, and perhaps all peoples, conceive of their culture as encapsulated in specific cultural forms which can be exhibited in "cultural performances" to outsiders and to themselves.[29] One may perhaps analyze how elements of high tradition are communicated to the villager in these cultural forms, and how the elements are modified as they are taken into the local culture.

Or it may become possible and important to study particular "cultural institutions," those activities and personnel that exist for the purpose of communicating the great tradition. In India it should be possible, as Marriott suggests, to study a temple at its points of contact with pilgrims or one of those many regional shrines which house the images of those deities that are intermediate between great and little traditions, being local forms of the one and universalized forms of the other. Where a fairly limited community contains institutions of formal instruction, the social organization of tradition can be studied, I should imagine, in those institutions.

The Muslim school differs from the Hindu temple as a religion based on fidelity to an ultimate perfect revelation recorded in one book differs from a religion of polymorphous symbolic expression of levels of the same truth. From what I read,[30] the Magreb of Morocco even today provide an instance of an ancient and little changed structure of Islamic sacred tradition. We are told by Professor Le Tourneau that there is practically no difference there between a work written in the sixteenth century and one written in the twentieth, newspapers are unknown, and the intellectual life is confined to a small elite who are concerned ever with the same problems of interpreting Muslim orthodoxy. The peasant in the village is connected with Muslim orthodoxy by koranic teachers and minor administrative employees; such people are taught in mosque-schools in the minor cities; a few then attend the mosque to learn Muslim law or elements of Arabic grammar; and a very few go to Muslim universities in Fez or Tunis. Here the stable connections between village and city life with regard to the cultivated sacred tradition can be defined.

In India one might study one of the subcastes whose functions are to cultivate the history and genealogy of their caste, or one might study a caste composed of entertainers and singers who sing traditional stories from the *Ramayana* or the *Mahabharata* to their patrons.[31] Such castes are corporate groups relating great and little traditions to each other. It seems that in India the structure of tradition is very complex indeed and provided with a great variety of specialists, often caste-organized, for communicating the greater traditions to the lesser. Milton Singer says that in Madras he finds three major groups of specialists associated with the Sanskritic tradition: the priests supervising domestic and temple rites; reciters, singers, and dancers who convey the popular Purānic culture; and

Sanskrit pundits and scholars who cultivate different branches of Sanskritic learning.

Looked at in this way, the interaction of great and little traditions can be regarded as a part of the social structure of the peasant community in its enlarged context. We are concerned with those persisting and important arrangements of roles and statuses, in part appearing in such corporate groups as castes in sects, that are concerned with the cultivation and inculcation of the great tradition. The concept is an extension or specialization of the concept of social structure as used by anthropologists in the study of societies that are more nearly self-contained than are peasant villages. We turn now to consider, for the compound peasant society, a certain kind of the persisting social relations, a certain part of the social structure. The relations between Muslim teacher and pupil, between Brahman priest and layman, between Chinese scholar and Chinese peasant—all such as these that are of importance in bringing about the communication of great tradition to the peasant or that, perhaps without anyone's intention, cause the peasant tradition to affect the doctrine of the learned—constitute the social structure of the culture, the structure of tradition. From this point of view a civilization is an organization of specialists, of kinds of role-occupiers in characteristc relations to one another and to lay people and performing characteristic functions concerned with the transmission of tradition.

We might, as does Professor Raymond Firth, reserve the phrase "social organization"[32] in connection with concrete activity at particular times and places. Social organization is the way that people put together elements of action so as to get done something they want done. Social structure is a persisting general character, a "pattern" of typical relationships; social organization is described when we account for the choices and resolutions of difficulties and conflicts that actually went on in one particular situation. Accordingly we might withdraw the title of this chapter from its wider use and reserve it for the way in which elements of action are put together in any particular case of transmission of tradition. Thus we shall be studying the social organization of tradition when we investigate the way in which the school day is arranged in the conservative Islamic school, or when we study the way in which the festival of Ram Lila is brought about in an Indian community, the peasants and the literate pundit co-operating to the end that the sacred stories are acted out to the accompaniment of readings from the sacred text of the higher tradition. If there are problems of adjustment between what the more learned man would like to see done and what the lay people of the village think proper or entertaining, these cases of social organization of tradition will be the more interesting. I remember lost opportunities to study the social organization of tradition in my own field work, especially one occasion when the Catholic parish priest and the local shaman of the Maya tradition took part, successively, in a ceremony of purification in a Guatemalan village. There were then many pushings and pullings, many matters of doubt, conflict, and compromise, which I failed to record. In that case there were, of course, two more esoteric traditions, in some degree of conflict with each other, and both requiring some adjustment to the expectations of the villagers.

So we come to develop forms of thought appropriate to the wider systems, the enlarged contexts, of our anthropological work. In studying a primitive society, in its characteristic self-containment, its societal and cultural autonomy, we hardly notice the social structure of tradition. It may be present there quite simply in a few shamans or priests, fellow-members of the small community, very similar to others within it. In a primitive and preliterate society we cannot know much of the history of its culture. The structure of tradition in early Zuni is seen as a division of function within the tribal community and is seen as something now going on, not as a history. But a civilization has both great regional scope and great historic depth. It is a great whole, in space and in time, by virtue of the complexity of the organization which maintains and cultivates its traditions and communicates them from the great tradition to the many and varied small local societies within it. The anthropologist who studies one of these small societies finds it far from autonomous and comes to report and analyze it in its relations, societal and cultural, to state and to civilization.

IV

THE PEASANT VIEW OF
THE GOOD LIFE

The anthropology of the early twentieth century stressed the differences among peoples rather than the resemblances. Primitive societies, especially those distant from each other, were shown to exhibit contrasting customs, opposing views of the good life. Two neighboring tribes of the Plains may be similar, but the Canadian Kwakiutl have a way of life very different from that of the Zuni and yet more different from that of the Melanesian Dobu.[1] We learned that people with roughly similar ways of getting a living may nevertheless have different moral systems and world views. The Australian food gatherers and those of aboriginal California would not feel at home each in the company of the other, and the agricultural Zuni and the agricultural tribes of northern Luzon are notably different kinds of people. Even as between tribal peoples living in the same part of the world, marked differences in value-orientation have been reported.[2]

On the other hand, whatever anthropologists may think about it, there is a common impression that peasantry are much the same over very wide regions, even the whole world over. Oscar Handlin, reviewing the peasant qualities that immigrants brought to North America, asserts that "from the westernmost reaches of Europe, in Ireland, in Russia in the east, the peasant masses had maintained an imperturbable sameness."[3] He then describes that sameness: everywhere a personal bond with the land; attachment to an integrated village or local community; central importance of the family; marriage a provision of economic welfare; patrilocal residence and descent in the male line; a strain between the attachment to the land and the local world and the necessity to raise money crops; and so on. An observer of East Indian peasant life finds in these peasants "the real link between East and West." "He represents a way of life as old as civilization itself" with "an underlying unity which makes peasants everywhere akin."[4] The same impression is reported by a recent French writer, who thinks that peasantry are so much the same everywhere that he calls them "a psycho-physiological race," and declares that peasant and remote peasant are more alike than are city man and peasant in the same country. And he also mentions features he thinks present among peasantry everywhere: the family as a social group, the mystic attachment to the farm, the emphasis on procreation.[5] The impression that peasantry are somehow a type of mankind is strengthened when one finds in a Latin writing of the fourth century a description of the peasantry of that time and place that could be substituted for Handlin's words about other and later peasants.[6]

This impression became my own personal experience when in reading about peasant societies in many places and times I came to feel that much that I read was already familiar to me from what I had experienced in peasant communities of Maya Indians in Yucatan. In Reymont's novel[7] about Polish peasants, in Chinese villages, in recent accounts of Latin-American and European country people, I felt this "imperturbable sameness." And I began to wonder of what this sameness consisted and whether or not it could be shown to be a fact.

In a paper published nine years ago, Professor E. K. L. Francis suggested that the sameness might consist of "an integrated pattern of dominant attitudes"[8] of "a distinct peasant substratum of society in widespread areas of the globe."[9] Professor Francis proceeded to identify this integrated pattern of dominant attitudes as it appeared to him from a study of the oldest book we have about peasant life: Hesiod's *Works and Days*. Hesiod had enough urban sophistication to go to law with his brother in disputing an inheritance and to learn poetic art from books and so go on to win prizes at poetry-writing, but he did for years live with peasants.

Professor Francis' summary of what Hesiod tells us was so well done and so suggestive of other peasantry that it occurred to me to look for similar things in some other peasant communities. Invited to contribute to a series of lectures on "The Good Life," I adopted this phrase for the "integrated pattern of dominant attitudes," especially as representing the value-orientations of people, and made a brief comparison of Hesiod's description of Boeotians of the sixth century B.C. with the Maya Indians of recent Yucatan (because I knew them directly) and with the simple rural people of Surrey as described by George Sturt.[10] Sturt (who wrote under the name of George Bourne) also directs our attention toward dominant attitudes or ideas as to how life ought to be lived, in this case those of English peasants transformed into rural people after the inclosure of the commons in 1861 and the later coming to the countryside of people from towns and cities. George Sturt witnessed many of these changes.

In the course of my little comparison of these three peoples, so separate in space and time, I found so much likeness that I wrote that "if a peasant from any one of these three widely separated communities could have been transported by some convenient genie to any one of the others and equipped with a knowledge of the language in the village to which he had been moved, he would very quickly come to feel at home. And this would be because the fundamental orientations of life would be unchanged. The compass of his career would continue to point to the same moral north." And I went on to particularize the resemblances that I found.[11] The rest of this chapter is about these particularizations as to peasant attitudes and values and especially about what became of them as they were examined and tested by other evidence.

The lecture in which I came to this conclusion was not written as a contribution to science but merely to suggest to an audience that peasants have something that one would want to call a view of the good life. To declare important similarities, with no attention to differences, as to qualities only vaguely defined as among peoples so widely separate in time and space as the ancient Boeotians, the recent English countrypeople, and the remade Indian peasantry of present-day Yucatan, is not good science, but it is a good way to get a discussion going. There is so much about the comparison that may be challenged. The meaning of the phrase, "the good life," and of other words used to describe peasant values, the validity of comparisons based on such different kinds of sources of information on such widely separated peoples, and the worth of generalizations offered after brief examination of only three out of thousands of more or less peasant peoples, all invite criticism.

The criticism came. It was provoked and guided through the kindness and skill of Professor F. G. Friedmann, himself a student of the peasants of southern Italy and long interested in those aspects of the life of simple peoples that anthropologists call "value orientations" or perhaps "ethos." As a philosopher and humanist, he called these orientations more simply, "way and view of life," and he brought about a discussion, by exchange of letters, of my lecture and of the topic generally. About a dozen persons who had studied peasant peoples in one part of the world or another contributed to this little symposium. In what follows I draw very largely on the contributions of these other students, and in connection with particular issues mention their names. I am very grateful to them all and hope that they will further correct and develop the small beginnings I make here in reporting some of the results of the discussion. I use their contributions not so much to provide a description of peasant values as to support an opinion that the problem is a real one. The effect of the discussion, as far as it has gone, seems to me to intensify the impression that the circumstances of peasantry tend to bring about in such peoples views of life that have some similarity: that the view of life of one peasant people will be found to have resemblances to that of some others, but not always at the same points of resemblance. Further, I believe that as terms come to be better defined and as facts are more sharply reported and brought more definitely to bear on more restricted questions, some of these points of resemblance or difference will be provided with explanations, with statements of particular circumstance which account for them. In short, this excursion into problems of peasantry as a human type, an attitude toward the universe, seems to me to be one of the consequences of that enlargement of the anthropological subject matter which is the subject of these four chapters. Not much is known about these problems as yet. I think that the discussion led by Professor Friedmann has shown them to be accessible to more considered examination and investigation.

I begin now with the first three generalizations I offered in that early offhand comparison and say what became of them in the discussion that followed. Among peasants of nineteenth-century England, present-day Yucatan, and ancient Boeotia, I seemed to find a cluster of three closely related attitudes or values: an intimate and reverent attitude toward the land; the idea that agricultural work is good and commerce not so good; and an emphasis on productive industry as a prime virtue. As to the intimate and reverent attitude toward the land, the injunction of Hesiod chimed in closely with many a piece of advice I had heard the Yucatecan agriculturalist give to his son or offer to me, the recording ethnologist. The Maya farmer teaches his boy how to use the ax and the machete, while also he sees to it that the youth bows his head in prayer when the forest is cleared for planting and that he always treats the maize plant with reverence and the maize field as something of a holy place. In Hesiod's pages too I found this mixture of prudence and piety as to the agricultural life, and I concluded that for ancient Greek as for recent Maya, nature is man's and gods' both; nature is wrought upon, but decent respect attends the work; farming is practical action suffused with religious feeling. In the book about the Sussex countryman I found no explicit religious expressions with regard to agriculture, but quoted George Sturt to the effect that there too prevailed a similar feeling of intimacy with nature and reverence for it. There, although the formal expressions of religion-in-agriculture are lacking, there remains what Sturt calls "the faint sense of something venerable" in the landscape and in agricultural activity.

I went on to declare the peasant's emphasis on agricultural industriousness as a prime virtue and suggested that this emphasis is supported by three principal considerations: security, respect, and the religious feeling already noted. I quoted Hesiod again as to the security and respect that comes to a man who is industrious, and I reported how the rural Yucatecan also taught his children to work hard on the land, because both his livelihood and his reputation depended on it and because the gods expected it. I showed that in a Maya village I knew some men continued to practice agriculture although economically disadvantageous because to plant a cornfield was essential to participating in the moral and religious life of the community.

Further, I mentioned the scorn exhibited by the rural Maya toward the townsman as a creature easily tiring and unable to sustain the labor which was the necessity and pride of the villager and quoted George Sturt to similar effect in connection with the Sussex countryman. This contrast, to the advantage of himself, the rural

Mayan, and the Boeotian, extends also to the man of commerce. In Yucatan commerce became something of a game and venture to the later peasantry but never came to have anything like the importance and seriousness of agriculture. Similarly, Hesiod's advice is unfavorable to business ventures; his section on the subject begins with the words, "If you turn your misguided heart to trading. . . ." In summary, I thought I found in the three peoples I reviewed a sober attitude toward work, a satisfaction in working long and hard in the fields, a disinclination to adventure or to speculate. I thought all this in striking contrast (as Francis and others have noted) to the view and ideals of such warrier-chieftains as are described in the *Iliad* or the *Mahabharata*.

And how did this characterization fare in the discussion? At first some corroboration appeared. Professor Irwin T. Sanders had already described the Bulgarian peasant as putting forward among chief values "land ownership, hard work, frugality."[12] Professor Donald Pitkin remarked, from his reading, that to the Irish countryman and to the French Canadian peasant also "the emphasis on productive industry as a prime good and central duty would ring true."

But it soon appeared that not all the people we find it easy to call peasants feel this way about their land and work. Pitkin told us that the peasant of southern Italy works because one must in order to eat but feels that it is better to work with one's head than with one's hands and better yet not to work at all. And Friedmann does not find find that the impoverished southern Italian takes that reverent attitude toward the land which is so marked among the Maya and was at least recognizable among the late peasantry of England according to Sturt.

Why are the southern Italian peasants different in this respect? And what other peasantry or near-peasantry also feel that the land is just something on which one works as a necessity, not as a virtue? Looking further, I find that the town-dwelling Andalusians recently reported by J. A. Pitt-Rivers lack a mystical attitude toward the land; they go out to cultivate the land, but they do not love it.[13] Labor on the land is no prime virtue with them. And a French author whom Pitt-Rivers quotes in his book says that much the same may be said of the Syrian peasant: "The fellah cultivates . . . with regret . . . he works for himself and not for the land; he does not feel that the land is an extension of himself" ("Il ne sent pas que celle-ci le dépasse et le prolongue").[14] This appears to be a real difference: the Maya, and I think the French Canadian, and the old-fashioned rural Englishman, did feel that the land was an extension of himself.

Professor Tullio Tentori, another student of Italian peasantry, and also Donald Pitkin have proposed that those peasants who emphasize labor on the land as a virtue have enough land and security so that agricultural work does, in fact, result in an existence with some dignity, not "just a sort of desperate scrounging for existence" (Pitkin). The economic condition of the south Italian is certainly bad, and one can see that there, where also examples of wealth and of pleasanter urban living are present, the wish to escape agricultural toil might easily develop. I am not so sure that the same explanation will serve for the Spanish mountain-dwelling agriculturalist, who is apparently better off economically than is the south Italian.

I begin to wonder if it is a mere accident that those European peasant villages where the dignity of agricultural work is recognized are, so far as these reports go, some distance from the Mediterranean. It is the Bulgarian, the Irish countryman, the Englishman, who are reported as showing the feeling of dignity in work on the land. It is the south Italian, the Andalusian, the Syrian, who do not. Pitt-Rivers says that the attitude he found in the Andalusian town "is typical of the whole Mediterranean, though it contrasts with the north-west of the Iberian peninsula."[15] This sounds as if the differences in attitude might in part reflect some ancient regional differences of culture. One recalls the emphasis on town-dwelling throughout the ancient Mediterranean area as contrasted with the more tribal and migratory character of the ancient people of northern and eastern Europe. The Andalusian thinks of himself as a townsman although he works the land and belongs culturally to a class inferior to the more educated elite. The possibility presents itself that around the Mediterranean Sea the prestige of the town, the *polis*, carried with it at an early date the peasant's distaste for agricultural life. But does not this possibility seem less likely when one recalls Hesiod's injunctions as to agricultural industry? Or do his words express a time and place when and where rural Greeks had not come to form a distaste for farming? Or is it that Hesiod is not to be read as evidence of a sense of virtue in performing agricultural work?

It may be that both kinds of explanations, historical and ecological-economic, for peasant attitudes toward land and labor are valid with different weights and effects in different parts of the world. To the Maya Indian labor on the milpa is dignified by its connections with religion and manly virtue; and, in fact, he does earn himself a decent way of life by agricultural toil. The religiousness of his agriculture arose in primitive life and has not been destroyed by a more secular civilization. The sentimental and moral attachments of the old-fashioned English peasant to his land are farther away from such primitive involvements of religion and agriculture. The Maya is a primitive agriculturalist who, having been something of a peasant to his indigenous elite, has become a peasant to the Spanish-Maya elite of the present day. The English countryman ceased to be a more secular kind of peasant while it was yet possible to earn a life of dignity in rural labor. The south Italian may bring a distaste for rural life down from ancient times, while he also is influenced by the fact that he now lives in hardship in contrast to the life of the gentry and the rich.

The case of the rural Paraguayans described by Elman and Helen Service is interesting and suggests possible directions in which explanations for resemblances and differences in these attitudes may be found. The Paraguayans live on scattered farms as squatters. Their agricultural resources are not closed: the people can get more land by making an effort to reclaim waste for agriculture. We are told that these people, who have important relationships of power and status with an educated elite, have "typical peasant attitudes" in that, at least, they farm to keep themselves fed and as a way of life and not as a business enterprise. These Paraguayans do not regard ownership of land as particularly desirable; they get along all right without owning it, for they control the land on which they live without legal right. When they work for hire, they regard their relationship to their employer as personal, and their work as the performance of a favor to a friend. It is not clear from the account just how they value their own labor on the land. But one gets the feeling that to understand the attitudes of these Paraguayans one must take into account both the fact that land resources are not strictly limited and the fact, historical rather than environmental or ecological, that they came to Paraguay as pioneers and did not bring with them such religion and social systems centered around agriculture as grew up in America among the Maya.

Up to this point the attempt to reconcile the somewhat conflicting accounts of the attitudes peasants have with regard to the land and their work upon it has proceeded on the assumption that the different accounts are equivalent, that is, that all these writers provide us with reliable answers to the same question: Do these peasants think labor on the land is good? It is doubtful that they do. What is meant by "think good"? Apparently the contributors to the symposium all understood that what was under discussion was the peasant's view of what is good, not the good as judged by the observer and outsider. But the "good" of the peasant is of several kinds or dimensions. Dr. Börje Hanssen, in writing of old-time Swedish peasants, brought this to the fore by pointing out that physical vigor and endurance are "goods" in that it is a desirable and necessary thing to have these powers; on the other hand, labor on the land is not desired: the peasant prefers "his resting place by the warm stove more than any kind of hard work." One imagines that it could be truly said of more than one peasant that hard work in the fields is a virtue taught and respected, while at the same time rest and leisure are not merely desired but desirable—that is, within some limits of disapproved idleness, it is thought good in the nature of things not to work but to be free from work. Dr. Hanssen has also raised the point that the good (the desirable?) for the individual may be distinguishable from the good for the community, that is, there may be a certain inconsistency among elements of the desirable.

This turn in the discussion demands a reconsideration of our sources and a re-examination of our concepts. Maybe the sources are talking of different aspects of "the good." It may be that Friedmann, Tentori, and Pitkin could tell us something about the positive value placed on industriousness in the field in the face of the south Italian's wish to escape his little-rewarding toil, while it yet remains true that labor has more dignity in French Canada and in Yucatan than it has in Calabria. My report of Maya attitudes is on the whole an account of values these peasants see in agriculture; it does not report—something which is also a fact—that leisure is also desirable and that hard work is, if possible, to be escaped. Hesiod's account does not amount to proof that his peasantry were entirely content with their lot:[16]

much of *Works and Days* is as didactic as *Poor Richard's Almanac;* he is telling his neighbors how to make a success—practical and religious—of farming. The sources are not equivalent. In some there is an emphasis on the reverence or religious feeling in the agricultural activity; in others on the preferences for rest or leisure; in others on the teaching of industry as an admirable habit. In part these emphases conform, I imagine, to differences between the communities reported; but in part, I also suppose, they arise from choices made by observers and writers as to an aspect of a social situation to be stressed.

Nor is it sure that all these reporters from Hesiod to Professor Friedmann's band of irregulars have described, in the same sense, a view of "the good life"—a phrase brought into the discussion through the title put upon my lecture by the organizer of a series of addresses to general audiences in Chicago in 1953. Within any investigation as to what the "goods" (values) of certain other people are, at least three questions are implied: What do these people desire? What qualities, at least as a matter of prudence, do they try to bring about in their children? To what kind of life do they attach highest esteem—whether or not they foresee it for themselves and whether or not it is what they desire? I should think that there might be considerable discrepancy among the answers to these three questions about any particular peasantry.

If we could become sure that we were all asking the same question of the facts about particular peasants, and that the answers reported were of equivalent validity, we might reach conclusions as to the conceptions of goodness and badness that attach to land and labor in peasant societies. Even through the many uncertainties, I think I see in the discussion that has been carried on among a few of us the probability that many peasants share, not identically but with some notable resemblances, a cluster of attitudes or values in this part of their experience. Perhaps it will prove convenient to recognize such a cluster in the first instance only in cases of peasantry in long-standing and stable relationship to limited land and to a little-changing gentry or elite. For such peasants the cluster may include an involvement of agricultural labor with traditional, often reverential, sentiments about the land; the connection of that labor with ideals as to personal worth; the inculcation in the young of endurance and hard work rather than a disposition to take risks and to perform personal exploits; the acceptance of arduous labor, yet with great enjoyment of its surcease. Because of regional differences in traditional attitudes that come to prevail through a history special to that region, we may find it better to characterize the peasant values for one part of the world at a time. And then we may further come to see how this cluster or these clusters of goodness and badness in agricultural labor have, in particular cases, been pulled into some different direction of emphasis because of something peculiar to the ancient history of those people or because of such more recent events as a sudden increase in the burden of poverty or the appearance of an opportunity to escape it.

I turn now to another group of characteristics possibly attributable to peasantry and discussed in the interchange led by Professor Friedmann. In reviewing Hesiod's account of Boeotian views of marriage and the family, Francis had emphasized the practical disposition toward such personal matters and the economic values seen in marriage and in children: the ancient peasant chose a bride because she had a reputation for industry, and children were welcomed because they made more hands for work. In reviewing also the Surrey rural people and the Maya I knew, I made a wider generalization as to prevailing values or cast of character. I wrote: "It is . . . the state of mind at once practical and reverent, the inseparable mixture of prudence and piety, which gives the essential character to peasant life. . . . In this scheme of values sobriety is the chosen mode. The peasant values decorum and decency. Passion is not to be exhibited. A man does not flaunt his appetites, or make a show of his emotions."

And I thought I found in Hesiod and in Sturt evidence of a scorn for sentiment, an earthy matter-of-factness, a masking of tenderness and restraint of passion that to me contrasted with the behavior of the warriors of the *Iliad* or the chieftains of the Viking age.

In particular I saw this temper of mind and feeling manifest in the practical attitudes toward sex and marriage in the three peasant communities which I tried to compare. I recalled a Maya villager's remark to me that "one should care for the land as for a wife and family" when I read the parallel injunction in Hesiod: "First of all get a house and a woman and an oxe for the plough."[17] In Chan Kom, in rural Surrey as described by Sturt, and in Hesiod's pages I seemed to find similar prudential views for getting a wife and for living with her; in all three communities, I ventured to say, one marries as a part of the work and the piety of life. Sturt's characterization of the marriage of the old English countrypeople as "a kind of dogged partnership"[18] seemed to me to fit Maya and ancient Greek as well, and so I was led to write that "the peasant would not approve of the careless raptures of some urban marriages and would make no sense of the action of the Plains Indian brave, who, to show his manly independence and scorn of pleasant comforts, might, if he chose, publicly cast off a good wife only because he suffered a slight smart at the hands of his parents-in-law."[19] This line of thought led me into some generalizations as to the place of sex experience in the peasant scheme of values: In peasant life, where work and practical good sense join with a spirit of decent restraint, there is little room for sexual exploit as a sport or for bravado. The cultivation of amorous adventure, as practiced in not a few Polynesian societies, or among some modern Western groups, is hardly possible in peasant communities. Before marriage sexual experiment is common, yes, and may receive some public approval or at least licensed regulation (as in the custom of bundling). But adultery is not looked on with favor. Bourne say of his Surrey people that "it scandalizes them to hear of it. They despise it."[20] And Hesiod puts a large part of the reason for this attitude pithily: "Do not let a flaunting woman coax and cozen and deceive you—she is after your barn."[21] In Chan Kom too the occasional adultery, when brought to a public issue, exposed the principal parties as figures almost as comic as reprehensible.

With these assertions that the three peasants were similar in minimizing sexual experience as a good in itself or as a sport or manly achievement I connected what I took to be another characteristic: a distaste for violence, a disfavor of prowess in any form of conspicuous aggressiveness. And again, as in the case of what I had said as to the attitudes connected with agricultural labor, other men who know other peasants challenged the scope of the generalizations, and again it was the south Italian who provided evidence to support the challenge. Professor Tentori reported that to those rural people sexual experience is highly valued. "It is the only way," a peasant told him, "that we know to enjoy life." And I was referred to the statement by Signor Nitti, himself from southern Italy, as to "the violence of the carnal instinct" in that part of the rural world. Also I was reminded of the violence of which Mediterranean peasantry are capable when revenge is involved. At once I recalled much of what had been written about Mediterranean peoples: the expression of passion, the disposition to use violence to redress personal wrong, and the role of sexual exploit in conceptions of manhood. There are indeed, even at this first glance, differences among peasant peoples as to these matters of violence and emphasis on sexual exploit.

But again it is not yet clear just what these differences are or to what they are to be attributed. In part the difference may be only apparent and arise from a report which emphasizes an ideal of good conduct with which, perhaps, other concepts of good present in the same society are in some conflict. Or it may in part be the difference between saying what certain peasants will tell you ought to be man's conduct and what they tell you they enjoy. But there may here be real differences between the habits of mind and character that have come to be established in one part of the world as compared with those that have developed in another. And some of such differences may perhaps be compatible with the common circumstances of peasant life.

There is such a thing as ethnic temperament. The group-personality of the Chinese is something to investigate and describe, and the results will not correspond with the results of investigations of the group-personality of south Italians. The Maya Indians, peasantry remade, have a group-personality which in important degree must have come about before ever they began to come into relationship with the Spanish-American gentry of the present-day towns. Yet in their case the group-personality that had been developing before the Conquest was already congenial, one may perhaps think, to the conditions of peasant life and, indeed, had partly been developed in the course of their relationships to their own priestly elites. The Comanche if moved to Yucatan would have had to change very much more to become peasantry. So it may turn out that the general circumstances of peasant life do not set aside other influences on character but yet do dispose a people toward the more restrained and sober valuation of sex and violence which I first tried to describe.

Possible explanations of peasant values appear to be numerous and complicated. Even in this brief discussion as to what peasants think of sexual prowess or manly aggressiveness, and as to whether the tone of their lives is sober or passionate, one sees that several explanations might be seriously considered. It may be that the characteristics of peasant life do on the whole dispose people to a sober temper unfavorable to individual exploit in any field of action. It may also be that even within such generally conforming circumstances old-established characteristics of the modal personality may be more congenial to such a result in one place than in others. And it may also be that in some parts of the world the peasantry have been strongly influenced by the gentry and elite with whom their lives are completed and entertain views of what is good, desirable, and ideal that they have taken over from examples provided by the gentry. Is it not the gentry of Spain, for instance, that exhibited most markedly that value called *hombría* which involves a certain approval of male sexual exploit and a touchy pride and use of violence in defense of honor? And yet do not the peasantry also show it? Certainly the rural townspeople of Andalusia show it.[22] Do (or did) the peasants or the gentry in Italy show the satisfactions in sexual exploit and in manly violence which Professor Tentori calls to our attention? The extent to which a gentry ideal has influenced a peasantry probably differs from one part of the world to another: I imagine the influence to have been stronger in Spain than in Poland or Russia. At any rate, I am glad to remind myself by one fact I know well of the obvious importance of differences in historic heritage in explaining differences in peasant value-systems: In rural western Guatemala the Indian peasant or almost-peasant lives beside another peasant, the man called a *ladino*, whose ancestry is partly Spanish and whose language and culture are Spanish. The two rural agriculturalists work side by side and have similar material conditions of life, but they are notably different in manners and character: the *ladino* shows much of the formal courtesies of Castile and exhibits the remnants of *hombría*, manly pride; the Indian does not.

It becomes, then, impossible justly to explain the ideals of peasantry without considering the kind and duration of the relationships those peasants have had with their gentry. I think that it is in the relations between the peasant and his gentry or townsman that we shall find much of what makes a peasant different from a primitive person. There is very much in peasant life which is also in primitive, tribal life. Peasant activity too is so organized as to provide for what the people there accept as a good life. A structure of meanings gives the pleasure that comes from a life well lived with little. Satisfactions come from the exercise of unquestioned virtues and the enjoyment of one's own skills and the fruits of one's own labor. What Sturt says about the good life of the English peasantry he knew could be said as well of many an African or American Indian primitive: "By their own skill and knowledge they formed the main part of their living out of . . . their own neighborhood. And in doing so they won at least the rougher consolations which that mode of life had to offer. Their local knowledge was intensely interesting to them; they took pride in their skill and hardihood; they felt that they belonged to a set of people not inferior to others . . . ; and all the customs which their situation required them to follow contained their belief in the ancestral notions of good and evil."[23]

As with other long-established people, peasants find in life purpose and zest because accumulated experience has read into nature and suffering and joy and death significance that the peasant finds restated for him in his everyday work and play. There is a teaching, as much implicit as explicit, as to why it is that children come into the world and grow up to marry, labor, suffer, and die. There is an assurance that labor is not futile; that nature, or God, has some part in it. There is a story or a proverb to assure one that some human frailty is just what one ought to expect; there are in many cases more serious myths to explain the suffering of the innocent or to prepare the mind for death. So that although peasants and primitives will quarrel and fear, gossip and hate, as do the rest of us, their very way of life, the persisting order and depth of their simple experiences, continue to make something humanly and intellectually acceptable of the world around them.

And yet the peasant is differently situated from the primitive because peasants know of and are dependent upon more civilized people. There is another dimension of life, outside the village, in that powerful manor or that alarming town. The peasant has given his hostage to the fortunes of a society and mode of life that is both like his and yet alien to it. He keeps the integrity of his traditions by making compromises: by selling his grain in the town, paying his taxes, respecting the priest or the political leader, acknowledging that there are things out there that are perhaps better than his own village. He is not self-sufficient in his moral or intellectual life. Out there, he knows, are people who will baptize my child; people who will, in their courts of law, get me my rights or deprive me of them. There, in that town, or in the person who comes to me from the town, is one who can tell me more than I know of the life and death of Christ, or of the teaching of Confucius, or of Rama and Sita and the great struggle with the evil being, Ravana. There, in that outsider's keeping and understanding, is the holy tale or the book, the book that, read by those who can, gives knowledge about what I already know, a deeper, better knowledge. And perhaps, if I scrape and sacrifice, my son can go to that man or town and learn that deeper knowledge too. When George Sturt says that the English peasants felt they belonged to a set of people not inferior to others, he adds the qualification, "albeit perhaps poorer and ruder."[24] Yes, every peasant finds his self-respect, his contentment, qualified by the knowledge that he is poorer and ruder than the gentry, those people of the towns.

So it seems that in extending his studies of values to peasant peoples the anthropologist encounters another "heteronomous" characteristic: the value-orientation, the view of the good life, of peasantry, is not to be understood solely from consideration of the way the people of the village look upon themselves. The townsman or the gentry form an aspect of the local moral life—form it by reflection, by the presence of example, by the model these outsiders offer, whether that model be one the peasant seeks to imitate or to avoid, or whether he merely recognizes both its likeness to and its difference from its own ideals.

In the peasant's view of the good life do the townsman and the gentry occupy such a place that the characteristics of this relationship are much the same everywhere? In writing the lecture which later came into discussion I was struck by statements that in European history up to very recent times no peasant revolt had revolution for its goal, and that the prevailing relation between the peasant and his gentry has not been one of oppressor and oppressed but rather that the peasant has thought that the rich should be generous and the powerful should not abuse their power.[25] The occasional resentment of or hatred for a rich and powerful man seemed to me on the whole to represent cases where someone had failed to preserve the traditional and approved roles and statuses of gentry and peasantry.

Beyond this fact—if it is a fact—of acceptance of these relative positions of power, one wants to find out about the resemblances and the differences in content of culture and conceptions of the good between peasant and gentry. Is there indeed a guidance in the moral sphere[26] which the elite exert upon the peasantry? Is the gentry imitated or is his example avoided? The discussion on which this chapter has so largely drawn has not reached very far into this question. Dr. Hanssen tells us that the Swedish peasant of a hundred or more years ago regarded, more or less, every representative of the gentle folk as a foreigner, and that this attitude slowed while it did not prevent the interchange of ideas and forms between the two classes. In the French village of Nouville (Seine-Inférieure) at the present time the difference between the peasant and the bourgeois is marked; the peasant puts his daughter to work with the bourgeois "so that she will learn good manners"; but he does not expect his child to become bourgeois. "The idea of *becoming* (such a one) does not exist. What exists is the idea of *being*."[27] Many of the facts from India mentioned in the preceding chapter indicate how strongly there influences from intellectuals outside of the local community influence its moral life; they do not show the peasant rejecting these influences nor, on the other hand, do they show him trying to become something different from what he has been. Nevertheless, we know that in some parts of the world, in China for example, at certain periods occasional peasants, by act of will and through success in the examinations, become something other than—and better than—peasants. These few considerations suggest that the relations with elites of various kinds are essential parts of peasant life and that they take different forms in different times and places.

Nowadays they are indeed taking new and different forms. Looking back on history one may justly see the peasant as on the whole and for thousands of years little changing and somehow typical. He came about indigenously as cities and civilizations rose in the Old World, and today more peasants are made as Indian or Chinese civilization moves into the communities of tribal peoples. As European civilization spread to the New World, secondary peasantry, with roots of culture different from that of the invaders, came and still come to be made.

In every part of the world, generally speaking, peasantry have been a conservative factor in social change, a brake on revolution, a check on that disintegration of local society which often comes with rapid technological change. And yet in our days many peasants are changing very rapidly. For the future it may be said that peasantry are ceasing to be. The troubles of the anthropologist in taking account of compound societies and cultures in the Far and Near East and in Latin America are made greater by the fact that what was stable is no longer so. In many a peasant village where the anthropologist works the peasant is going to town to become a factory worker, even a member of the urban middle class. Peasants now want to be something other than peasants. They are pulled by the city into industrial work. The promises and the pressures of communism, while they meet great resistance in peasant communities, do succeed in unmaking peasants.

These are times in which even the isolated and the backward experience discontent. Quite plain people want to be different from what they have always been; peasantry develop aspirations. The desires attending peasantry are of two kinds. The old stable, landed life is attractive to that rural man who has no land and wants only the security of having land. In many a peasant society many people are landless laborers who cannot be practicing peasants because they have not the ancestral land that would make it possible. This is true in Calabria and Lucania, in south China, in parts of India. In such rural communities there are people seeking to become peasants and there are people seeking to escape from peasant life. "We can today see land-hunger and land-flight next to each other. Sub-peasants seek to get in while peasants seek to get out" (Friedmann). The anthropologist on such a scene will find himself not only studying the ways in which the incomplete cultural, societal, and value systems of the peasants are completed by the relations and conceptions which the gentry and the town provide. He will find himself also devising ways to study the transformation of peasantry into kinds of peoples—industrial workers, urban social classes, proletariats, marginal peoples of one sort or another—that have had little or no attention here.

The peasant and the anthropologist are both changing, and it is the changes in the anthropologist rather than those in the peasant that have been the subject of these pages. Of some of them the peasant, as subject matter of new and greater interest for anthropology, is a cause. I have tried to show here some of the ways in which the thoughts and procedures of anthropologists are growing as they study people whose ways of life are only in part present in the small communities in which they live and in which anthropologists are accustomed to work. I have looked for the developing attention given to the "heteronomous" features of community life, be that life conceived as social relations, as culture, or, more specially, as a value-orientation.

This last chapter is concerned with an anthropological frontier not only because the subject matter, peasantry, is such, but also because ethos or value-orientation has only recently become a matter of serious anthropological attention.[28] Anthropologists are only now learning how to think about and how validly to report the basic values of primitive and self-contained communities. Perhaps they are not ready for further complexity: the interdependence of gentry ethos and peasant ethos, this relation between a widespread tradition of the town and priest and a local tradition of the village.

The question which set in motion the preliminary discussion reported in this chapter is put at too ultimate, inclusive, and vague a form to serve the needs of science, a science that grows, on the whole, upward from its base, in small increments of new knowledge. Here the topic has been considered at a level of abstraction remote from the terrain of particular research. Even at this misty upper level, I do think that something remains of the assertions made as to the peasant view of the good life; but others might not accept even the following modified statement of peasant values: an intense attachment to native soil; a reverent disposition toward habitat and ancestral ways; a restraint on individual self-seeking in favor of family and community; a certain suspiciousness, mixed with appreciation, of town life; a sober and earthy ethic. The characterization is no doubt too vague and impressionistic to serve the methods of the more scientific kinds of inquiry. For serious work in the establishment of truth by precise definition and close comparison, the study of peasant values will attack much more particular questions, such as the effects of changes in land tenure on family relations and attitudes,[29] or the question whether many children are wanted where there is abundant land, as among the Maya, and not wanted where limited land must be divided among heirs (as Hanssen reports for eighteenth-century Sweden).

Such advances in more precise knowledge will be welcome. Yet they will destroy, as science always does, something of the integrity of the concrete reality: that way of life of just those peasants. It is no harm and some good that more speculative and perhaps philosophically inclined thinkers, such as some of those whom Professor Friedmann brought together, also turn their minds to what is, in spite of all difficulties in the way of precise knowledge of the subject, a recognizable and long-enduring human type. To reach for a much higher generalization about the way of life of that human type, with some control on the results from facts as to particular peasants, helps to open the area of investigation and to suggest the more particular questions while retaining something of the natural integrity of peasant life. Vision and craftsmanship are mutually helpful indispensable parts of the effort toward understanding of truth. All who make that effort use both in some degree, though the proportions of one to the other vary greatly. The perception of resemblance and of natural unity needs to work its way down to precise words and procedures that yield generally accepted proof. On the other hand, the wide perception may quicken the developing procedure, the growing edge of science, and help guide it to the light.

NOTES

NOTES TO CHAPTER I

1. A. L. Kroeber, in *Method and Perspective in Anthropology*, ed. Robert F. Spencer (Minneapolis: University of Minnesota Press, 1954).

2. Graham Wallas, *The Great Society* (New York: Macmillan Co., 1914).

3. A. R. Radcliffe-Brown, "The Methods of Ethnology and Social Anthropology," *The South African Journal of Science*, XX (October, 1923), 143.

4. A. R. Radcliffe-Brown, "The Meaning and Scope of Social Anthropology," *Nature*, Vol. CLIV, No. 3904 (August 26, 1944).

5. E. E. Evans-Pritchard, *Social Anthropology* (London: Cohen & West, Ltd., 1951), pp. 10–11.

6. W. Lloyd Warner, "Introduction," in *The Irish Countryman*, by Conrad M. Arensberg (New York: Macmillan Co., 1937), p. viii.

7. Ralph L. Beals, "Urbanism, Urbanization and Acculturation," *American Anthropologist*, LV, No. 1 (January–March, 1951), 1–10.

8. Raymond Firth, *Malay Fishermen: Their Peasant Economy* (London: Kegan Paul, Trench, Trubner & Co., 1946).

9. Edmund R. Leach, *Political Systems of Highland Burma: A Study of Kachin Social Structure* (London: London School of Economics and Political Science, 1954).

10. Elman R. and Helen S. Service, *Tobatí: Paraguayan Town* (Chicago: University of Chicago Press, 1954).

11. Morton H. Fried, *Fabric of Chinese Society: A Study of the Social Life of a Chinese County Seat* (New York: Frederick A. Praeger, Inc., 1953).

12. Horace Miner, *St. Denis: A French-Canadian Parish* (Chicago: University of Chicago Press, 1939).

13. H. H. Turney-High, *Château-Gérard: The Life and Times of a Walloon Village* (Columbia: University of South Carolina Press, 1953).

14. James West, *Plainville, U.S.A.* (New York: Columbia University Press, 1945).

15. E. E. Evans-Pritchard, *The Senusi of Cyrenaica* (Oxford: Clarendon Press, 1949).

16. Ruth Benedict, *The Chrysanthemum and the Sword* (Boston: Houghton Mifflin Co., 1946).

17. Robert H. Lowie, *Toward Understanding Germany* (Chicago: University of Chicago Press, 1954).

18. Henri Mendras, *Études de sociologie rurale: Novis et Virgin* ("Cahiers de la Fondation Nationale des Sciences Politiques" [Paris: Librairie Armand Colin, 1915]).

19. Julian Steward *et al.* (forthcoming).

20. Iwao Ishino and John W. Bennett, *The Japanese Labor Boss System: A Preliminary Sociological Analysis* (Ohio State University Research Foundation and Department of Sociology, Report No. 3 [Columbus, April, 1953]).

21. A. L. Kroeber, in *An Appraisal of Anthropology Today*, ed. Sol Tax *et al.* (Chicago: University of Chicago Press, 1953), p. 360.

22. Margaret Mead, "National Character," in *Anthropology Today*, ed. A. L. Kroeber (Chicago: University of Chicago Press, 1953), p. 653.

23. Robert Redfield, "The Folk Society," *American Journal of Sociology*, LII, No. 4 (January, 1947), 293–308; "The Natural History of the Folk Society," *Social Forces*, XXXI, No. 3 (March, 1953), 224–28.

24. Paul Kirchhoff, in "Four Hundred Years After: General Discussion of Acculturation, Social Change, and the Historical Provenience of Culture Elements," *Heritage of Conquest*, ed. Sol Tax *et al.* (Glencoe, Ill.: Free Press, 1952), p. 254.

25. Pedro Armillas, "The Mesoamerican Experiment," in "The Ways of Civilization," ed. Robert J. Braidwood, MS.

26. Kalervo Oberg, "Types of Social Structure among the Lowland Tribes of South and Central America," *American Anthropologist*, LVII, No. 3, Part I (June, 1955), 472–87.

27. Daryll Forde, "The Conditions of Social Development in West Africa, Retrospect and Prospect," *Civilizations*, III, No. 4 (1953), 471–89.

28. Firth, *op. cit.*, p. 49.

29. Laura and Paul Bohannon, *The Tiv of Central Nigeria* (London: International African Institute, 1953); *Akiga's Story*, trans. and annotated by Rupert East (London: Oxford University Press, 1939).

30. E. E. Evans-Pritchard, *The Nuer* (Oxford: Clarendon Press, 1950).

31. *Seven Tribes of British Central Africa*, ed. Elizabeth Colson and Max Gluckman (London: Oxford University Press, 1951), pp. 39 ff.

32. E. Jensen Krige and J. D. Krige, *The Realm of a Rain-Queen: A Study of the Pattern of Lovedu Society* (London: Oxford University Press, 1943).

33. Melville J. Herskovits, *Dahomey: An Ancient West African Kingdom* (New York: J. J. Augustin, 1938).

34. Forde, *op. cit.*

35. Paul Honigsheim, "Max Weber as Historian of Agriculture and Rural Life," *Agricultural History*, XXIII (July, 1949), 179–213.

36. Charles Wagley and Marvin Harris, "A Typology of Latin American Subcultures," *American Anthropologist*, LVII, No. 3, Part I (June, 1955), 428–51.

37. Robert Redfield, *Tepoztlán, A Mexican Village: A Study of Folk Life* (Chicago: University of Chicago Press, 1930), p. 217. The suggestion made in this passage that "folk" be used for such intermediate societies and cultures has lately been revived by Foster (note 41 below). I later used the word for the "abstract conceptual model."

38. Robert Redfield, "Introduction" to *St. Denis: A French-Canadian Parish*, by Horace Miner (Chicago: University of Chicago Press, 1939).

39. John Gillin, *Moche: A Peruvian Coastal Community* (Smithsonian Institution, Institute of Social Anthropology, Pub. No. 3 [Washington, D.C.: Government Printing Office, 1945]); "Modern Latin American Culture," *Social Forces*, XXV, No. 3 (March, 1947), 243–48.

40. Beals, *op. cit.*

41. George M. Foster, "What Is Folk Culture?" *American Anthropologist*, Vol. LV, No. 2, Part I (April–June, 1953).

42. Steward, *op. cit.*

43. Eric R. Wolf, "Types of Latin American Peasantry: A Preliminary Discussion," *American Anthropologist*, LVII, No. 3, Part I (June, 1955), 452–71.

44. Wagley and Harris, *op. cit.*

45. C. von Dietze, "Peasantry," *Encyclopaedia of the Social Science.*

53. ". . . it is difficult to define the term, while the construction of a coi sive theory of peasantry is wellnigh impossible, . . ." (p. 50).

46. Raymond Firth, *Elements of Social Organization* (London: Watts 1951).

47. *Ibid.*, p. 102.

48. *Ibid.*, p. 88.

49. Wolf, *op. cit.*

50. Gideon Sjoberg, "Folk and Feudal Societies," *American Journal of Sociol ogy*, LVIII, No. 3 (November, 1952), 231–39.

51. *Ibid.*, p. 234.

52. A. L. Kroeber, *Anthropology* (New York: Harcourt, Brace & Co., 1948), p. 284.

53. Rushton Coulborn (ed.), *Feudalism* (Princeton, N.J.: Princeton University Press, 1956).

54. George Bourne, *Change in the Village* (New York: George H. Doran & Co., 1912).

55. Von Dietze (*op. cit.*) remarks that although in Europe the peasant has changed from being an inferior rustic with an essentially maintenance economy to something of an entrepreneur with full civil and political rights, yet he retains his ethos: "intense attachment to his native soil and family tradition, which, even in the economic sphere, takes precedence over his desire for individual gain and advancement" (p. 50).

56. Helen and Elman Service, *op. cit.*

57. James B. Watson, "Way Station of Westernization: The Brazilian Caboclo," *Brazil: Papers Presented in the Institute for Brazilian Studies* (Nashville: Vanderbilt University Press), pp. 9–58.

58. Oscar Lewis, *Life in a Mexican Village: Tepoztlán Restudied* (Urbana: University of Illinois Press, 1951).

59. Oliver La Farge, *Santa Eulalia: The Religion of a Cuchumatán Indian Town* (Chicago: University of Chicago Press, 1947); Charles Wagley, "The Social and Religious Life of a Guatemalan Village," *American Anthropologist*, Vol. LI, No. 4, Part 2, Memoir No. 71 (October, 1949); Ruth Bunzel, *Chichicastenango: A Guatemalan Village* ("Publication of the American Ethnological Society," Vol. XXII [New York: J. J. Augustin, 1952]).

60. Kroeber, *op. cit.*, p. 361.

NOTES TO CHAPTER II

1. Robert Redfield, *The Little Community: Viewpoints for the Study of a Human Whole* (Chicago: University of Chicago Press, 1955).

2. Raymond Firth, "Social Organization and Social Change," *Journal of the Royal Anthropological Institute of Great Britain and Ireland*, LXXXIV, Part 1 (January–June, 1954), 1–17.

3. Melville Herskovits, *Dahomey: An Ancient West African Kingdom* (New York: J. J. Augustin, 1938).

4. Julian H. Steward, *Area Research, Theory and Practice* (Social Science Research Bull. 63 [New York: Social Science Research Council, 1950]).

5. Julian H. Steward *et al.* (forthcoming).

6. J. A. Barnes, "Class and Committees in a Norwegian Island Parish," *Human Relations*, VII, No. 1 (1954), 39–58.

7. In Steward's words, the local units are "vertical" and the groups formed by common occupation, caste, etc., are "horizontal sociocultural subgroups." Appar-

ently some groups are both vertical and horizontal: in Bremnes the local fishermen's associations are territorially defined. In many an East Indian village the caste groups are also neighborhoods.

8. Barnes, *op. cit.*, p. 42.

9. Ruth Bunzel, *Chichicastenango: A Guatemalan Village* ("Publication of the American Ethnological Society," Vol. XXII [New York: J. J. Augustin, 1952]).

10. J. A. Pitt-Rivers, *The People of the Sierra* (London: Weidenfeld & Nicolson, 1954), pp. 32-33.

11. Irwin T. Sanders, *Balkan Village* (Lexington, Ky.: University of Kentucky Press, 1949).

12. Barnes, *op. cit.*, p. 41.

13. *Ibid.*, pp. 41-42.

14. Max Weber, *General Economic History* (Glencoe, Ill.: Free Press, 1950).

15. R. H. Tawney, *Religion and the Rise of Capitalism* (New York: Harcourt, Brace & Co., 1937).

16. A. R. Radcliffe-Brown, *The Andaman Islanders* (Glencoe, Ill.: Free Press, 1948), p. 42.

17. Bunzel, *op. cit.*, pp. 67 ff.

18. Robert Redfield, "Primitive Merchants of Guatemala," *Quarterly Journal of Inter-American Relations*, I, No. 4 (October, 1939), 42-56.

19. Sanders, *op. cit.*, pp. 105-6.

20. Robert Redfield, *The Folk Culture of Yucatan* (Chicago: University of Chicago Press, 1941), p. 163.

21. Börje Hanssen, *Österlen* (Stockholm: L. T.'s Förlag, 1952).

22. Webster McBryde, *Sololá* (New Orleans, La.: Department of Middle American Research, Tulane University, 1933).

23. Conrad Arensberg and Solon T. Kimball, *Family and Community in Ireland* (Cambridge: Harvard University Press, 1940), chap. xiii.

24. Barnes, *op. cit.*, p. 43.

25. *Ibid.*, p. 44.

26. A. R. Radcliffe-Brown, *The Social Organization of Australian Tribes* ("Oceania Monographs," No. 1 [Melbourne: Macmillan Co., 1931]), p. 95.

27. Barnes, *op. cit.*, p. 44.

28. Horace Miner, *St. Denis: A French-Canadian Parish* (Chicago: University of Chicago Press, 1939), pp. 69-70.

29. A. M. Shah, "A Dispersed Hamlet in the Panchmahals," *Economic Weekly* (Bombay) (January 26, 1955), p. 115.

30. Marian W. Smith, "Social Structure in the Punjab," *Economic Weekly* (Bombay), II, No. 47 (November 21, 1953), 1297.

31. McKim Marriott, "Little Communities in an Indigenous Civilization," *Village India* (Chicago: University of Chicago Press, 1955), p. 175.

32. Bernard Cohn, "Changing Status of a Depressed Caste," *Village India*, p. 57.

33. Herskovits, *op. cit.*, p. 57.

34. Wilbert E. Moore, *Industrialization and Labor* (Ithaca: Cornell University Press, 1951).

35. Max Gluckman, "The Lozi of Barotseland in Northwestern Rhodesia," in *Seven Tribes of British Central Africa*, ed. Elizabeth Colson and Max Gluckman (London: Oxford University Press, 1951).

36. Gideon Sjoberg, "Folk and Feudal Societies," *American Journal of Sociology*, LVIII, No. 3 (November, 1952), 234.

37. Donald Pierson (with the assistance of Levi Cruz *et al.*), *Cruz das Almas* ("Smithsonian Institution, Institute of Social Anthropology Publications," No. 12 [Washington, D.C.: Government Printing Office, 1948]).

38. Sanders, *op. cit.*, p. 11.

39. Miner, *op. cit.*, pp. 250–51.

40. "Thus a hundred and fifty years ago there were in each rural parish one or two bureaucrats living at a much higher standard from the rest of the population, speaking a different language, and moving from post to post without developing marked local affiliation. Below them in status were a few traders, usually burghers of a town; they had more local ties and were not so mobile as the bureaucrats. The rest of the population were peasants . . ." (Barnes, *op. cit.*, p. 56).

41. Pitt-Rivers, *op. cit.*

42. *Ibid.*

43. Sjoberg, *op. cit.*, p. 234.

NOTES TO CHAPTER III

1. "Acculturation: An Exploratory Formulation" (The Social Science Research Council Summer Seminar on Acculturation, 1953 [Members: H. G. Barnett, Leonard Broom, Bernard J. Siegel, Evon Z. Vogt, James B. Watson]), *American Anthropologist*, LVI, No. 6 (December, 1954), 974.

2. George M. Foster, "What Is Folk Culture?" *American Anthropologist*, LV, No. 2, Part 1 (April–June, 1953), 169.

3. *Ibid.*, p. 164. In quoting this passage I venture to substitute "peasant" for "folk" to make the terminology fit that chosen for these chapters. I think Foster's "folk societies" are much the same as those I here call "peasant societies."

4. *Ibid.*

5. Of course there may be several great traditions, as Islam and Sanskritic Hinduism are present in India, and there may be numerous subdivisions of a great tradition: I speak of "two" for simplicity.

6. *Akiga's Story*, trans. and annotated by Rupert East (London: Oxford University Press, 1930), p. 11.

7. Elsdon Best, *Maori Religion and Mythology* (Dominion Museum Bulletin No. 10 [Wellington, N.Z.: W. A. G. Skinner, Government Printer, 1924]), pp. 31–32. See also B. Malinowski, "Baloma: The Spirits of the Dead in the Trobriand Islands," in *Magic, Science and Religion* (Glencoe, Ill.: Free Press, 1948), pp. 125–227, 231 ff.

8. Melville Herskovits, *Dahomey: An Ancient West African Kingdom* (New York: J. J. Augustin, 1938), Vol. II, chap. xxvi.

9. Marcel Griaule, *Dieu d'Eau* (Paris: Les Éditions du Chêne, 1948).

10. Pedro Armillas, "The Mesoamerican Experiment," in "The Ways of Civilizations," ed. Robert J. Braidwood, MS.

11. Julian H. Steward, "Evolution and Process," in *Anthropology Today: An Encyclopedic Inventory*, ed. A. L. Kroeber (Chicago: University of Chicago Press, 1953), p. 323; "Cultural Causality and Law: A Trial Formulation of the Development of Early Civilizations," *American Anthropologist*, LI, No. 1 (January–March, 1949), 1–27.

12. *Studies in Chinese Thought*, ed. Arthur F. Wright. "Comparative Studies in Cultures and Civilizations," ed. Robert Redfield and Milton Singer (Chicago: University of Chicago Press, 1953).

13. Swami Nikhilananda, *The Upanishads: A New Translation* (New York: Harper & Bros., 1949).

14. Wing-tsit Chan, *Religious Trends in Modern China* (New York: Columbia University Press, 1953), pp. 141 ff. The distinction between the lay and hierarchic levels of Chinese religion and philosophy is made by Wolfram Eberhard, in a review article in the *Archiv für Religionswissenschaft*, XXXIII, No. 3 (1936), 304–44. For religions of the Middle East it is recognized by Raphael Patai, "Re-

ligion in Middle Eastern, Far Eastern, and Western Culture," *Southwestern Journal of Anthropology*, X, No. 3 (Autumn, 1954), 239–41.

15. V. Raghavan, "Adult Education in Ancient India," *Memoirs of the Madras Library Association* (1944), pp. 57–65; "Methods of Popular Religious Instruction, South India," MS; "Variety and Integration in the Pattern of Indian Culture," MS.

16. Raghavan, "Methods of Popular Religious Instruction, South India," MS.

17. G. von Grunebaum, "The Problem: Unity in Diversity," in *Unity and Variety in Muslim Civilization*, ed. G. von Grunebaum (Chicago: University of Chicago Press, 1955), p. 28.

18. *Ibid.*, pp. 28–29.

19. Edward Westermarck, *Ritual and Belief in Morocco* (London: Macmillan & Co., Ltd., 1926).

20. Derk Bodde, "Harmony and Conflict in Chinese Philosophy," in *Studies in Chinese Thought*, ed. Arthur F. Wright (Chicago: University of Chicago Press, 1953), p. 79, n. 46.

21. Stella Kramrisch, *The Art of India through the Ages* (London: Phaidon Press, Ltd., 1954).

22. For this way of contrasting the two kinds of studies, I am indebted to Milton Singer.

23. Norvin Hein, "The Ram Lila," *The Illustrated Weekly of India*, October 22, 1950, pp. 18–19 (provided by McKim Marriott).

24. Oscar Lewis, *Life in a Mexican Village: Tepoztlán Restudied* (Urbana: University of Illinois Press, 1951), pp. 273 ff.; John Gulick, *Social Structure and Culture Change in a Lebanese Village* ("Viking Fund Publications in Anthropology," No. 21 [New York: Wenner-Gren Foundation for Anthropological Research, Inc., 1955]), pp. 92 ff.

25. M. N. Srinivas, *Religion and Society among the Coorgs of South India* (Oxford: Clarendon Press, 1952). See also Bernard S. Cohn, "The Changing Status of a Depressed Caste," in *Village India*, ed. McKim Marriott ("Comparative Studies in Cultures and Civilizations," ed. Robert Redfield and Milton Singer [Chicago: University of Chicago Press, 1955]).

26. McKim Marriott, "Little Communities in an Indigenous Civilization," in *Village India*, pp. 171–222.

27. Mr. Marriott kindly tells me something of the strong evidence for the conclusion that Laksmi has entered the great tradition relatively late and from the folk cultures of India. He quotes Rhys Davids, Renou, and Filliozat to this effect. It appears that this deity was absent from early Vedic literature, that early statues to her were set in places reserved for popular deities, and that the Buddhist canon castigates Brahmans for performing nonsensical, non-Vedic rituals such as those to Siri Devi (Laksmi), etc.

28. Marriott tells me that in "Kishan Garhi" the more learned villager takes, in short, quite distinguishable positions toward great and little traditions. The latter, which he sees manifest in the doings of the uneducated villagers, is a matter of practice, of ignorance or fragmentary knowledge; it is confusion or vagueness and is expressed in concrete physical or biological images. The great tradition, which he thinks of himself as representing in larger degree, is theory or pure knowledge, full and satisfying; it is order and precision and finds for its expression abstractions or symbolic representations.

29. Personal communication.

30. Roger Le Tourneau, "The Muslim Town: Religion and Culture," MS.

31. Shamrao Hivale, *The Pardhans of the Upper Narbada Valley* (London: Oxford University Press, 1946).

32. Raymond Firth, *Elements of Social Organization* (London: Watts & Co., 1951), chap. ii, pp. 35 ff.

NOTES TO CHAPTER IV

1. Ruth Benedict, *Patterns of Culture* (New York: Penguin Books, Inc., 1946).

2. Margaret Mead, *Sex and Temperament in Three Primitive Societies* (New York: William Morrow & Co., 1935). The opposite demonstration—of resemblance in value-orientations between distant and otherwise very different peoples —is illustrated in Walter Goldschmidt, "Ethics and the Structure of Society: An Ethnological Contribution to the Sociology of Knowledge," *American Anthropologist*, LIII, No. 4, Part 1 (October–December, 1951), 506–24.

3. Oscar Handlin, *The Uprooted* (Boston: Little, Brown & Co., 1951), p. 7.

4. Malcolm Darling, *Rusticus Loquitur: The Old Light and the New in the Punjab Village* (London: Oxford University Press, 1930), p. x.

5. René Porak, *Un village de France: Psycho-physiologie du paysan* (Paris: G. Doin & Cie, 1943).

6. "Rusticam plebem, quae sub divo et in labore nutritur, solis patiens, umbrae negligens, deliciarum ignara, simplicis animi, parvo contenta, duratis ad omnem lanorum tolerantium membris; cui gestare ferrum, fossam ducere, onus ferre consuetudo de rure est" (Vegetius *Epitoma Rei Militaris*, i. 3, quoted in Darling, *Rusticus Loquitur*, p. x).

7. Ladislas Reymont, *The Peasants* (4 vols.; New York: Alfred A. Knopf, 1925).

8. E. K. L. Francis, "The Personality Type of the Peasant According to Hesiod's Works and Days: A Culture Case Study," *Rural Sociology*, X, No. 3 (September, 1945), 278.

9. *Ibid.*, p. 277.

10. George Bourne, *Change in the Village* (New York: George H. Doran Co., 1912).

11. In a lecture delivered at University College of the University of Chicago, May 14, 1954.

12. Irwin T. Sanders, *Balkan Village* (Lexington, Ky.: University of Kentucky Press, 1949), p. 147.

13. J. A. Pitt-Rivers, *The People of the Sierra* (New York: Criterion Books, 1954), p. 47.

14. J. Weulersse, *Paysans de Syrie et du Proche-Orient* (Paris, 1946), p. 173.

15. Pitt-Rivers, *op. cit.*, p. 47, n. 1. Yet Hamed Ammar in *Growing Up in an Egyptian Village, Silwa, Province of Aswan* (London: Routledge & Kegan Paul, Ltd., 1954) tells us the fellah has strong emotional attachment to his land. Also he tells us that to be an industrious farmer attending to his business is a good qualification for a youth about to get married (p. 35) and stresses "the dignity of farmwork compared to other occupations" (p. 39).

16. Work "is felt as a definite burden imposed by the gods and—regretted." "The cycle of the seasons itself occasionally admits full enjoyment of a happy time of rest, which Hesiod depicts with a poetical verve . . ." (Francis, *op. cit.*, p. 284).

17. Hesiod *The Homeric Hymns and Homerica*. With an English translation by Hugh G. Evelyn-Whyte (London: William Heinemann; New York: Macmillan Co., 1914), p. 55.

18. Bourne, *op. cit.*, p. 44.

19. Robert H. Lowie, *The Crow Indians* (New York: Farrar & Rinehart, 1935), p. 57.

20. Bourne, *op. cit.*, p. 41.

21. Hesiod, *op. cit.*, p. 31.

22. Pitt-Rivers, *op. cit.*, chap. vi.

23. Bourne, *op. cit.*

24. *Ibid.*

25. "The agrarian revolutions of 1917–19 in Eastern Europe . . . were quite different from earlier revolts, such as the Peasants' War of 1524–25 in south and central Germany or the peasant movements in the early years of the French Revolution, which aimed primarily at reducing or abolishing the oppressive services and dues exacted by landlords" (C. von Dietze, "Peasantry," *Encyclopaedia of the Social Sciences*, XII, 50). "Hesiod apparently takes domination by feudal lord and the stratification of society for granted. What he resents is abuse of power, although he makes no attempt to remedy that, except by persuasion and reference to divine sanction" (Francis, *op. cit.*, p. 293). "The deep differences among peasants and between the peasants and other groups was not a cause for envy. This was the accepted configuration of society. The lord was expected to be proud and luxurious, but humane and generous, just as the peasant was expected to be thrifty and respectful. Even bitterly burdensome privileges were not open to dispute" (Handlin, *op. cit.*, p. 23). Karl Marx himself wrote that French peasantry were incapable of revolution because they had no common sense of oppression.

26. Gideon Sjoberg, "Folk and 'Feudal' Societies," *American Journal of Sociology*, LVIII, No. 3 (November, 1952), 235.

27. Lucien Bernot et René Blancard, *Nouville, un village français* (Paris: Institut d'ethnologie, 1953), p. 282.

28. *Stanford Humanities-Anthropological Conference, Santa Barbara, May 16, 17, 1947* (mimeographed); David Bidney, "The Concept of Value in Modern Anthropology," in *Anthropology Today*, ed. A. L. Kroeber (Chicago: University of Chicago Press, 1953), pp. 682–99; "Values" in *An Appraisal of Anthropology Today*, ed. Sol Tax *et al.* (Chicago: University of Chicago Press, 1953), chap. xviii, pp. 322–41; Clyde Kluckhohn, "Values and Value-Orientations in the Theory of Action" in *Toward a General Theory of Action*, ed. T. Parsons and E. Shils (Cambridge: Harvard University Press, 1951), pp. 388–433; and papers published or forthcoming of the study, under Kluckhohn's direction, of values in certain communities of the Southwest; A. L. Kroeber, "Reality Culture and Value Culture" in *The Nature of Culture* (Chicago: University of Chicago Press, 1952), pp. 152–68.

29. Donald S. Pitkin, "Land Tenure and Family Organization in an Italian Village" (Ph.D. thesis, Harvard University, 1954).

INDEX

Acculturation, 15

Africa: "networks" in, 35; states in, 13–14, 35–36; studies of, 12, 36–37

Agriculture: for the market, 29; as mode of life, 29, 63 ff.; and peasantry, 18

Amazon, 32

Andalusia, 27–28, 37, 39, 66, 73

Andaman islanders, 10, 11, 29, 40, 41, 43

Anthropology: definitions of, 9–10; field experience basic to, 6–7; interests in all of a culture, 8–9; as natural history, 6; studies civilized communities, 13–14, 24–25, 26; studies compound societies, 12, 16, 24–25; studies peasants, 14 ff.; studies social systems, 23 ff.; studies urban communities, 24; as study of primitive or of all peoples, 9–10, 39, 77; views the small community, 23

Aranda, 40, 60

Armillas, Pedro, 12

Australia, 41, 60

Balkans, 28

Barnes, J. A., 25–26, 36; quoted, 28, 30, 31, 32

Barnot, Lucien, quoted, 76

Beals, Ralph, 10, 23

Benedict, Ruth, 10, 23

Bernot, Lucien, quoted, 76

Blancard, René, quoted, 76

Boas, Franz, 7

Boeotians, 62, 63, 65, 70

Bourne, George, quoted, 71

Brazil, 21, 36

Bremnes, 26, 28, 31, 34

Buddhism, 47

Bulgaria, 28, 29, 36–37

Caboclo, 21

Calabria, 68, 77

California, 60

Cambodia, 48

Caste, 34, 53, 57

Chan Kom, 70–71

Chichen Itza, 46

Chichicastenango, 29

China, 28, 45, 46–47, 76, 77

Christ, 75

City, and countryside, 12

Civilization, 59; European, 76; Maya, 44–46; in Meso-America, 44–46; and peasantry, 19–20, 40 ff.; primary and secondary, 45–46, 76–77

Classification of cultures and societies, 16–17

Coba, 46

Comanche, 72

Comparisons of cultures, 15

Compound societies, 12, 76; as civilizations, 41–42

Confucianism, 47

Confucius, 42, 75

Coorgs, 53

Copan, 45

Culture and cultures: as autonomous system, 40, 59; civilization as compound, 41–42; concept of a, 40; folk and peasant among the Maya, 44–45; hierarchic and lay, 41, 47–

PHOENIX BOOKS

in Sociology

PHOENIX BOOKS
in Anthropology

PHOENIX BOOKS
in Archeology

PHOENIX BOOKS
in History